I PREDICT!

I PREDICT!

WHAT 12 GLOBAL EXPERTS BELIEVE YOU WILL SEE BEFORE 2025!

DR. THOMAS R. HORN
The Final Roman Emperor & the Vatican's Last Crusade

JOEL RICHARDSON
Islamic Antichrist & Apollyon Rising

MARK BILTZ
The Man of Sin Arrives

CARL GALLUPS
Wars & Rumors of Wars: The Brink of World War III

JOSH TOLLEY
Collapse of the Global Economy

DEREK GILBERT
The Ark of the Covenant & the Third Temple

JOSH PECK
Angels Everywhere

LARRY SPARGIMINO
The Next Great Awakening

TROY ANDERSON
The Rise of a Final End-Times Global Government

DR. GORDON MCDONALD
The Age of Convergence

SHARON GILBERT
The Hybrid Age Begins

PAUL MCGUIRE
America & Coming Revival

"Men's hearts failing them for fear, and for looking after those things which are coming on the earth..."
LUKE 21:26

DEFENDER

CRANE, MO

I PREDICT!: What 12 Global Experts Believe You Will See
Before 2025!
Defender
Crane, MO 65633
©2016 by Thomas Horn
All rights reserved. Published 2016.
Printed in the United States of America.

ISBN: 978-0-996-4095-5-1

A CIP catalog record of this book is available from the Library of Congress.

Cover illustration and design by Jeffrey Mardis.

All Scripture quotations from the King James Version; in cases of academic comparison, those instances are noted.

Contents

The Final Roman Emperor and the Vatican's Last Crusade

By Dr. Thomas R. Horn

(EDITOR'S NOTE: The following is largely adapted from the new book by Thomas Horn and Cris Putnam, *The Final Roman Emperor, the Islamic Antichrist, and the Vatican's Last Crusade*)

Many years ago, I (Tom Horn) died and woke up in heaven. Contemplating my surroundings, I wondered where I was, where I had come from, and why I had no memories of getting here—wherever *here* was.

At that moment, before it was shortly confirmed, I knew this was no dream; it was too vivid to be anything less than real. In fact, it felt *realer* than any previous *reality* I had known.

I became aware of these uncanny surroundings when abruptly I found myself standing somewhere before a spectacular pillar of light *(or was it a throne?)*. It was so bright, so intense, and penetrating—glistening with vibrant streams of silver, blue, and gold emanating with the most unexplainable yet awe-inspiring presence—that I could hardly keep my eyes open or my face toward the radiance.

I was exclaiming something, and didn't know why I was saying it: "Please, Lord, don't let me forget! Please don't let me forget! IT'S TOO WONDERFUL!"

How long had I been here and what was I talking about? Why was I so desperate to recall something I had obviously been told I would forget? And how did I know I was standing before the LORD?

Suspended there like a marionette on wires, I somehow was aware that "memories" from moments before (but were there "moments" or "time" in this place?) stood just beyond my ability to reckon them back into my conscious mind again.

But I *had* known something, something about the future. *I had seen it, and then I had been told I would not remember the details.* But why? What would be the purpose of that?

Something else had happened, too. Somehow I knew that a scroll of some kind had unrolled before me…with scenes of a future, *my future*, playing out on what looked like a silvery parchment. It had been as clear and as believable as if I were watching a movie, with rich depictions of a destiny, or a possible future, where something extraordinary and miraculous was taking place—a cinematic conveyance of a personal fate, a "potential existence" that had been downloaded into my subconscious mind, or soul, and then…for some reason…had departed my intellect. Had a revelation of some type been sealed inside me? Something for a later time?

My thoughts raced, and I started to repeat, "Lord, please, don't let me forget," but I stopped short, as just then, a deep, still, small voice countered, *"You will not remember…and it is time for you to go back now."*

Then I heard a thunderclap…and found myself falling backward, drifting swiftly, as if I had been dropped out of an airplane window or let loose by some heavenly hands that had been holding me above, my arms and legs gliding up and down now against a cloudless sky.

As I fell, I gazed unblinkingly upward in amazement. The brilliance that had just been in front of me was moving rapidly away into the distance, and yet I wasn't afraid. A high-pitched whistling sound began rushing in around my ears, and I thought it must be the air carrying me aloft as I plummeted toward the earth. A moment later, I watched as the oddest thing happened: The roof of my house literally enveloped me as I passed effortlessly through it, and then it felt as if I had landed on my bedroom mattress with a THUD!

I sat straight up, took a desperate, shuddering, deep inhalation, and slowly let it out, realizing that something extraordinary had occurred. Wherever I had been, whatever I had seen, I was back now to the so-called real world, and this material substance straightway felt far less authentic to me than the other place I had been.

It was the middle of the night, and I sat there for a few seconds, possibly in shock, trying to determine what had happened.

I could feel my chest burning…then I heard something.

Sobbing…right next to me…my young wife, Nita, with her head in her hands.

As my eyes adjusted to the darkness, I found her isolated stare. She looked as if she had been crying desperately, and she had an unfamiliar expression conveying what I somehow already understood: We had both experienced something far more irregular than we ever could have prepared for.

"Nita," I said softly, "what's going on? Why are you crying?"

It took a while for her to collect herself, but once she did, she tearfully described how she had awakened to find me dead. No pulse, no breath, no heartbeat. I had been cold to the touch—and not just for a few seconds, either. I had remained in that condition for approximately fifteen minutes while she had screamed for me to wake up, pounded on my chest, and attempted CPR.

We didn't have a phone in those days, and since it was in the middle of the night, Nita had been unsure of what to do. She was about to try pulling me outside to the car to take me to the hospital when I jerked up, took in a deep breath, and looked at her.

For the reader, no matter how incredible the narrative above seems, this really did happen to me a long time ago. Later, and since then, I have understood why God allowed my wife to wake up to find me in that condition. Without her eyewitness account that night, uncertainties about the supernaturalism of the experience would have undoubtedly crept into my mind over the years. Also, that I had been dead for a significant period of time, not breathing and therefore not taking in oxygen, and yet experiencing no brain damage (though I'm sure some would argue otherwise) also attested to the preternatural virtues of the event.

But why would God show me something and then not allow me to remember it? What would be the point of that, right? I can tell you that this was *the* question pressing me in the days immediately following the event, and in my youthful naïveté and impatience, I first went about trying to find the answer to that mystery in the wrong way. I learned a valuable and biblical lesson as a result. In fact, that early mistake is why most have never heard this story until now.

What happened next was this: A couple of days after my death and return from "over yonder," I told the pastor of our local church that I had an important question to ask him. In private, I recounted the events of earlier that week and probed what it could possibly mean. "Why would God show me something then tell me I would not remember the vision?" I had inquired earnestly. His response was shocking for an honest and sincere young Christian man. Basically, he offered that I had probably eaten too much spicy food, or maybe had accidentally been poisoned, and was therefore delusional or had a vivid dream.

No kidding.

Of course, I wasn't yet familiar with such admonitions as, "Give not that which is holy unto the dogs, neither cast ye your pearls before swine, lest they trample them under their feet" (Matthew 7:6). I am not saying that my pastor back then was a dog, you understand, but that this was a lesson I would not soon forget about sharing sacred holy things with those who have not had similar supernatural experiences and therefore cannot appreciate or understand the otherworldly significance. In fact, besides my closest friends and family, from that day forward, I kept the event (and what I would soon understand about its measurable implications) a secret between me and them. Then, just a few years ago, well-known television personality Sid Roth asked me to repeat the story on his syndicated program, *It's Supernatural.* Because Sid, unlike some preachers, actually BELIEVES in the miraculous, I agreed that it was time to tell at least a part of that history. Albeit, as legendary radio broadcaster Paul Harvey used to ponder, what was the rest of the story?

After the disappointing experience following my pastor's less-than-enthusiastic response to my question, I struggled to make sense of what had obviously been an extraordinary incident in my and Nita's life. I prayed daily, seeking understanding, and during this same period (undoubtedly God had all this timing in control from the very beginning), I happened to be reading the Bible from cover to cover for the first time in my life. I had made it to the book of Job when, one day, my eyes suddenly fell upon Job 33:15–17. The Word of God dramatically came to life in what some charismatics might call a *rhema* moment, a time in which the Scripture went from being ink on paper to being *the living Word of God!* The text that instantly conveyed the dynamic truth behind what had happened to me that fateful night read:

> In a dream, in a vision of the night, when deep sleep falleth upon men, in slumberings upon the bed; Then he openeth the ears of men, and **sealeth their instruction** [within them], That he may withdraw man from his purpose, and hide pride from man. (emphasis added)

Though I was a very young and inexperienced believer, I clearly understood what this text was saying to me. Like the apostle Paul who could not tell whether he was "in the body...or out of the body" when he was "caught up to the third heaven" (2 Corinthians 12:2), God, on that momentous night, had taken me to a heavenly place and sealed "instructions" within me. These directions would be there when I needed them during life, as they were like a roadmap that the Holy Spirit would "quicken" when, at different times, I needed guidance or information. Nevertheless, I was not to remember these details ahead of time; otherwise, I might be drawn away into my "own purpose" and lifted up in "pride," according to this oldest book in the Bible—Job.

In other words, if, as a young believer, I had seen the ministries that God would later allow me and Nita to participate in—from pastoring large churches to owning a Christian publishing house and syndicated television ministry, to speaking at major conferences as a best-selling author, or any of the other opportunities He would give us permission to be associated with—I very likely would have made two huge mistakes. First, I would have immediately aimed at these later ministries and started working to try to make them happen all without the benefit of the struggles, trials, setbacks, side roads, and experiences that are necessary for "seasoning" and (hopefully) qualifying one to eventually operate in them (thus God "withdrew me from *my* purpose"). Second, I would have been tempted by pride to think of myself as more than I should have as a young man, if I had seen myself ending up in high-profile ministries. So God, in His benevolence, also "hid pride" from me by keeping the revelations sealed until the appropriate times.

The Quickenings

In the Bible, it is clear that God does "seal" knowledge, wisdom, and revelations in the hearts of those who follow Him, and that these concealed truths can be "quickened" or made alive at the right moments as they are needed. This is depicted in such texts as Matthew chapter 10, where Jesus says to His disciples: "But when they deliver you up, take no thought how or what ye shall speak: *for it shall be given you in that same hour* what ye shall speak. For it is not ye that speak, but the Spirit of your Father which speaketh *in you*" (Matthew 10:19–20, emphasis added). That this reflects a deep partnership between our personal devotions and studies (2 Timothy 2:15; Psalms 119:11) and the indwelling Holy Spirit as part of the mystical union God has with all members of the true Church—the Body of Christ—can also be seen in Proverbs 3:6, which says, "In all thy ways acknowledge him [that's us doing our part], and he shall direct thy paths" [His part]. Again, the book of John (6:63) refers to the Holy Spirit as the one "that quickens" (Greek: *z opoie* , "to cause to live, to make alive at that moment") the Word of God as well as those "sealed instructions" that Job talked about.

I'm not sure how this experience plays out for others, but several times in my life and at times completely unexpected (always at night when I am asleep), I have been jolted from bed with an extraordinary glimpse that I believe is taken from that original storyboard God gave me years ago, and about which I begged Him not to "let me forget." One time, for example, I was shaken from sleep by a very powerful and detailed list of things that would happen in the former religious institution in which I had been an executive. I jumped from bed, wrote down the vision as I had seen it—including names of people who would be involved, exactly what they would do, and how it would greatly damage the ministry if the district leaders did not intervene (they didn't, and it did)— then I sent that detailed letter to the state superintendent, plus gave a copy to my son, Joe Ardis, and to my wife, Nita. Within three years, everything played out exactly as I had seen it, down to the smallest details. In fact, it was so precise that it shook Joe up, causing him to come to me after the fact to express his utter amazement as to how it could have been possible for me to foresee such comprehensive events that accurately.

A more recent "quickening" revelation is one that the world kinda-sorta knows about now involving how me and Cris Putnam were able to very precisely predict the historic resignation of Pope Benedict in our book *Petrus Romanus: The Final Pope Is Here,* as well as on television and radio a year in advance.

This began with a series of preternatural events too long to list in this book, but which ultimately brought Cris and me together to investigate and write our first best seller, *Petrus Romanus*. During the research phase of that work, Cris uncovered the obscure manuscript of a Belgian Jesuit name Rene Thibaut, who predicted sixty years in advance that the papacy would change hands in 2012 based on his understanding of the nine-hundred-year-old prophecy by Saint Malachy that we were studying. Cris worked diligently to translate Thibaut's work into English and to verify his mathematical (and mystical) calculations using a software spreadsheet and language translator.

At first, we found Thibaut's speculations interesting, partly because of the year 2012, which the world was abuzz about in the lead-up to that date. But as we made inroads behind the scenes with Catholic academics and historical artifacts, we began to believe something much bigger was afoot, and that either the Malachy prophecy was genuine (that is, it was either divinely or demonically inspired) or that some of the cardinal electors *believed* it was genuine and were therefore electing popes down through the years who could somehow be seen as fulfilling their lines in the prophecy; therefore, it had become a self-fulfilling oracle.

During this time, one night I was, once again, rattled from sleep and instantly convinced that Cris had been led by God to make this discovery and that in fact Pope Benedict would indeed step down in April 2012 using "health reasons" as a cover for his abdication. We went on television and radio in 2011 (and out on a limb, quite frankly) as the book was being written and rushed through editing, typesetting, and print so that it could be in stores before the anticipated resignation of the pope. We wrote specifically on page 470 of *Petrus Romanus* that Pope Benedict would "likely" step down in April 2012, but in media (which people can watch on YouTube in numerous interviews from 2011), we were more insistent that not only "could" it happen, but, we predicted, it would.

As the year 2012 came and went, and neither Pope Benedict nor the Vatican made any announcement that he was stepping down, I thought perhaps for the first time since I had woken up dead in heaven years earlier, the "sealed," Job-like "instructions" mechanism either had not worked or I had been mistaken. Yet, as the months passed, I somehow remained convinced that we had seen the vision correctly! I would email Cris and say, "It's not over till it's over," while at the same time saying to myself, *What are you talking about? Benedict is still the pope!*

Then something happened that the world knows about now—on February 28, 2013, at 8:00 PM, the resignation of Pope Benedict was announced by the Vatican, which immediately gave the *New York Times* an interview in which it made the astonishing admission: Pope Benedict had SECRETLY AND OFFICIALLY resigned to select members of the Curia in April 2012, just as Cris Putnam and I (and Thibaut *and the quickening!*) had said he would. This was immediately confirmed by Giovanni Maria Vian, the editor of the official Vatican newspaper, *L'Osservatore Romano,* who wrote that the pope's decision "was taken many months ago," after his trip to Mexico and Cuba ended in March 2012, "and kept with a reserve that no one could violate"[1] (meaning it was to remain top secret and was to be known only to a handful of trusted Vatican cardinals until preparations for Benedict's housing and the public announcement was ready).

This revelation was astounding! Cris Putnam had been led by God to uncover the trail, Thibaut had mystically speculated the event sixty years in advance, and "the quickening" had confirmed for me this historic event with pinpoint accuracy all ahead of time. Media everywhere went crazy! My office phone did not stop ringing for weeks, with top media from around the world (including Rome) wanting to interview us to ask who our "insider at the Vatican" was. CNN begged me to come on their program, which I declined. The History Channel pleaded with us to participate in a special series, and Putnam agreed, and so on. But why am I talking about this now? Is it so we can pat ourselves on the back and brag about how incredibly accurate our prediction was?

No.

I'm raising this issue now because there has been another "quickening," and this time it involves the current Pope Francis (the last Pope, Petrus Romanus, according to the Malachy list [OR IS HE!? More on that question later])—and the revelation I will shortly detail as being much bigger and more concerning than the last one was, yet it is with the same level of confidence I had when we foresaw that Pope Benedict would step down (an event that had not happened for hundreds of years and one that everybody was telling us would never happen again…that is, until it did) that I will now convey what I (Tom Horn) predict is going to happen over the next few years.

Isis and the Final Roman Emperor

In the book, *The Final Roman Emperor, the Islamic Antichrist, and the Vatican's Last Crusade*, and in much greater detail than we will examine here, the apocalyptic beliefs—both Muslim and Catholic—of a final war between Islam and the "Army of Rome" are described as currently guiding the actions of some of the major global players in both of these institutions, and that is tied to a startling revelation that no other modern writers/researchers have made involving an ancient prediction about a "Last Roman Emperor." In summary, there is a role that ISIS is playing and will play in the prediction that I (Tom Horn) am set to make involving the "hows" and "whys" of our modern world's fears over this mysterious group called ISIS (Islamic State of Iraq and Syria; sometimes "ISIL": Islamic State of Iraq and the Levant). Our Facebook newsfeeds have been inundated with blurred images of bloody beheadings. When we visit YouTube, unsolicited videos pop up to the side of the screen with the latest reporting of death tolls by men in black clothing carrying threatening firearms with their faces covered. When we Google search something entirely unrelated, articles appear declaring that the seemingly unnecessary and irrational executions of non-hostile men in orange jumpsuits are still underway. Our confidence in national security has been rattled by the threat, the American collective consciousness lives in nail-biting suspense, and even our children have picked up on the fact that nameless and faceless "bad guys" are fulfilling repulsively dreadful feats of bloodshed that make the boogeyman look like a saint.

Unbelievably, however, a group of central questions remains at the forefront of our minds—questions that even our country's leaders have not been able to effectively answer: What is ISIS' motivation? Where did they come from? Why are they killing? And what in the world is the "Islamic State"?

Reasonable questions, no doubt, and simple enough to assume they would render equally simple answers. Despite convoluted explanations, however, our government, as well as the American public, is largely mystified. Though many theories have surfaced, some of which are popularized as the most likely, getting in touch with ISIS and understanding the purpose behind their mission is puzzling to even Maj. Gen. Michael K. Nagata, former US Army commander of the Special Operations Command Center, who said in an interview with *The New York Times*, "'We do not understand the movement, and until we do, we are not going to defeat it,' he said, according to the confidential minutes of a conference call he held with experts. 'We have not defeated the idea. We do not even understand the idea.'"[2] Former Defense Intelligence Agency spokesperson Michael T. Flynn reacted to this comment: "The fact that someone as experienced in counterterrorism as Mike Nagata is asking these kinds of questions shows what a really tough problem this is."[3]

Firstly, the Islamic religion is monotheistic and Abrahamic, and it holds its roots in the Qur'an (Arabic: "the recitation"), which Muslims (followers of the Islamic faith) believe to be the exact and literal words of Allāh (Arabic: "the God [of Abrahamic religions]"). There are many common elements between fundamental Islam and Christianity, such as beliefs in only one God; the message and teachings of the prophets Noah, Abraham, Moses, David (and others), as well as Christ; Christ as a prophet (but not divine in Islam); Old and New Testaments are holy; wickedness of Satan; appearance of Antichrist; and heaven and hell... and so on. A peaceful start, one might think. However, just like there are different denominations within Christianity in which fundamental beliefs and lifestyle practices fluctuate, there are varying sects of Islam (Sunni, Shia, Sufi, Kharijites, Ahmadiyya, etc.), under each of which exist numerous different schools of thought—and all with their own views on violence.

To which does ISIS belong? It is said they subscribe to Wahhabism, a branch of Sunni Islam. Wahhabism is described by neutral and unbiased sources as a "religious reform movement...[in which] followers believe that they have a religious obligation...for a restoration of pure monotheistic worship."[4] Even among many Muslims, however, such as those behind the As-Sunnah Foundation of America (ASFA), whose mission statement on the front of their web page says, "Unity, Knowledge, and Understanding for the Muslim Community,"[5] Wahhabism is "[t]he most extremist pseudo-Sunni movement today."[6] The ASFA goes on to say, "Irrespective of what they think, they [Wahhabis] are not following the Islamic sources authentically."[7]

Other experts say the "best" way to describe ISIS' belief system is Salafist, a belief in the literal interpretation of the words and deeds of Muhammad and his early successors (*salaf* being Arabic for "ancestor"), and that while all Wahhabists are Salafists, not all Salafists are Wahhabists. In fact, "Wahhabi" is apparently considered an insult by Salafists.

"Wahhabism," referring to the subset of Salafism founded by Muhammad ibn 'Abd al-Wahhab (d. 1792), was allied to the House of Saud in the late eighteenth century and still is today. In a nutshell, Wahhabism rejected modern influences on Islam.

Salafism emerged at al-Azhar University in Cairo (according to Tim Furnish, the most influential Islamic academic institution in the world) in the second half of the nineteenth century. Contra the Wahhabists, Salafists tried to reconcile Islam with modernism. ISIS rejects leadership of the House of Saud because they are not the religious or political heirs to Muhammad. (ISIS declared war on Saudi Arabia in December, and the Saudis have been building a high-tech fence along its border with Iraq.)

What they have in common is a "fundamentalist" interpretation of the Qur'an and hadiths, a belief that mainstream Sunnis have been wrong about their faith for about a thousand years. And both see themselves as the legitimate "true" Muslims. ISIS especially engages in *takfiri*, the practice of excommunicating those who aren't with the program, but for both groups, Shias are right-out, absolute heretics.

In 2010, Abu Bakr al-Baghdadi became the leader of ISIS, and has since strived for domination. Aggressively, he has led ISIS to control huge land masses in Iraq, Syria, Libya, Nigeria, and Afghanistan, among many other territories of Asia and Africa. In 2014, official ISIS spokesman Abu Muhammad al-Adnani declared Baghdadi the "Caliph Ibrahim":

> Adnani demanded that all jihadi factions, not only those in Iraq and Syria, but everywhere, pledge allegiance to the Islamic State, for the "legality" of their organizations is now void. He stated: "Indeed, it is the State. Indeed, it is the khilāfah. It is time for you to end this abhorrent partisanship, dispersion, and division, for this condition is not from the religion of Allah at all. And if you forsake the State or wage war against it, you will not harm it. You will only harm yourselves."[8]

Many may read these words and believe they are—*at least*—the most emphatic definition of hubris fathomable, if not complete totalitarianism. Nevertheless, though the world caliphate is a self-proclaimed authority (which numerous Muslim groups find controversial), and though Baghdadi is the self-proclaimed caliph (of whom numerous Muslim groups deny support), ISIS continues to gain assistance from fellow terrorists-in-training; American intelligence officials have estimated that one thousand foreign fighters *per month* travel to Iraq and Syria to join ISIS,[9] with Baghdadi now standing as dictatorial commander over every Muslim community in the world.

While their clandestine motives—political and religious—have baffled even US intelligence officials, their actions are loud and clear. They may be reclusive in keeping communication lines limited to themselves, allowing the rest of the world to draw whatever conclusions they will about the *whys*, but leaders of ISIS are social media savants, and at every turn they have blasted the Internet with execution videos, propaganda videos, rejections of peace, articles of demands, photos of their destruction of Christians, artifacts, and buildings, etc. Genocide, the likes of which this world has not seen since the domination of Nazi Germany, is one of ISIS' goals:

> The Nazi destruction of stolen art was an act of gratuitous violence against Europe's cultural heritage, undertaken in service to a demented ideology... Similarly gratuitous destruction of ancient cultural centers and artifacts is now underway wherever the black flag of the Islamic State, ISIS, is raised in Iraq and Syria. And so is another genocide, this time of Christians....
>
> As the indefatigable human rights campaigner Nina Shea wrote...the wanton destruction of a sacred place is also a metaphor for "the genocide of Iraq's Christian people and their civilization."[10]

Nina Shea is not the only one who sees this horror for what it is. For example, the European Parliament "passed a resolution declaring that the Islamic State terror group...'is committing genocide against Christians and Yazidis...(and) other religious and ethnic minorities.'"[11] Even Democratic presidential candidate Hillary Clinton said a few months ago, "I am now sure we have enough evidence, what is happening is genocide deliberately aimed at destroying lives and wiping out the existence of Christians and other religious minorities."[12]

Is ISIS so far off in left field that their cries for dominance are driven by an apocalyptic landscape? Some rational minds would believe this to be an immediately sensationalistic notion, but if we look at how dramatic ISIS is in every other aspect, we begin to not only accept, but *expect*, their ideologies to be ceaselessly and recklessly grandiose...and we are not alone. ISIS is in fact driven by very specific and ancient eschatological apocalypticism.

To begin, Islam's central figure, the prophet Muhammad, allegedly predicted the invasion and defeat of both Constantinople and Rome. The first of these two cities fell into the hands of the Muslims in the 1400s, bringing the prophecy to fruition. Rome has yet to be dominated. Sheikh Yousef Al-Qaradhawi, "one of the most influential clerics in Sunni Islam,"[13] explained this prophecy:

> The Prophet Muhammad was asked: "What city will be conquered first, Constantinople or Romiyya?" He answered: "The city of Hirqil [i.e., the Byzantine emperor Heraclius] will be conquered first"—that is, Constantinople.... Romiyya is the city called today "Rome," the capital of Italy. The city of Hirqil [that is, Constantinople] was conquered by the young 23-year-old Ottoman Muhammad bin Morad, known in history as Muhammad the Conqueror, in 1453. The other city, Romiyya, remains, and we hope and believe [that it too will be conquered].[14] (brackets and ellipses in original)

The idea that ISIS plans to wage war against Rome is more than clear through all of their speeches, posts, articles, and propaganda. To quote

Baghdadi himself in a speech to fellow Muslims just two days after he was pronounced the caliph (translated by ISIS' subsidiary media company Al-Hayat; as quoted by the Middle East Media Research Institute):

> So congratulations to you, O slaves of Allah, as Allah has allowed you to reach this noble month. Praise Allah and thank Him for having granted you long lives, thereby giving you a chance to correct your past deeds.... As for the religion of Allah, then it will be victorious. Allah has promised to bring victory to the religion....
>
> So take up arms, take up arms, O soldiers of the Islamic State! And fight, fight!... So raise your ambitions, O soldiers of the Islamic State!...
>
> Soon, by Allah's permission, a day will come when the Muslim will walk everywhere as a master, having honor, being revered, with his head raised high and his dignity preserved. Anyone who dares to offend him will be disciplined, and any hand that reaches out to harm him will be cut off.
>
> So let the world know that we are living today in a new era. Whoever was heedless must now be alert. Whoever was sleeping must now awaken. Whoever was shocked and amazed must comprehend. The Muslims today have a loud, thundering statement, and possess heavy boots. They have a statement that will cause the world to hear and understand the meaning of terrorism, and boots that will trample the idol of nationalism, destroy the idol of democracy, and uncover its deviant nature....
>
> So listen, O ummah [Arabic: "community"] of Islam. Listen and comprehend. Stand up and rise. For the time has come for you to free yourself from the shackles of weakness, and stand in the face of tyranny, against the treacherous rulers—the agents of the crusaders and the atheists, and the guards of the Jews....
>
> O Muslims everywhere, glad tidings to you... Raise your

head high, for today—by Allah's grace—you have a state and caliphate, which will return your dignity, might, rights, and leadership....

Therefore, rush, O Muslims, to your state. Yes, it is your state. Rush, because Syria is not for the Syrians, and Iraq is not for the Iraqis. The Earth is Allah's... The State is a state for all Muslims. The land is for the Muslims, all the Muslims....

Know that today you are the defenders of the religion and the guards of the land of Islam. You will face tribulation and epic battles....

So prepare your arms, and supply yourselves with piety. Persevere in reciting the Koran [Qur'an] with comprehension of its meanings and practice of its teachings.

This is my advice to you. If you hold to it, you will conquer Rome and own the world.[15]

Besides the aforementioned parallels between Nazi Germany and ISIS' genocidal agenda are the blatantly obvious parallels between Hitler's declaration-of-war speeches and this—Baghdadi's declaration of war against Rome and all enemies of Islam. His intonations are sometimes so Hitlerian that one could swap out the relative ethnic groups and enemy groups and post it online as a "lost speech by Hitler" and people would believe it. But I digress...

Under the leadership of Baghdadi, radical Muslim terrorist factions are, *in fact*, "raising up arms" for war. Islamic eschatology (from the Hadith) points to the town of Dabiq, Syria, as a fester-pot of the Muslim *Malahim* (apocalypse; Armageddon). The "Romans" (or "Roman Christians," as some scholars put it) will "land" in Dabiq, wage war against the Muslim soldiers, the Muslims will win, and the "Last Hour" heralds the arrival of Isa (Christ) and Dajjal (Antichrist). (Note, also that ISIS' official magazine is also called *Dabiq*.) From "The Only Quran" website, the prophecy reads:

Abu Huraira [Muhammad's recorder and companion] reported Allah's Messenger (may peace be upon him) assaying: The Last Hour would not come until the Romans would land...in Dabiq. An army consisting of the best (soldiers) of the people of the earth at that time will come from Medina (to counteract them).... They will then fight and a third (part) of the army would run away, whom Allah will never forgive. A third (part of the army), which would be constituted of excellent martyrs in Allah's eye, would be killed and the third who would never be put to trial would win... And as they would be busy in distributing the spoils of war (amongst themselves) after hanging their swords by the olive trees, the Satan would cry: The Dajjal [Antichrist] has taken your place among your family. They would then come out, but it would be of no avail. And when they would come to Syria, he would come out while they would be still preparing themselves for battle drawing up the ranks. Certainly, the time of prayer shall come and then Jesus [Isa] (peace be upon him) son of Mary would descend and would lead them in prayer. When the enemy of Allah [Dajjal; Antichrist] would see him, it would (disappear) just as the salt dissolves itself in water and if he (Jesus) were not to confront them at all, even then it would dissolve completely, but Allah would kill them by his hand and he would show them their blood on his lance (the lance of Jesus Christ). [16]

For some time, ISIS has been goading worldwide military powers to bring vicious attacks against Dabiq, believing that the Muslims will win, and subsequently take the battles therefore outward to Rome. These provocations have been seen in a number of recent terrorist activities, and now they have raised the incitement even higher, baiting up to sixty countries across the globe.

Not long ago, a serious ISIS threat-video was released called *See You in Dabiq*, relating imagery of this upcoming war. Since the war has not yet happened, the media specialists in ISIS used some digitally altered stock footage as well as original footage from Iraq to make the film. At one point in the video, the ISIS flag is raised over sixty other nations' flags, representing its domination over opposition. Another scene shows an armored battle tank driving toward the Roman Coliseum, with the voiceover saying, "This is your last crusade, the next time it is us who will take the battle on your own land."[17] From *Heavy News*:

> In the video, tanks can be seen driving towards the Colosseum crumbled in the sand. Footage then cuts to outside buildings of the Italian capital, before zeroing in on the Vatican....
>
> The film's dialogue makes claims that the "Dabiq Army" will race into Rome, destroy crucifixes, and enslave Christian women.[18]

This video trails another, which was released last December (2015). Two ISIS radicals sit on a peaceful beach, facing the camera. One speaks in (somewhat broken) English, regarding the November 2015 ISIS terrorist attacks in Paris, France, and goes on to list other targets, including the US:

> It is a state [referring to the Islamic State]. When you violate its right, your hand is bound to get burned.... All you Crusaders, you claim to want to degrade and fight the Islamic State, while you fail to secure your nations and your capitols. How come shall you degrade us? You call your armies, like France called their armies in the streets of Paris, but rest assured, they will avail them nothing. We will come to them from where they do not expect.... The revenge has started, and the blood will flow. France was the beginning. Tomorrow will be Washington. It will be New York, and it will be Moscow. You Russians, don't you

think that we forgot you! Your time is coming! It is coming! And it will be the worst…. You will not have safety in the bedroom of your houses…. Allah! This event healed our hearts.[19]

The article, "ISIS Release Chilling New 'End of the World' Video Showing Final Battle with Crusaders," from *Mirror News,* has no problem linking all of their past violence to their latest unsettling "See You in Dabiq" bait, calling forth all powers of the world to challenge them on their own soil, and then taunts that nonbelievers will "burn on the hills of Dabiq."[20]

How the Vatican Is—and Will— Play Right into Isis' Hands

Over the last few years and on more than one occasion, Pope Francis, as well as top Vatican diplomats and spokespersons, have argued in favor of a coordinated international force to stop so-called Islamic State atrocities against Christians and other minorities throughout the Middle East. In 2015, this included Italian Archbishop Silvano Tomasi calling on the United Nations to "stop this kind of genocide…. Otherwise we'll be crying out in the future about why we didn't do something, why we allowed such a terrible tragedy to happen."[21] Pope Francis himself has tried to parse words between "stopping" ISIS and distancing himself from US-led bombing sorties; yet he, too, has used very specific language in recent days that has not gone unnoticed by these writers, hermeneutical efforts undoubtedly cultivated for theologians and knowledgeable persons to encourage them to see beneath his judiciously chosen phrases to his deeper, *sotto-voce* ("under-voice") communication, which clearly expresses his and Rome's intentions to sanction a coming war, using terms like "unjust aggressor," "genocide," and even the very idiom, "Just War,"[22] which are directly connected not only to specific activities of

ISIS, but are particular vocabulary extracted from "Just War theory" and "Just War doctrine" (the latter is derived from *Catholic Church 1992 Catechism*, paragraph 2309, which lists strict conditions for "legitimate defense by military force").

Both Just War traditions mentioned above (thoroughly examined by Cris Putnam in *The Final Roman Emperor, the Islamic Antichrist, and the Vatican's Last Crusade* as it involves definitions by theologians, policy makers, and military leaders) repeatedly employ the very terms "unjust aggressor" and "genocide" for the purposes of ratifying those doctrines whenever "war is morally justifiable through a series of criteria, all of which must be met for a war to be considered *just*. The criteria are split into two groups: 'the right to go to war' (*jus ad bellum*) and 'right conduct in war' (*jus in bello*). The first concerns the morality of going to war and the second moral conduct within war," which postulates that war, "while terrible, is not always the worst option. There may be responsibilities so important, atrocities that can be prevented or outcomes so undesirable they justify war."[23] The fact that Pope Francis and other high-ranking churchmen have explicitly used precise Just War terms is telling, and supports the PREDICTION made later in this chapter, as well as clarifies why Archbishop Tomasi, in his call to the UN for greater military action against ISIS, admitted his request for engagement was derived from "a doctrine that's been developed both in the United Nations and in the social teaching of the Catholic Church."[24] This is the dictum I (Tom Horn) believe certain power brokers at the Vatican (what Father Malachi Martin called the Masonic "Superforce") and the pontiff will knowingly use to eventually engage the self-proclaimed caliph of the ISIS regime, who wants nothing less than a final, end-times holy war leading to the arrival of the Islamic Mahdi (Messiah). Once the proper balls are rolling, both ISIS and the Vatican will see themselves in the midst of unfolding prophecy. For their part, all the Vatican needs at this moment are the right trigger events. This is where my prediction comes in.

I PREDICT—Weapon of
Mass Destruction and Prophetic War

Sometime over the next forty-eight months, the Islamic State and/or its associates are going to use a weapon of mass destruction (WMD). It will be of such scope and impact as to raise the international outcry sufficient for Rome to play its first card, which, as we noted above, has been primed by subtle references to Just War theory in the lead-up to this predicted event. When this WMD (electromagnetic pulse, biological weapon, chemical weapon, dirty radiological bomb, or nuke that causes widespread damage) is used by ISIS, the Roman pontiff will—in one way or another—call for the revitalization of the Christian rules for Just War. A coalition army similar to the 2003 invasion of Iraq will be formed to seriously engage the Islamic radicals. Geopolitics aside, the jihadis will see the Vatican's sanction of war as a new and final religious crusade—indeed, an actual fulfillment of their thirteen-hundred-year-old hadith, which allegedly quotes the sayings of the Prophet Mohammed concerning a last-days caliphate that goes up against "the army of Rome" to initiate *Malahim*—the equivalent to Armageddon in Christian teachings, a battle that ISIS believes they will ultimately win. This war will, according to ISIS, provoke the coming of Mahdi (their Messiah), the Al-Masih ad-Dajjal (Antichrist), and Isa (Jesus), who spears the Antichrist figure and fights on behalf of the Muslim army.

It is this author's (Tom Horn) belief that Pope Francis likewise will view himself—and Rome—as amidst unfolding prophecy, which the pope has alluded to on several occasions, including connecting ISIS terrorism with the end of the world.[25] Francis has even recommended that people read *Lord of the World*—a related 1907 book by Monsignor Robert Hugh Benson that depicts the reign of Antichrist and the Vatican's relationship to the end of the world, which both Francis and emeritus Pope Benedict have called prophetic. This is not surprising, as the reigning pope is an avowed prophecy believer and knows that he is

"Petrus Romanus," the final Pope (#112) from the famous Prophecy of the Popes attributed to Saint Malachy (that is, unless Francis was NOT canonically elected, which we will briefly mention later in this chapter, an intriguing possibility that presents additional strange and prophetic alternatives to the narrative). The best-selling work by Cris Putnam and myself titled *Petrus Romanus: The Final Pope Is Here* thoroughly and critically dissected this mystical prophecy and found widespread support for the document from Catholics and even evidence that, down through the years, cardinals elected popes who could somehow be viewed as fulfilling their line in this prophecy. As it involves Pope Francis, here is what the final line in the prophecy says:

> In the extreme persecution of the Holy Roman Church, there will sit Peter the Roman [Pope #112, Petrus Romanus], who will pasture his sheep in many tribulations, and when these things are finished, the city of seven hills will be destroyed, and the dreadful judge will judge his people. The End.

When elected Pope #112, Jesuit Jorge Mario Bergoglio (Pope Francis) immediately did several fascinating things to wrap himself in his "Peter the Roman" title.

First, he took as his namesake Saint Francis of Assisi, an Italian (Roman) friar whose original name was Giovanni, but that was later changed to Francesco di Pietro (Peter) di Bernardone—a man whose name can literally be translated "Peter the Roman" from the final line of the Prophecy of the Popes.

Second, Pope Francis knows that Francis of Assisi was a prophet and that he predicted this final pope would "be raised to the Pontificate, who, by his cunning, will endeavor to draw many into error and death…for in those days Jesus Christ will send them not a true Pastor, but a destroyer." It is astonishing that Francis would pick as a namesake a man who foretold this of the final pope.

Third, Pope Francis named Pietro Parolin as the Vatican's new secretary of state—a man who could sit on the throne of Peter if Pope Francis retires like Benedict did, dies, or is killed, and whose name can also be viewed as "Peter the Roman." If Francis was not canonically elected, Pietro Parolin would actually become the real Pope #112 under that scenario.

Then there are those famous last words from the Prophecy of the Popes itself: "When these things are finished, the city of seven hills will be destroyed, and the dreadful judge will judge his people." This idea, that the city of Rome will be destroyed during the reign of Pope #112 (and just ahead of the Second Coming of Jesus Christ as Judge), is a vision repeated in numerous ancient prophecies from Greek, Jewish, Catholic, and Muslim cultures. This includes what ISIS draws from their hadith—that they will go to war against the army of Rome and destroy the Vatican's headquarters. ISIS has even produced a movie that depicts this apocalyptic event culminating in the destruction of Rome.[26] In tandem with the prediction, they have threatened to kill Pope Francis,[27] and the pontiff has responded by saying he is willing to be assassinated if that is God's will; he just hopes it doesn't hurt.[28] As this narrative continues unfolding toward the conflict I am predicting, it becomes increasingly clear that both Pope Francis and ISIS believe they are engaged in an end-times scenario, making some of what Francis has said and done since his "election" clearer within a larger oracular context.

For example, in addition to what the ISIS hadith and the Prophecy of the Popes says about the destruction of Rome, shortly after he accepted the pontificate, Pope Francis consecrated the world to Our Lady of Fatima during Mass in Saint Peter's Square.[29] Francis knows the prophecies and controversies connected to Fatima, including the vision of the "Holy Father" (Pope) walking among a destroyed city (the Vatican) when ISIS-like fighters run in and kill him. Francis believes in this prophecy (obviously why he dedicated the world to precisely this Marian apparition), and ISIS vows to make it happen. In *Petrus Romanus,* we noted:

> The third part of the Secret of Fatima, which was supposedly released in total by the Vatican June 26, 2000, seems to echo the visions of Pius X. A section of the material reads:
>
> ...before reaching there the Holy Father passed through a big city half in ruins and half trembling with halting step, afflicted with pain and sorrow, he prayed for the souls of the corpses he met on his way...on his knees at the foot of the big Cross he was killed by a group of soldiers who fired bullets and arrows at him, and in the same way there died one after another the other Bishops, Priests, men and women Religious, and various lay people of different ranks and positions.[30]

It's interesting, given the prediction from Fatima, that Pope Francis has also reached out to Kabbalist rabbis, who in their Zohar (the most important work of Jewish Kabbalah, which was written in medieval Aramaic over seven hundred years ago) also foretell this destruction of Rome (Vaera section, volume 3, section 34) in connection with "Messiah's" secret arrival in the year 2013 (is this why top rabbis in Israel are saying Messiah's presentation to the world is imminent?) and, after this "Messiah" makes himself known to the international community, "the kings of the world will assemble in the great city of Rome, and the Holy One will shower on them fire and hail and meteoric stones until they are all destroyed."[31]

The deepness to which Pope Francis can be thought of as a mystic and believer in such prophecy involving the coming destruction of Rome may also be connected to his knowledge of the Cumaean Sibyl, whose prophecy about the return of the god Apollo (identified in the New Testament as the spirit that will inhabit Antichrist) is encoded on the Great Seal of the United States as well as in Catholic art, from altars to illustrated books and even her appearance upon the ceiling of the Sistine Chapel, where four other sibyls join her (Paul cast a demon out of one such prophetess in the New Testament) and the Old Testament prophets in places of sacred honor. Yet this Cumaean—who sits so prominently inside Catholicism's most celebrated chapel—gave forth other famous and forgotten prophecies, which we examine in *The Final Roman Emperor, the Islamic Antichrist, and the Vatican's Last Crusade* to show how she was quoted by early Church Fathers and actually connected the end-times Islamic Mahdi with a "Last Roman Emperor" (who arguably developed into the "Holy Pope" legend)—eschatological figures whose time, and whose catastrophic war, may now have arrived.

Will Pope Francis be the one to play the role of the last Roman emperor? Or will it be another pontiff? Was there something strange about the conclave from which Pope Francis emerged to the pontificate? Something mentioned earlier in this chapter that suggests he was not actually "canonically elected?" Even some Catholics think "illegitimate" activity may have gone on behind closed doors during the last conclave[32] and that, for reasons we do not yet understand, Francis was put in as a temporary "placeholder" until the real Pope #112 (Petrus Romanus) could be installed. This, too, might echo the choice of Saint Francis of Assisi as a namesake, as the ancient friar did predict, "a man, not canonically elected, will be raised to the pontificate." The mysterious reasons surrounding a "placeholder" pope—a false pope—is largely unknown to the public, but was foreseen by such mystics as Father Herman Bernard Kramer in his work, *The Book of Destiny*. During an unusual interpretation he made of the twelfth chapter of the book of Revelation concerning "the great wonder" mentioned in verse 1, Father Kramer wrote:

> The "sign" in heaven is that of a woman with child crying out in her travail and anguish of delivery. In that travail, she gives birth to some definite "person" who is to RULE the Church with a rod of iron (verse 5). It then points to a conflict waged within

the Church to elect one who was to "rule all nations" in the manner clearly stated. In accord with the text this is unmistakably a PAPAL ELECTION, for only Christ and his Vicar have the divine right to rule ALL NATIONS.... But at this time the great powers may take a menacing attitude to hinder the election of the logical and expected candidate by threats of a general apostasy, assassination or imprisonment of this candidate if elected.[33]

Although we disagree with Kramer's interpretation of the book of Revelation, his fear that "great powers may take a menacing attitude to hinder the election of the logical and expected candidate" echoes the sentiment of priests mentioned elsewhere in our book *Petrus Romanus*, who see a crisis for the Church coming, and the Final Roman Emperor (Antichrist) rising as a result. As we move through 2016, Pope Francis is publically looking for a global political authority (such as the UN) to come alongside him to implement his religious and social agenda, President Barack Obama has just set his eyes on becoming the UN Secretary General following the US presidential election,[34] and Israeli President Benjamin Netanyahu is very concerned about the ramifications of both. Will the Pope or ex-president step forward to fulfill the Cumaean Sibyl's prophecy...or are there others waiting in the wings? Either way, I predict that an ISIS WMD and a call by Rome to sanction war will soon result in both Muslims and Romans engaging in their own apocalyptica.

Oh...and one final thought to consider. Nearly a decade ago, a major Islamic website set the date on which this war and its Mahdi would unfold: "Based on our numerical analysis of the Quran and Hadith," they concluded, "the official beginning of the End of Time and the coming of the Imam Mahdi will most likely be in...2016."[35]

[2]

Islamic Antichrist
and Apollyon Rising

By Joel Richardson

Anyone who is a student of the end times is probably aware that the majority of prophecy teachers and books, as well as those infamous Christian end-time movies, tends to depict the Antichrist emerging as a young, suave, European politician. His religion is often portrayed as something that will bring all of the major religions together under one umbrella. Whatever it will be, it will be new: a religion that doesn't exist yet, at least not in any organized manner. Such portrayals have been repeated so many times that any suggestions to the contrary are often met with great suspicion or even resistance from certain Christians. So it should not have been a big surprise that, when I first published my book, *Islamic Antichrist,* in 2006, many Christians very strongly objected. I was arguing, after all, that the Antichrist would come out of the Middle East, and his religion would be Islam. Today, however, just a little more than a short decade later, many of those same people who attacked the idea have actually come to embrace and espouse it themselves. Among students and teachers of the end times, this view has actually become quite widely accepted. No doubt, world circumstances—the rise of global jihad and groups like ISIS—have contributed to this. But ultimately, for the Christian, understanding the future should not be primarily determined by present world circumstances, as these things can change overnight. Instead, our understanding of the future must be based on Bible—the Word of God.

The purpose of this chapter, therefore, is twofold. First, we will summarize just a few of the biblical arguments for the Islamic Antichrist theory. By no means is this short chapter a comprehensive discussion of the issue. If you are interested in a much more thorough presentation, I would encourage you to consider reading my book, *Mideast Beast*. The second purpose of this chapter is to discuss what series of events I increasingly suspect will come next on the prophetic timeline leading to the rise of the Islamic Antichrist. Let's begin with biblical basis for an Islamic Antichrist.

It's All about Israel

Anyone who wishes to properly understand the story of the Bible absolutely must grasp a very basic but profound point. Simply stated, geographically speaking, the story of the Bible is thoroughly centered on Israel and Jerusalem. The culmination of the story in particular revolves around this very specific piece of land and this very specific city. Jerusalem, after all, is the location where Jesus will return and reestablish the throne of David. It is from Mount Zion that Jesus will rule the nations. As difficult as it might be for some Americans to grasp, the United States is not the center of God's unfolding story. Throughout the Scriptures, the world outside of the Middle East and North Africa is most often referred to in such vague terms as "the coastlands," "far off," or even "the ends of the earth." Now, this isn't to say that those who live outside of the biblical world are less important in God's eyes. Of course not. But in terms of the prophetic story that is unfolding, it revolves around Israel. Any effort to understand the story of the end times must begin by grasping this simple reality. This is the context of the Bible.

The Surrounding Nations

Understanding this fact then, which nations do the Bible say will, in the last days, under the leadership of the Antichrist, attack and attempt to take control of Jerusalem? Repeatedly, throughout the Scriptures, it is "the surrounding" nations or peoples. Let's consider just a few examples.

Speaking of the armies of the Antichrist, the prophet Joel said:

> Hasten and come, all you surrounding nations, and gather yourselves there… for there I will sit to judge *all the surrounding nations.* (Joel 3:11–12, emphasis added)

Through the prophet Zechariah, the Lord said:

> I will gather all the nations against Jerusalem to battle…. Behold, I am about to make Jerusalem a cup of staggering to *all the surrounding peoples.*… On that day I will make the clans of Judah like a blazing pot in the midst of wood, like a flaming torch among sheaves. And they shall devour to the right and to the left *all the surrounding peoples.* (Zechariah 12:2, 6, 16, emphasis added)

Ezekiel also could not have been clearer, as he wrote of the day when the people of Israel will no longer be surrounded by people who despise them:

> And for the house of Israel there shall be no more a brier to prick or a thorn to hurt them among *all their neighbors* who have

treated them with contempt. Then they will know that I am the Lord GOD. (Ezekiel 28:23–24, emphasis added)

The phrase translated here as "all their neighbors" is the same word used in both Joel and Zechariah. It is the Hebrew word *cabiyb*, which refers to those nations that are around Israel: her neighbors. So let us now ask this simple question: Are Israel's neighbors the nations of Europe, or are they the nations of the Middle East and North Africa?

The Nations of the Antichrist

This simple, yet critical, point cannot be emphasized enough. Throughout the Scriptures, consistently, whenever the nations of the Antichrist are mentioned, they are *all* Middle Eastern and North African nations. Did you catch that? Every time the Bible mentions, lists, or names the nations, peoples, tribes, or groups that will attack Israel in the last days, they are always—down to the very last name—Muslim-majority nations. Conversely, there is not a single mention by name of a European or non-Muslim majority nation being judged in the Day of the Lord for attacking Israel. Now, that isn't to say that none will do so. What I am saying is that since the Bible overwhelmingly, repeatedly, and consistently names and emphasizes nations from the Middle East and North Africa, we should also emphasize those nations. And where the Bible is silent, we must be extremely careful not to add our own assumptions. When Bible teachers tell you that we should not look to the Middle East, or even consider this part of the world as potentially producing the Antichrist and his system, they are simply not being true to the Scriptures. We should emphasize that which the Bible emphasizes. We should focus on that which the Bible focuses on. I hope we are all in agreement on this point.

The Messiah Will Crush His Enemies

Now we will begin to get a bit more specific. We all know the story of the disobedience of Adam and Eve, of course. No sooner did the fall of mankind take place than the Lord began pointing to His solution. In the midst of the story of Adam and Eve and Satan the serpent, in one simple verse, God gave an overview of how He would eventually come to crush His adversary. Speaking directly to the serpent, the Lord said:

> I will put enmity between you and the woman, and between your offspring and her offspring; he shall bruise your head, and you shall bruise his heel. (Genesis 3:15)

According to this prophecy, through history, Satan's seed would be at war with *the* "Seed," which is the Messiah, and those who follow Him. In the end, however, Jesus the Messiah will crush Satan's head—as well as all of Satan's followers. God declared that Eve's "Seed," the Messiah, will make right all of the damage done on that very dark day in the Garden. It is appropriate, then, that this prophecy is sometimes referred to as "the mother prophecy."[36]

Picking up on the theme of the Messiah someday crushing Satan and his followers, in the book of Numbers, chapter 24, we find another critical prophecy about Jesus. This is the story of Balak, King of Moab, and the prophet Balaam. In this passage, Balak and Balaam are standing on a high overlook, gazing down over the Hebrews as they encamped in a vast valley below. The Exodus from Egypt had just occurred, and God's people were making their way into the Promised Land. Balak, however, was greatly disturbed by the fact that such a vast people group was encroaching upon the borders of his kingdom. Therefore, Balak had actually hired Balaam to pronounce a curse on the Hebrew people. But instead, as they stood there together, under the inspiration of the Holy

Spirit, Balaam began to utter a profound end-time prophecy. Looking down at the Hebrews, he declared to Balak:

> Come, I will let you know what this people will do to your people in the latter days. (Numbers 24:14)

This phrase, "latter days," in the Hebrew is *acharyith yawm*, literally meaning "the last days." Balaam then continued, making one of the most important messianic prophecies in the whole Torah:

> I see him, but not now; I behold him, but not near: a star shall come out of Jacob, and a scepter shall rise out of Israel; it shall crush the forehead of Moab and break down all the sons of Sheth. Edom shall be dispossessed; Seir also, his enemies, shall be dispossessed. (Numbers 24:17–19)

Balaam declared that in the end times, a king would arise out of Israel. From very early on, Jewish interpreters understood this passage to be a prophecy concerning the King Messiah. What does the passage say the Messiah will carry out when He returns? What did the Holy Spirit emphasize would be the primary accomplishment of the Messiah on that day? Expanding on "the mother prophecy" of Genesis 3, the Messiah is once again described as crushing the head of the seed, or followers, of Satan. This time, however, Satan's followers are actually named. The Messiah will come back and crush the heads of Moab, Edom, Seir, the sons of Sheth, and the Amalekites. Who do these names refer to? The Moabites and the Edomites were a people who lived to the east of modern-day Israel in what is today the nation of Jordan. Mount Seir was the most prominent mountain within the territory of Moab. Thus, the references to Moab, Edom, and Seir all point to the same general region. Likewise, the Amalekites were a people group that lived throughout the greater region to the east of Israel. All of these peoples, throughout biblical history, carried a deep hatred toward the Hebrew people. What about this term, the "sons of Sheth"? The ancient Jewish interpretation, as found in the Jerusalem Targum, translates it as "all the sons of the East."[37]

Now, the question must be asked: If we take this passage at face value, is it more reasonable and responsible to interpret these references to Edom, Moab, and the Amalekites as pointing us to the Middle East, or Germany, Italy, and England, as so many teachers of prophecy today would argue?

Crushing Moab into the Dung

A verse frequently read at funerals is Revelation 21:4, which reads:

> There will be no more death or mourning or crying or pain, for the old order of things has passed away.

Few are aware, however, that the book of Revelation actually borrowed this passage from the prophet Isaiah. In Isaiah 25, we are told that the Lord will not only wipe away tears and destroy death, but He will also remove the disgrace of His people Israel from the earth. But how does He do this? By destroying Israel's enemies. Let's look at the passage.

> He will swallow up death forever; and the Lord GOD will wipe away tears from all faces, and the reproach of his people he will take away from all the earth, for the LORD has spoken. It will be said on that day, "Behold, this is our God; we have waited for him, that he might save us. This is the LORD; we have waited for him; let us be glad and rejoice in his salvation." For the hand of the LORD will rest on this mountain [Zion], and Moab shall be trampled down in his place, as straw is trampled down in a dunghill. And he

will spread out his hands in the midst of it as a swimmer spreads his hands out to swim, but the LORD will lay low his pompous pride together with the skill of his hands. (Isaiah 25:8–11)

Now, obviously, God has not yet wiped away every tear, and death certainly still exists. This prophecy is clearly yet to be fulfilled. Like the passages we have already looked at, the context is the future, after the return of Jesus. Thus, once again, at the end of the age, the Lord says His hand of blessing and protection will rest on the head of Zion, His people, while His foot will crush the head of Moab, His enemy. In this passage, however, the Lord is crushing Moab's head face down into a pile of dung. Once more, we must take note that it is not a vague or universal enemy of God's people that is specified. As in Numbers 24, it is "Moab" whom Jesus the returning Messiah will judge.

So once again I ask, according to this passage, at the time of the Lord's return, are the primary recipients of His judgment described as those from Europe, or is the text once again pointing us to the anti-Semitic sons of the East? Again, common sense clearly tells us that it is the latter.

The Nations of the Antichrist in Ezekiel

In Ezekiel 25:12-17, another clear prophecy speaks of the Lord's divine judgment directed against Ammon, Moab, and Edom, because of how they treated "the house of Judah." Again, these three kingdoms inhabited what is modern-day Jordan. The prophet says that by executing undue "vengeance" against His chosen people, He Himself is "greatly offended." For this reason, the Lord will judge them with "wrathful rebukes."

But the text speaks of much more than just Ammon, Moab, and Edom. It also mentions Dedan, a city located in what is now central Saudi Arabia, known in modern times as *Al-'Ula*. The prophecy also goes on to mention the Philistines and the Cherethites, pointing to regions that are today associated with the Gaza strip. A few chapters later in Ezekiel 30, many other nations are specified as being marked for judgment at the Day of the Lord:

> The word of the LORD came to me: "Son of man, prophesy, and say, Thus says the Lord GOD: "Wail, 'Alas for the day!' For the day is near, the day of the LORD is near; it will be a day of clouds, a time of doom for the nations. A sword shall come upon Egypt, and anguish shall be in Cush, when the slain fall in Egypt, and her wealth is carried away, and her foundations are torn down. Cush, and Put, and Lud, and all Arabia, and Libya, and the people of the land that is in league, shall fall with them by the sword." (Ezekiel 30:1–5)

The ultimate context of the passage is the Day of the Lord and Christ's return. And here, as in so many other passages, the Messiah comes to execute judgment against the enemies of His people, Israel. Included in the list of those marked for judgment are Egypt, Cush (Sudan), Put, (North Africa), Lud (Turkey), Arabia, and Libya.

The Nations of the Antichrist in Zephaniah

Following in the footsteps of all the other prophets, Zephaniah prophesied that on "the day of the LORD's anger" (2:3, NKJV), Gaza, Ashkelon, Ashdod, Ekron, the Cherethites, Canaan, and the land of the Philistines will all be utterly ruined. Together, these names point us to the whole region around the Gaza Strip. But beyond judgment against Gaza, the prophecy continues with a warning concerning the future of Moab, Ammon, Cush (Sudan), as well as Assyria and Nineveh:

> "I have heard the taunts of Moab and the revilings of the Ammonites, how they have taunted my people and made boasts against

their territory. Therefore, as I live," declares the LORD of hosts, the God of Israel, "Moab shall become like Sodom, and the Ammonites like Gomorrah, a land possessed by nettles and salt pits, and a waste forever. The remnant of my people shall plunder them, and the survivors of my nation shall possess them.... You also, O Cushites [Sudan], shall be slain by my sword. And he will stretch out his hand against the north and destroy Assyria [Syria, Turkey, Lebanon, and Iraq], and he will make Nineveh a desolation, a dry waste like the desert." (Zephaniah 2:8–9, 12–13)

We've already discussed the location of most of these peoples, but during Zephaniah's day, Assyria straddled the borders of modern-day Turkey, Syria, Lebanon, and Iraq. The ancient city of Nineveh, now called Mosul, at least at the time of this writing, is in the hands of the Islamic State.

Of course, it all goes without saying that all of these nations and regions are dominated by Islam. So again, if the Lord repeatedly and consistently emphasizes Muslim majority nations as being singled out for judgment at the Day of the Lord, then why do so many resist the idea that the Antichrist will come from this part of the world?

Treading the Winepress of the Wrath of God Almighty

Finally, we come to the book of Revelation. It is here, in chapter 19, that we find arguably the most well-known passage concerning Christ's return in the entire Bible. In dramatic imagery, Jesus bursts forth from heaven with eyes of fire, riding upon a white horse with "the armies of heaven" following Him:

Then I saw heaven opened, and behold, a white horse! The one sitting on it is called Faithful and True, and in righteousness he judges and makes war. His eyes are like a flame of fire, and on his head are many diadems, and he has a name written that no one knows but himself. He is clothed in a robe dipped in blood, and the name by which he is called is The Word of God. And the armies of heaven, arrayed in fine linen, white and pure, were following him on white horses. From his mouth comes a sharp sword with which to strike down the nations, and he will rule them with a rod of iron. He will tread the winepress of the fury of the wrath of God the Almighty. On his robe and on his thigh he has a name written, King of kings and Lord of lords. (Revelation 19:11–16)

Most Christians are familiar with this passage. Yet few are aware whose blood is soaking Jesus' robes. Many think is Jesus' own blood, or the blood of the martyrs. But the real answer is found in Isaiah 63. Let's look at the passage:

Who is this who comes from Edom, in crimsoned garments from Bozrah, he who is splendid in his apparel, marching in the greatness of his strength? "It is I, speaking in righteousness, mighty to save." Why is your apparel red, and your garments like his who treads in the winepress? "I have trodden the winepress alone, and from the peoples no one was with me; I trod them in my anger and trampled them in my wrath; their lifeblood spattered on my garments, and stained all my apparel. For the day of vengeance was in my heart, and my year of redemption had come." (Isaiah 63:1–4)

In this dramatic passage, Isaiah the prophet is looking eastward from Jerusalem. He sees a majestic and determined figure—Jesus the Messiah—marching victoriously toward His throne in Jerusalem. Jesus is marching out from Bozrah, the capital city of ancient Edom. Today it is called Petra, in modern-day Jordan. Few are aware that this passage is where the concept of Jesus treading "the winepress of the fury of the wrath of God the

Almighty" comes from. For here, Isaiah informs us that Jesus, the victorious Warrior—the Lion of the tribe of Judah—will actually crush the enemies of God like grapes, soaking His robes with their blood.

Do you truly grasp what is being conveyed here? When Jesus returns, "the mother prophecy" of Genesis 3 will come full circle and find its ultimate fulfillment. Though Satan has struck the heels of God's people throughout history, when He returns, Jesus will not only crush Satan, but Satan's followers as well. He will tread the winepress of the wrath of God Almighty. This is a profound point. But we also must not miss the fact that it will specifically be in Edom where God's enemies will be crushed. Let me restate this: When Jesus returns, the Bible describes Him as destroying His enemies, specifically in what is today southern Jordan and northwest Saudi Arabia.

So, to summarize, as we have seen throughout the Bible, repeatedly and abundantly, whenever specific nations are named and highlighted for the judgment of God when Jesus returns, it is always regions or nations that are today vastly dominated by Islam. This is the part of the world the Bible is screaming at us to look to. It is no surprise, then, that today this part of the world is where hatred of the Jewish people and a lust to possess the Promised Land is absolutely thriving.

The Pillars of the European Antichrist Theory

Moving on, let us now consider a few other truly critical passages. If we search through the many works over the years that present a European Antichrist, we will find the same passages cited over and over again. These pillars upon which the entire theory is supported are the following:

1. Daniel 2: Nebuchadnezzar's dream of a giant metallic statue
2. Daniel 7: Daniel's vision of four beasts
3. Daniel 9:26: "The people of the prince to come"

Amazingly, although these three passages are looked to as the primary supporting pillars of the European Antichrist perspective, none of them actually offers any real support. In fact, any careful examination of these passages will lead us not to Europe at all, but rather to the Middle East. Let's take a look.

The Fourth Kingdom

Together, both Daniel 2 and Daniel 7 prophesy concerning the kingdom or empire that will eventually produce the Antichrist. This kingdom, referred to in both chapters as a "fourth kingdom," is never actually named. Most commentators, however, have assumed this fourth kingdom to be the historical Roman Empire, which will be revived in the last days. It is from this assumption that many have arrived at the idea that the Antichrist would come from Europe. We must note here that ever since the birth of the European Union, most of the prophecy-watching world has been looking exclusively to Europe. The idea, however, that the Roman Empire and Europe are synonymous is partially true at best. As any map will show, the Roman Empire included much of the Middle East and North Africa. Yet, for some reason, if one even suggests that the Antichrist will come from anywhere other than Europe, in some circles, this is viewed as being unorthodox. This can only be explained by the tendency of some Christians to become fantastic students of their teachers, but not such excellent students of the Scriptures.

So, do the prophecies of Daniel 2 and 7 really point to the Roman Empire, as is commonly assumed? As we will see, a more careful examination of the texts will reveal just the opposite. Let's look at the evidence.

Daniel 2 and 7

As the story of Daniel 2 begins, we find Nebuchadnezzar, the king of the Babylonian Empire, who, having dreamt a dream, is deeply disturbed by what he saw. In his dream, he was shown a towering statue divided into four (or arguably five) distinct sections. Each section was composed of a different metal or element. Determined to understand the dream's meaning, he consulted all of his wise men, priests, and astrologers, but none was able to offer him any understanding concerning the dream. Daniel, however, when called upon, was able to do what none of the other "wise men" could do. After Daniel sought the God of Israel in prayer, the Lord revealed Nebuchadnezzar's dream to Daniel. And so, standing before the king, Daniel described the statue that Nebuchadnezzar saw in his dream. Clearly, Daniel had the king's attention. Then he went on to explain what it meant. The first section, the head of gold, Daniel explained, represents Nebuchadnezzar's Babylonian kingdom (vv. 36–38). The sections of the statue that follow represent three other kingdoms that would succeed Babylon, each possessing its former dominion. The first two kingdoms are understood to be Medo-Persia and then Greece. In fact, both are later mentioned by name in Daniel (8:20–21; 10:20). Christian commentators agree that the fourth kingdom, represented by the legs of iron and feet of mixed iron and clay, represents the kingdom of the Antichrist. As we already mentioned, this fourth kingdom, however, is never actually named. Despite this fact, many Bibles, so confident of the Roman identity of this fourth kingdom, actually add the name "Rome" into the subheadings. Yet as surprising as this claim may be to many, the various criteria contained within the text, as well as the clear testimony of history, make it impossible to identify the fourth kingdom as the Roman Empire. Instead, as we will see, the Islamic caliphate, the only other possible candidate, meets all the scriptural criteria perfectly.

The Islamic caliphate is simply the historical Islamic government or empire, which began in AD 632, shortly after the death of Muhammad, the founder of Islam, and culminated in the Ottoman Empire, which officially came to an end in 1923.

The Rise of the Fourth Kingdom

The first problem with the Roman identification of the fourth kingdom is that the Roman Empire does not meet the requirements of Daniel 2:40. This verse, speaking of the nature of the rise of the fourth kingdom, says that when it arose, it would crush all three of the other kingdoms:

> And the fourth kingdom shall be as strong as iron…and like iron that crushes, that kingdom will break in pieces and crush all the others. (NKJV)

Later, in Daniel 7, speaking of this same fourth empire, we find an almost identical statement:

> [There] will be a fourth kingdom on the earth, which will be different from all the other kingdoms and will devour the whole earth and tread it down and crush it. (v. 23)

Again, to reiterate, the other three kingdoms that would be trampled and crushed were Babylon, Medo-Persia, and Greece. The text is clear that the fourth kingdom would "crush," trample, or conquer all three of these other empires. The three empires never existed at the same time, of course, and thus the crushing must simply refer to a conquering of their territories. The Roman Empire, however, only conquered roughly one-third of the regions controlled by these other three empires. Roughly two-thirds of the regions controlled by these empires was left entirely untouched by Rome. In fact, the Roman Empire never even reached the two Persian capital cities of Ecbatana and Persepolis.

Consider the following modern equivalence: If an invading nation conquered Boston, but never came close to reaching New York or Washington, DC, it would hardly be accurate to say that such a nation "crushed" all of the United States. Neither would it be correct to say that the Roman Empire crushed the all of the Babylonian, Medo-Persian, or Grecian empires. Yet the text is clear: to fulfill Daniel 2:40, an empire must crush all three of these. The Roman Empire simply does not fulfill this requirement. The historical Islamic caliphate fully, on the other hand, absolutely, completely conquered all their territories.

Borders, Language, Culture

What if we expand the definition of "crush" to include more than mere geography? Consider the description of the fourth kingdom as described in Daniel 7:

> It had great iron teeth; it devoured and broke in pieces and stamped what was left with its feet. (v. 7)

As we read this description, it certainly seems to be pointing to much more than merely gaining control over territories. I believe this description points us to the fourth kingdom actually devouring and crushing the actual culture, religion, and languages of those it conquers. With this expanded definition in mind, what happens when we compare the Roman Empire to the Islamic caliphate?

There is no question that the Roman military was a powerful fighting force. But when we consider the nature of the Roman Empire and the manner in which it exerted dominance over the people it conquered, once again, it is very difficult to make the Roman Empire fit the descriptions of the prophecy. The Roman Empire is actually quite well known for being a nation-building force of the ancient world. When the Roman

Empire conquered a people, rather than destroying the culture, abolishing its religion, and imposing a new language, it generally tolerated these things while adding law, building roads and infrastructure, and creating order. The famous Roman roads reached every corner of the Roman Empire. These were well-built, stone-covered roads laid on very solid foundations. Through the famous Roman roads, trade prospered, which in turn brought in more taxes. Eventually, every town and city of the empire was connected by an elaborate system of these roads. This led to the famous phrase, "all roads lead to Rome." Rome's law and the protection of its military also created a peace and stability that came to be famously known as the *Pax Romana*. Rather than being a crushing and devouring force, the Roman Empire was often quite the opposite to its conquered peoples. Even John Walvoord, the late former dean of Dallas Theological Seminary, recognized and wrestled with this problem, stating, "There is apparently little that is constructive of this empire in spite of Roman law and Roman roads and civilization."[38]

By ancient standards, the Romans were also often a tolerant empire compared to many other ancient empires. Under Roman authority, during Jesus' day, the Jewish Temple stood prominently in Jerusalem, and the Jews openly practiced their own religion. Roman law actually protected the Jews' right to do so. While there were certainly exceptions, such as under Emperor Caligula, throughout much of its reign, the Roman Empire was relatively forbearing. When we ponder the idea of the fourth kingdom being a culturally destructive entity, it becomes apparent that this serves as a problem when associating the Roman Empire with Daniel's fourth kingdom. Consider, for example, the relationship of the Roman Empire to Greek culture. Rather than crushing Greek culture, as the text demands, much of the Roman Empire was overwhelmed by Greek ways. Under Roman rule, during Jesus' day in the first century, Greek was the dominant language throughout much of the empire. With regard to religion, much of the Roman culture adopted the pagan Greek pantheon of gods. While the names were changed, the basic pantheon remained the same. Zeus became Jupiter, Artemis became Diana, and so on. In considering the Bible's description of this culturally destructive force, it would seem apparent that the Roman Empire was not the crushing power referenced in Daniel 2:40.

The Islamic Caliphate

On the other hand, the Islamic caliphate from its very inception was an Arab-Islamic-supremacist force that crushed and erased the cultures and religions of the peoples it conquered. This is due to the deeply totalitarian nature of Islam. Islam is the very epitome of a totalitarian ideology. Its name actually means "submission." Consider what life is like under the Taliban or Islamic State. Wherever Islam spread, it brought with it this oppressive ideology. Not only did Islam conquer all the territories of Babylon, Medo-Persia, and Greece, but it also imposed the Arabic language onto much of the peoples it conquered. Think about this. Today, in Jordan, Iraq, Syria, Lebanon, and throughout much of North Africa, the people speak Arabic. As an imperial force, Islam imposed Arab religion and culture onto all of its dominated peoples while erasing previous religions and cultures. An entire book could be written listing the endless examples of crushing and erasing the cultures it conquered. Today in the ancient heartland of the early Church, the Christian community is but a struggling minority, often fighting for its very survival. While the cities of Antioch, Alexandria, and Jerusalem were once the thriving missionary-sending capitals of the Church, today the indigenous Christian communities there are a shadow of what they once were. Since the establishment of the ISIS, hundreds of churches throughout the region have been destroyed. Where crosses once adorned the roofs of churches, the flag of ISIS now waves, declaring, "There is no god but Allah, and Muhammad is his messenger." Ancient shrines and museums have been blown up or smashed with sledge hammers. The same thing could be said of the effort of the Muslim waqf in Jerusalem as they have sought to deny and erase any historical Jewish connection or presence on the Temple Mount.

A list of such examples could literally fill volumes. Wherever Islam has spread, the conquered culture is gradually erased, the symbols and evidences of that former culture destroyed. The religion of the subjugated peoples is most particularly targeted. This is Islam's heritage, the perfect fulfillment of Daniel's predictions (cf. 2:40; 7:7, 19). While the Roman Empire has a very difficult time fitting into these descriptions, the Islamic caliphate fulfills the biblical descriptions to a T.

The "Mixed" Fourth Kingdom

Another interesting hint regarding the ethnic base of the final phase of the fourth kingdom is found in Daniel 2:43:

> As you saw iron mixed with ceramic clay, they will mingle with the seed of men; but they will not adhere to one another, just as iron does not mix with clay. (NKJV)

Three times, this verse uses the same word translated as "mixed," "mingle," and "mix." Few are aware that this is the Aramaic word `arab. In the ancient Middle East, the Arabs were viewed as the mixed desert peoples. In Hebrew, the word is `ereb and in Aramaic `arab. Because the descendants of Ishmael and Esau had so intermarried among the various desert pagan tribes, they had become known collectively as "the mixed ones." The first reference in the Bible to the "mixed ones" is found in the book of Nehemiah. After the Book of the Law had been rediscovered, all of Israel gathered together to hear the word read publicly:

> On that day they read from the Book of Moses in the hearing of the people, and in it was found written that no Ammonite or Moabite should ever come into the assembly of God.... So

it was, when they had heard the Law, that they separated all the mixed multitude [`ereb*] from Israel. (13:1–3)

After reading the Law, the Jews realized that it was forbidden for them to take wives from the mixed pagan peoples of the desert. Specifically mentioned are the Ammonites and the Moabites, who lived in what is today the Hashemite Kingdom of Jordan. Essentially, the verse is saying that when the people heard this law, they excluded from Israel all who were `ereb*. Again, in the ancient Near East, the words "mixed" and "Arab" were synonymous. The very name "Arab" in its etymological origins refers to the mixed people who lived primarily to the east of Israel. A literal translation of Daniel 2:43, then, is:

As you saw iron mixed with ceramic clay, they will be Arab; and will thus not remain united, just as iron does not mix with clay.

The riddle-like nature of this verse, pointing to the primary peoples from which the fourth empire would arise, is very reminiscent of another episode in Daniel 5, where Daniel interpreted the writing on the wall as pointing to the fall of the Babylonian Empire to the Medes and the Persians. Daniel read the word *peres*, which means "divided," and interpreted it as reference to the *paras*, or the Persians.

Crumbling Pillars

As we have seen, although Daniel 2 and 7 have been looked to as two of the most important pillars of the European Antichrist perspective, a more careful examination points us instead to the Middle East and the religion of Islam. This is where we begin to recognize that the case for a European or Roman is built on a truly weak foundation. But what about the final pillar of Daniel 9:26? Let's turn now to that passage.

The People of the Prince to Come

Over the past several years, as I have attempted to articulate and explain the scriptural basis for the Islamic Antichrist theory, I've had the opportunity to discuss these things with various internationally known prophecy teachers who espouse the European Antichrist theory. Universally, the passage that every teacher has cited as the basis for rejecting the Islamic Antichrist theory is Daniel 9:26, which speaks of "the people of the prince to come."

While varying interpretations have been offered as to the exact meaning of this verse, most hold that this prophecy is telling us that the specific people (or peoples) who destroyed Jerusalem and the Temple in AD 70 are the ancestors of the "people" who will comprise the primary followers of the Antichrist ("the prince to come"). According to this position, then, the verse should be understood as follows: "The people—that is, the primary followers—of the prince (the Antichrist) to come in the last days, shall destroy the city (Jerusalem) and the sanctuary (the Jewish temple of the first century)."

Despite the fact that this is only one verse, the weight it carries in the minds of many as proving a Roman Antichrist is profound. However, after having examined this passage inside and out for years, and after having consulted numerous commentaries and considered all options, I can say with confidence that the traditional European, or Roman-centric interpretation of Daniel 9:26 is in error. Please bear with me as I explain.

As I said, most believe the destruction of "the city and the sanctuary" to be a reference to the destruction that occurred in AD 70 when the Roman legions under General Titus destroyed both the Jewish capital city of Jerusalem and its Temple. Because the soldiers were Roman citizens, many conclude that the primary followers of the Antichrist in the last days will be Europeans in general or Italians specifically. The problem, however, is that the historical testimony and the consensus of modern scholarship tell us that very few of the soldiers who destroyed the Temple and Jerusalem in AD 70 were actually Italians or even Europeans. In fact, as we will see, the historical facts reveal a dramatically different picture.

A brief bit of history is in order. Before the Roman Empire became an empire, it was called the Roman Republic. In the early days of the Republic, as it was evolving into the Empire, the majority of the soldiers recruited to serve in the Roman legions were Italians from Rome and the outlying suburbs. However, as the Empire vastly expanded, it became next to impossible to man the entire Empire with soldiers only from Italy. There were just not enough Italian men to spread all over Europe, Northern Africa, and a large swath of the Middle East. Thus, at the beginning of the first century, Emperor Augustus made a series of sweeping reforms that led to significant changes in the ethnic makeup of the Roman armies. After Augustus's reforms in AD 15, the only portion of the Roman army that continued to consist largely of Italians was the Praetorian Guard, an elite military unit that protected the emperor. The remainder of the army was increasingly composed of "provincials," citizens who lived in the provinces—the outer fringes of the Empire, away from the capital of Rome. The "provincialization" of the army was true for all of the Roman legions of this time period, but it was most clearly and markedly the case for the eastern legions that were used to attack Jerusalem. Both ancient historical records and modern scholarship clearly confirm this.

Publius Cornelius Tacitus, a senator and Roman historian, in speaking of the armies that attacked Jerusalem, said this:

> Titus Caesar...found in Judaea three legions, the 5th, the 10th, and the 15th.... To these he added the 12th from Syria, and some men belonging to the 18th and 3rd, whom he had withdrawn from Alexandria. This force was accompanied...by a strong contingent of Arabs, who hated the Jews with the usual hatred of neighbors.[39]

We can gain several important bits of information from this reference. First, we learn that the Roman legions had been stationed in Judea, Syria, and Egypt. Second, we learn that beyond the Roman legions, "a strong contingent of Arabs, who hated the Jews," accompanied the soldiers. Needless to say, little has changed since the first century regarding the regional hatred of the Jewish people.

Later, Flavius Josephus, another irreplaceable historian from this period, confirmed Tacitus' report: "So Vespasian sent his son Titus [who], came by land into Syria, where he gathered together the Roman forces, with a considerable number of auxiliaries from the kings in that neighborhood."[40]

Once again, Josephus revealed that the Roman legions used to attack Jerusalem were stationed in Syria. With these, Titus recruited a "considerable number" of auxiliaries, or volunteers, from the "neighborhood." Elsewhere, Josephus even described a great number of Arab soldiers who joined forces with the invading armies: "Malchus also, the king of Arabia, sent a thousand horsemen, besides five thousand footmen."[41] Mind you, six thousand men is the size of an entire legion. Malchus, who was only one of three different Arab kings to have sent volunteers, sent enough soldiers to compose a full legion. As I detail in my book *Mideast Beast*, modern scholars of Roman history are in full agreement that the majority of the "Roman" soldiers were ethnically Syrians and Arabs. Again, these were not the ancestors of modern Europeans. Rather, they were the ancestors of the modern-day inhabitants of the Middle East.

Although we can certainly understand how a hasty reading of Daniel 9:26 would lead one to conclude that the Antichrist's followers would be Europeans, doing just a little bit more homework and examining the evidence reveals something quite different from what has been commonly and popularly believed.

Conclusion

Let us then recap. First, we discussed the Israel-centricity of the Bible. We zeroed in on the actual geographic context of the great end-times wars and showed that they all center on Jerusalem. Then we examined several passages that specifically refer to the invading armies of the Antichrist as "the surrounding nations," or "neighbors," of Israel. Then we explored the fact that through the prophets, the Bible repeatedly names the nations that will follow the Antichrist. They are all Middle Eastern and North African Islamic nations. Finally, we examined the three primary supporting pillars of the European Antichrist theory. And despite the fact that most throughout Church history have assumed the kingdom of the Antichrist to be a latter-day, or revived, Roman Empire, instead, we saw that a far more solid case is made for a revived Islamic caliphate. When we understand that not only the prophet Daniel, but also all of the other prophets were speaking of the Islamic caliphate and not the Roman Empire, then suddenly numerous tensions within the Bible disappear. All of the major prophecies of the Bible suddenly flow together seamlessly. When we insert the key of Islam into the often-puzzling world of biblical prophecy, everything comes into alignment and suddenly makes perfect sense.

So What Comes Next?

Having laid the framework for a coming Islamic Antichrist, let us now turn our attention to what I suspect may be next, and how the Islamic Antichrist will arise. The key to understanding this may very well be found in Daniel chapter 8. Speaking of this chapter, one nineteenth-century biblical exegete said, "The right interpretation of this depends the correct meaning of the whole book [of Daniel]."[42] As we will see, the geopolitical and theological information contained in this vision is deeply relevant for multiple nations at this present moment.

Daniel 8

Daniel chapter 8 contains Daniel's second vision, which occurred just a few years after his first vision of the four great beasts, as recorded in chapter 7. Like so many other biblical visions and revelations, the chapter is divided between the actual vision and the interpretation, as given here by the famed messenger angel, Gabriel.

As the vision begins, Daniel sees two animals. The first is a two-horned ram, and the second is a male goat with only one very large horn. Later, the two animals are said to represent two empires: Medo-Persia and Greece (Hebrew: *Yavan*).

The action begins as the two-horned ram (Medo-Persia) is seen butting to the west, north, and south, greatly expanding its regional power. No one is able to stop the ram, and he is entirely successful in his regional expansion. But then, the goat with a single large horn (*Yavan*) retaliates, lunging fiercely toward the ram, breaking off its two horns, and brutally trampling it to death. No sooner has the goat conquered the ram that its large singular horn is broken off and replaced by four smaller horns.

The majority opinion among Christian exegetes is that the vision has been fulfilled historically. They understand the exchange between the two-horned ram and the goat as pertaining to the historical conquest of the Middle East and into Europe by the Medo-Persian Empire (two-horned ram) and their subsequent defeat by the Greek Empire (goat) led by Alexander the Great (the prominent singular horn). The four horns that emerged after the prominent horn was broken are interpreted as the most prominent of Alexander's successors (Greek: *diadochi*). Most, then, see the little horn spoken of in verses 9–12 and 23–25 as representing the historical tyrant, Antiochus IV Epiphanes, the eighth king of the Seleucid dynasty. Many commentators see Antiochus as a type or shadow of the ultimate meaning, fulfillment, and emphasis of the prophecy, which is the Antichrist of the last days. We believe, and will seek to briefly demonstrate, that both the text and the historical evidence demand that the prophecy is speaking of the Antichrist.

As we have said, the implications of this prophecy for the Middle East in the days we are now living and in the days ahead are absolutely profound. But before we consider these implications, let's examine the actual text more carefully.

Daniel's Vision in Iran

Chapter 8 begins with Daniel explaining that it was two years after he had received his previous vision of four beasts (as recorded in chapter 7) that he was given this next revelation:

> In the third year of the reign of Belshazzar the king, a vision appeared to me, Daniel, subsequent to the one which appeared to me previously. (v.1)

In this new vision, Daniel finds himself in, or by, the palace of Susa (Hebrew: *Shushan*), in the province of Elam. This corresponds with southeast modern-day Iran, roughly 250 miles east of the ancient city of Babylon (modern: *Hillah*), where Daniel resided:

> I looked in the vision, and while I was looking I was in the citadel of Susa, which is in the province of Elam; and I looked in the vision and I myself was beside the Ulai Canal. (v. 2)

The Ram

As Daniel begins describing the vision, the first thing he sees is the two-horned ram as it is seen "butting" to the west, to the north, and to the south:

[B]ehold, a ram which had two horns was standing in front of the canal. Now the two horns were long, but one was longer than the other, with the longer one coming up last. I saw the ram butting westward, northward, and southward, and no other beasts could stand before him nor was there anyone to rescue from his power, but he did as he pleased and magnified himself. (vv. 3–4)

The ram would seem to be an appropriate symbol for the ancient Medo-Persian Empire and would likely have been understand as such by Daniel and his contemporaries. The *Bundahis*, an ancient Persian Zoro-astrian text, portrays Persia through the metaphorical form of a ram.[43] And according to Ammianus Marcellinus, the fourth-century Roman historian, instead of a crown, the kings of ancient Persia wore a golden headdress modeled after a ram's head.[44] Various Persian coins from this period also featured a ram's head.[45]

The Goat

Following the violent regional expansion of the two-horned ram, a new animal emerges onto the scene. Daniel tells us that from the east comes a unicorn goat, a male goat with a single, prominent horn, charging with great rage. In his wrath, the goat completely crushes the ram and its two horns:

While I was observing, behold, a male goat was coming from the west over the surface of the whole earth without touching the ground; and the goat had a conspicuous horn between his eyes. He came up to the ram that had the two horns, which I had seen standing in front of the canal, and rushed at him in his mighty wrath. I saw him come beside the ram, and he was enraged at him; and he struck the ram and shattered his two horns, and the ram had no strength to withstand him. So he hurled him to the ground and trampled on him, and there was none to rescue the ram from his power. (vv. 5–7)

As we've already stated, most Christian and Jewish commentators understand this portion of the vision to refer to the historical conquests of the Greek armies over the Medes and the Persians, led by Alexander the Great, who is represented by the single prominent horn. The symbolism here of a goat would also seem to be very appropriate, as the goat was widely used as a symbol for the Greek Empire. The first Greek colony was allegedly founded when a pagan oracle, which called for using a goat as a guide, led to the location to establish a city. This city, the first Greek city, was called Aegae—"goat-city." To this day, the waters around Greece are called the Aegean Sea—the "goat-sea."

Four Conspicuous Horns and the Small Horn

No sooner does the goat defeat the ram and exalt itself, however, that its prominent horn is "broken," After this, four other horns grow up in its place. One of these horns in particular starts small, but eventually becomes exceptionally powerful, controlling much of the Middle East:

Then the male goat magnified himself exceedingly. But as soon as he was mighty, the large horn was broken; and in its place there came up four conspicuous horns toward the four winds of heaven. Out of one of them came forth a rather small horn which grew exceedingly great toward the south, toward the east, and toward the Beautiful Land. (vv. 8–9)

Again, as we have said, most Christian commentators agree that the four horns refer to the successor kingdoms of Alexander the Great, which came to divide control of his former dominion, with the small horn referring to Antiochus IV Epiphanes, the eighth king of the Seleucid Dynasty.

Casting Down the Stars of Heaven (v. 10)

The view that interprets the vision as being fulfilled in history runs into its first major problem in verse 10. There it is revealed that this individual, the small horn, causes "the host of heaven…and some of the stars to fall to the earth, and it trampled them down." Commentators who seek to interpret the small horn as being fulfilled in Antiochus IV Epiphanes, rather than the Antichrist, are forced to claim that the stars and host of heaven are human religious or political leaders of Israel. While references to the more generic "host," which follow in verses 12 and 13, are indeed pointing to earthly leaders of Israel, the efforts and arguments of those commentators who seek to argue that the "host of heaven" and the "stars" in verse 10 are also earthly leaders, are strained at best.

Christian commentator H. C. Leupold argues this case by pointing to Genesis 15:5, in which God told Abraham that his descendants would become as numerous as the stars: "That stars should signify God's holy people is not strange when one considers as a background the words that were spoken to Abraham concerning the numerical increase of the people of God."[46] But in this passage, the Lord simply said that Abraham's descendants, like the stars (as well as the sand on the seashore), would become too vast to count. The people themselves, however, are never actually called stars. Others have offered a slightly better support by citing Daniel 12:3, where we are told that in the last days, "They that turn many to righteousness [shall shine] as the stars." Again, however, this passage is simply using an expression similar to the modern expression, which references someone famous (primarily in pop culture) as "a star." In both passages, humans are simply described as being "like" or "as" stars—either through being numerous, or wise and righteous. But never are they actually called stars, even in a symbolic manner. In truth, there is little to no scriptural support to interpret stars, or "the host of heaven," as referring to mere men.

On the contrary, Isaiah uses this precise term to make a clear contrast between heavenly (angelic) and earthly (human) rulers:

> On that day the LORD will punish the *host of heaven*, in heaven, and the *kings of the earth*, on the earth. (Isaiah 24:21, ESV, emphasis added)

There are, in fact, many very clear scriptural references where angelic beings are referred to as "stars" or "heavenly host." In Job chapter 38, the Lord refers to the angels as "the morning stars" (v. 7) who rejoiced when He created the cosmos. The prophet Isaiah refers to Satan both as one who is fallen from heaven and as "the morning star" (Isaiah 14:12). In Revelation 1:20, in Jesus' hand are "the seven stars," which are said to represent "the angels of the seven churches." Finally, and most importantly, in Revelation 12, we have a passage that clearly parallels Gabriel's comments concerning the small horn:

> Then another sign appeared in heaven: and behold, a great red dragon having seven heads and ten horns, and on his heads were seven diadems. And his tail swept away a third of the stars of heaven and threw them to the earth...the great dragon was thrown down, the serpent of old who is called the devil and Satan, who deceives the whole world; he was thrown down to the earth, and his angels were thrown down with him. (Revelation 12:3–4, 9)

In this passage, it is Satan, the dragon, rather than the small horn, who causes the stars to fall from heaven. The "stars" here refer to rebellious angels who, along with Satan, will be cast out of heaven (by Michael the angel) during the last three and one-half years before the return of Jesus the Messiah. The end-time context is seen in that, upon the expulsion, a loud voice from heaven will declare:

> Now the salvation, and the power, and the kingdom of our God and the authority of His Christ have come, for the accuser of our brethren has been thrown down.... Woe to the earth and the sea, because the devil has come down to you, having great wrath, knowing that he has only a short time. (vv. 10, 12)

So, in Daniel 8, we have a reference to the small horn causing some of the angels in heaven to be cast down to the earth. Later we will see that this takes place, according to the angel Gabriel, specifically in the last days. In Revelation 12, it is Satan who causes the angels to fall to the earth, also in the last days. The two passages are clearly related. As G. H. Lang concludes, "The expulsion will so enrage the Devil that he will precipitate the end of the age, and will bring up the beast (Antichrist) as his great agent. In Isa[iah] 14 and Ezek[iel] 28 the descriptions of the heavenly being seem to descend to merge into that of a human being."[47]

Antiochus IV Epiphanes never caused any rebellious angels to fall to the earth. If we simply accept the prophecy at face value, we must conclude that the small horn spoken of in Daniel 8 is none other than the Antichrist, a human indwelt by Satan, who is yet to fulfill this prophecy in the days ahead.

Gabriel Reveals the Timing of the Vision

> When I, Daniel, had seen the vision, I sought to understand it; and behold, standing before me was one who looked like a man.

And I heard the voice of a man between the banks of Ulai, and he called out and said, "Gabriel, give this man an understanding of the vision." (vv. 15–16)

Shocked and overwhelmed by the encounter, Daniel falls to the ground into a deep sleep. But before succumbing to the great sense of awe and fear, Gabriel makes a most critical statement. What was the sentence that Daniel heard just before he lost consciousness?

Son of man, understand that the vision pertains to the time of the end. (v. 17)

If one claims that the concluding portion of the vision is pointing only to Antiochus IV Epiphanes, then one must also take the absurd position of placing "the time of the end" two hundred years before Jesus. We conclude, then, that this prophecy must be regarded as a reference to the end times as regarded in the traditional sense. The Hebrew phrase (*èth kets*) is used later in both Daniel 11:40 and 12:4, where it is directly connected to both the final period of Tribulation and the resurrection of the dead, obviously, both of which are yet future. This then is the most critical and clear indicator as to the timing and ultimate meaning of the vision. Gabriel declared in unequivocal and clear terms that the vision concerns the end times and the time of the Antichrist.

Upon hearing Gabriel's declaration, Daniel fell into a "deep sleep" with his face to the ground. Undeterred, Gabriel picked Daniel up and immediately returned to his previous statement, declaring a second time:

Behold, I am going to let you know what will occur at the final period of the indignation, for it pertains to the appointed time of the end. (v. 19)

"The final period of indignation" is a very specific reference to what Jeremiah calls "Jacob's distress" (30:7), and what Jesus refers to as "the great tribulation" (Matthew 24:21). It is the time that immediately precedes the return of Jesus. Thus, in only two sentences, Gabriel states three times that the vision would be fulfilled in the last days. Further, in verse 23, Gabriel says that the vision would be fulfilled "in the latter period," and in verse 26, he tells Daniel, "But keep the vision secret, for it pertains to many days in the future." Altogether, Gabriel states five different times that the vision concerns the far-distant future, the time of the end, or the final period that immediately precedes the return of Jesus.

Gabriel Reveals the Meaning of the Vision

Gabriel then begins to explain the meaning of the two-horned ram and the shaggy goat:

> The ram which you saw with the two horns represents the kings of Media and Persia. The shaggy goat represents the kingdom of Greece [Hebrew: *Yavan*], and the large horn that is between his eyes is the first king. (vv. 20–21)

Gabriel states outright that the ram and goat point to a Medo-Persian military expansion, followed by the conquest of the region by Yavan. After this, we are told:

> The broken horn and the four horns that arose in its place represent four kingdoms which will arise from his nation, although not with his power. (v. 22)

Surveying a vast number of modern commentaries, a large number state rather matter-of-factly that after Alexander died, his kingdom was divided among four of his generals, known in Greek as the *diadochi*, or "successors." This then becomes the second disastrous problem for the historical interpretation. In truth, the historical record is in stark conflict with this claim and with the text. Most modern Christian commentaries, for example, seem to be in relative agreement concerning the four historical kingdoms the passage is allegedly referring to. John Walvoord, representing this modern consensus, states, "Practically all commentators, however, recognize the four horns as symbolic of the four kingdoms." He then lists Cassander, Lysimachus, Seleucus, and Ptolemy.[48] Yet Walvoord's claim that virtually all commentators recognize this position is simply not true. For at least the first five hundred years of the Church, commentators pointed to a different group of men as the alleged four horns.

In AD 305, Hippolytus points to Alexander's "four Chiefs...that is Seleucus, Demetrius, to Ptolemy and to Philip."[49] In 355, Ephrem the Syrian listed these same four.[50] About the same time, Eusebius listed Ptolemy, Philip, Seleucus, and Antigonus.[51] In AD 407, Jerome followed Eusebius' list exactly.[52] And in 430, Theodoret of Cyrus chose Ptolemy, Seleucus, Antigonus, and Antipater, while qualifying his list with the comment: "or, as some historians think, Philip, who is also called Arrhideus."[53]

Among these early Christian writers—Hippolytus, Ephrem, Eusebius, Jerome, and Theodoret—the only two names that all agree on are Ptolemy and Seleucus. This great variety of opinion among early commentators shows that the claim that the identification of the four horns is obvious or clear from history is simply not true. When one actually reviews the various wars and events that followed Alexander's death and the numerous rulers who arose in his place during that period, there were far more than four prominent leaders who arose in his place. Let's very briefly review the facts.

The Wars of the Diadochi

After Alexander's death in June of 323 BC, a dispute immediately arose among two of his generals as to who should be his successor. General

Meleager thought the successorship should go to Alexander's half-brother, Philip (also called Arrhidaeus). General Perdiccas argued that they should wait until Alexander's child was born. If it was a boy, then he would become successor. By way of compromise, the two generals agreed that Philip-Arrhidaeus would become king, and if Alexander had a son, then the child and Philip would share the throne. Until that time, both General Meleager and Perdiccas would share regency, or temporary rule, of the empire. No sooner was this arrangement agreed upon, however, than Perdiccas devised a plot and had Meleager and many of his supporters murdered. Peridiccas, now the sole regent of the empire, installed many of his supporters as provincial rulers or "satraps" over the empire. Initially there were twenty-four of these provincial rulers.

In 322 BC, only one year after Alexander's death, Perdiccas sought to marry Alexander's sister, Cleopatra. This led to four of the satraps—Antipater, Craterus, Antigonus, and Ptolemy—to form a rebellion against Perdiccas. Soon thereafter, Perdiccas was killed by his own generals, Peithon, Seleucus, and Antigenes. The vast empire once controlled by Alexander was now completely splintered, with no singular regent. It was every man—or satrap—for himself.

For the next fifty years, a series of wars raged among the many provincial rulers. Historians refer to these wars as the "Wars of the Diadochi." It was not until 301 BC, twenty-two years after Alexander's death, that one of the primary rulers, Antigonus, was killed, leaving Ptolemy, Lysimachus, Cassander, and Seleucus as the dominant rulers of Alexander's former dominion that many modern commentators identify to as the four horns.

The glaring problem, however, is that even at this time, only Ptolemy and Seleucus were truly dominant, possessing more than 85 percent of Alexander's former empire, with Lysimachus and Cassander, Demetrius, son of Antigonus, and a few other small rules controlling the remaining 15 percent.

By 286 BC, Cassander had died and his son Demetrius was defeated by Seleucus. And by 281 BC, Seleucus also defeated Lysimachus. Thus, within forty-two years after Alexander's death, only Ptolemy and Seleucus remained as the two dominant rulers of Alexander's former dominion.

So, rather than speaking of four horns arising after Alexander's death, a much more accurate description would be to say that, at first, there was one regent—a very large horn, under which were twenty-four much smaller horns. These horns all began waging war among themselves. Within several years, there were five larger, primary horns and several other smaller horns. By 301 BC, the twenty-second year after Alexander's death, there were two large horns, two much smaller horns, and four much smaller horns still. And then, by 281 BC, there were only two dominant horns and a few much smaller horns as well.

Further complicating the historical interpretation is the fact that by the time Antiochus Epiphanes emerged in 175 BC, there most certainly were no longer four dominant horns, but only two. By the time Antiochus emerged, two of the horns, Lysimachus and Cassander, had been defeated and subsumed by the Seleucid Dynasty. This point must be emphasized: The passage portrays the little horn emerging out of a period when four relatively equal horns share power.

If we are to be honest, any serious survey of the events that followed Alexander's death will reveal that history simply does not conform to this portion of Daniel's vision, as many commentators claim. We can only conclude that the events that unfolded after Alexander's death were but of a type, a shadow, of the actual and ultimate fulfillment of the vision— a fulfillment that is yet to come, *perhaps in the not-so-distant future.*

He Will Oppose the Prince of Princes

Another significant reason to see the small horn as the Antichrist is found in a statement in verse 25: "He will even oppose the Prince of princes." As H. A. Ironside states, "Prince of princes can be none other than the Messiah; consequently, these words were not fulfilled in the life and death of Antiochus."[54] This can only be speaking of the Antichrist, who despite his opposition to Jesus, as the verse goes on to state, will be "broken without human agency." This is no doubt a reference to the destruction of the Antichrist that will take place after Jesus returns.

The Implications for Our Day

As we have already said, the prophetic implications of Daniel 8 for our day are profound and must be considered by all who revere the Word of God. Let us then summarize the key implications:

First, a regional military coalition of Iran (Persia) and the Kurds (Medes) will break out into the greater Middle East. We should note that it is the common practice of the prophets, when speaking of latter-day events, to use the regional names of their day to point to the latter-day counterparts. The equivalent to the Medes and the Persians would thus most likely seem to be the Kurds and Iran forming a unified coalition. This military excursion to the West, North, and South will be entirely successful. No foreign military will be able to stop them:

I saw the ram butting westward, northward, and southward, and no other beasts could stand before him nor was there anyone to rescue from his power, but he did as he pleased and magnified himself. (v. 4)

The ram which you saw with the two horns represents the kings of Media and Persia. (v. 20)

After an undefined period of time, a military response comes from *Yavan*. While most modern English Bibles translate Yavan as Greece, this is not a technically accurate term. Ancient Yavan included both the islands on the European side of the Aegean Sea as well as western Asia

Minor, or modern-day Turkey. If he was pointing to modern-day Turkey, of the names available to Daniel, Yavan would have been the best name. Daniel is pointing to Turkey or a perhaps a coalition of nations from the west, allied with Turkey. Although outside the parameters of this chapter, this is substantiated by the prophet Ezekiel, who refers to the Antichrist (Gog) as a ruler from Magog (Asia Minor). This Turkish response is entirely successful and the Iranian-Kurdish alliance is defeated. This will result in a new regional power, likely some form of Neo-Ottoman political structure in the region:

> While I was observing, behold, a male goat was coming from the west over the surface of the whole earth without touching the ground; and the goat had a conspicuous horn between his eyes. He came up to the ram that had the two horns, which I had seen standing in front of the canal, and rushed at him in his mighty wrath. I saw him come beside the ram, and he was enraged at him; and he struck the ram and shattered his two horns, and the ram had no strength to withstand him. So he hurled him to the ground and trampled on him, and there was none to rescue the ram from his power. (vv. 5–7)

Seemingly, immediately after his great military success, the prominent leader of this Turkish military response will die. We are not told how this occurs. The newly established Turkish dominion will be broken up into four distinct political entities governed by four distinct leaders:

> Then the male goat magnified himself exceedingly. But as soon as he was mighty, the large horn was broken; and in its place there came up four conspicuous horns toward the four winds of heaven. (v. 8)

After an unspecified period of time, out of one of these four divisions, the Antichrist shall arise. He shall grow in power to the south, the east, and toward the "beautiful land." This, of course, refers to the land promised to Abraham:

> Out of one of them came forth a rather small horn which grew exceedingly great toward the south, toward the east, and toward the Beautiful Land. (v. 9)

Conclusion

To be clear, I do not write this as a prophet. But as I said earlier, I increasingly suspect that Daniel 8 may indeed be best understood as pertaining entirely to the last days, and more specifically the days that are just before us. Time will tell, of course, but let the watchful among us remain in prayer. The Day of the Lord is indeed drawing close.

> The end of all things is near; therefore, be of sound judgment and sober spirit for the purpose of prayer. Above all, keep fervent in your love for one another, because love covers a multitude of sins. (1 Peter 4:7–8)

3

The Man of Sin Arrives

By Mark Biltz

The world, spiraling out of the control of mankind, is on a trajectory that will only lead to its self-destruction. Terrorism and extremism, many believe, are at the root of all our problems. Humanity is desperately seeking someone with a strong hand to take the helm and bring in world peace. Where is the leader who has the ability to compromise and appease every faction to stop the madness? What character traits are needed for someone to have the ability to navigate the strong currents of public opinion that shape the world we live in?

It is said that the one thing we learn from history is that we never learn from history. In Ecclesiastes, we read, "That which has been is that which shall be" (1:9). Many are looking for a type of Solomon who is willing to get into bed with multiple nations by entering strategic covenants to bring peace—but it will only bring a false sense of stability and a tentative peace. Our problem is that we have lost our bearings, our North Star, by throwing out our navigation control manual called the Torah. The Torah is the inspired Word of God, and no one should have the audacity or arrogance to feel that he or she has the authority or ability to edit God's Word or declare it null and void.

The Man of Sin or Lawlessness is just that! Second Thessalonians 2:8–10 tells us that there is a wicked one who will be revealed, whom the Lord shall consume with the spirit of his mouth, and shall destroy with the brightness of his coming. This wicked one will have all power, signs, and lying wonders, and because people do not have a love for the truth, God will send a strong delusion so they would believe a lie. The definition of the word "wicked" is one without Torah, or God's Law.

If someone performs all kinds of miracles and wonders, how do we know if he or she is from God or not? Does the performance of miracles by someone also imply that we should obey what he or she says? In the book of Revelation, we read of three unclean spirits coming out of the mouth of a dragon, a beast, and a false prophet who work all kinds of miracles going to the kings of the earth (Revelation 16:13). So, what is the test for a true prophet, anyway? Many state that the litmus test is whether the prophet's words come to pass or not. But that isn't the entire truth.

Let's go to God's Word to read what the true litmus test is and find out why so many will be deceived!

In the book of Deuteronomy, we are warned about a prophet who performs all kinds of signs and wonders—even the things he speaks of actually come to pass (see Deuteronomy 13:1–5). This is a big test to see whether we will believe and do what God says, or if we will obey a false prophet. The true test is whether the prophet tells us to act contrary to what God has already told us. Will we go after other gods and serve them, or will we walk after the Lord God of Israel and obey His voice? The Scriptures go on to say that the miracle-working False Prophet—even if what he said actually came to pass—was to be killed if he tried to make others walk contrary to God's instructions in the Torah. Think about this for a moment: Do you believe the Torah is the Word of God? Do you really?

Was Jesus a miracle-working, sign-delivering Prophet from God? Did whatever He said actually come to pass? Of course! He was the consummate Prophet from God performing all kinds of signs and wonders. But why don't the Jews today believe? Because mainstream Christians teach that Jesus not only violated the Torah, but also that the Torah is now null and void! God Himself mandated the Jews to kill Jesus if He taught them to violate the Torah!

Our current generation is so filled with the deception of hyper grace that pours forth from the pulpits, television, and the Internet that the Lawless One will easily have free reign over the minds of those who do not know the truth. The Lawless One already has control over the vast majority of humanity, and now only needs to convince those who believe in the God of Israel by proclaiming that He is God manifest!

I ask believers the difference between Haman in the book of Esther and Antiochus Epiphanes in the story of Chanukah. Haman was known for his desire to kill all the Jewish people, regardless. It was a matter of *annihilation*. But Antiochus was different. For him, it was a matter of *assimilation*. Of course, if you didn't assimilate, you would be annihilated. But the focus was assimilation. It will be the same with the wicked one. You will be able to keep your Jesus; just accept a universal god as well as a matter of compromise and peace, so that no one will be offended. It will be a unifying god, much like Chrislam today offers. It is total absurdity for Christians to believe that Allah of Islam and the God of the Bible are the same. The Muslims don't even believe that! According to Islam, Allah has no son. How in the world is that compatible with Christian beliefs?

We read in Matthew 24 about the questions Jesus' disciples had concerning the signs of Messiah's coming, the end of the world, and when those events might happen. Many people today don't realize that, as Yeshua was explaining to the disciples what would transpire, all contextually were seeing Chanukah happening again! Many of the events mentioned in Matthew 24 had happened during the time of Chanukah around 160 years earlier. Yeshua was saying that which had happened before is that which will happen again!

We also see in the book of Revelation that there will be a standoff between the Antichrist with the False Prophet battling the two witnesses on God's behalf (see Revelation 3:3). The two witnesses will be acting in the power of Moses and Elijah in their ability to stop rain, turn water into blood, and bring about unimaginable plagues. Imagine having no rain for three and a half years! We read how the Beast makes war against the witnesses, overcomes them, and kills them. The world rejoices over the death of the two witnesses/prophets, because the world considers them evil, as they are the ones who tormented the earth by all their plagues. The beast is considered to be the one who saves the world from these evildoers!

Could the two witnesses from God, who preach judgment and a return to Torah, and who bring about all kinds of plagues, be seen as the Antichrist and False Prophet? After all, they are so judgmental and not "seeker-friendly" at all! No one would dare let them speak in their church! Most churches have everything so dumbed down that they are more like Lot in Sodom than Abraham on the mountaintop interceding. The Antichrist and False Prophet will be seen by many as the true two witnesses operating in the spirit of Moses and Elijah. After all, the False Prophet brings down fire from heaven just as Elijah did (see 1 Kings 18:38; 2 Kings 1:10; and Revelation 13:13, 14).

I don't believe the Antichrist or the False Prophet is going to wear a name tag. Satan manifests himself as an angel of light. He wants to come across as holy. What if the Antichrist and the False Prophet played themselves off as if they were Moses and Elijah, and said that the two witnesses were acting like the Antichrist and the False Prophet? Revelation 11 states that the two witnesses will be operating out of Jerusalem. What are they going to be preaching? What will be on their agenda? Repentance! The last words of the prophet Malachi reveal to us their true mission (Malachi 4:4–6), which begins with a charge to remember the Torah. Then we have the sending of Elijah, who is to turn the hearts of the fathers to the children and the hearts of the children back to their fathers.

So, let's see just how deceptive this strong delusion will be. We will have the two witnesses, who are Jews, in Jerusalem—dressed in Jewish clothing, bringing judgment on the world through plagues and fire proceeding out of their mouths, and preaching a return to the Torah. They will be branded as the haters. All the anti-Semites will be cursing them, the Church will be screaming "legalism," and the ACLU will be yelling for a separation of church and state. Then we will have the False Prophet and the Antichrist appearing as angels of light in their Slick Willy suits, preaching the seeker-friendly message of hyper grace, assimilation, Chrislam, and "Just give love a chance."

The Antichrist and False Prophet will let you keep your Jesus. But for the sake of peace, everyone will have to also believe in another god—much like in the book of Daniel, in which everyone had to bow the knee to the image or face death. The Jews could keep their God, but they also had to bow to an idol. The strong deception will be that you can keep your Jesus, but must also bow down to a universal idol. The greasy-grace message and a false image of a Greek-minded Jesus who is not judgmental will cause many to believe they can bow down to an idol and still be forgiven. Surely Jesus would understand! Without having a Torah base, many will be led astray, because they have rejected the truth. In the book of Romans, we read that the wrath of God is revealed from heaven against all those who hold the truth in unrighteousness (see Romans 1:18). How do you hold truth in unrighteousness? This refers to a situation in which God is trying to open the door of truth to someone, but he or she doesn't want to hear it. The person feels that once he knows the truth, he will be accountable—so he stops up his ears.

The Antichrist will come as a Solomon, full of wisdom and bringing in a false peace through compromise, the building of pagan altars, and the continual breaking of God's covenant just as Solomon did. Many are looking for a Solomon-type character who can bring in world peace, but they will find they have fallen for the Man of Sin. But how could that be, they ask, especially if the Torah is done away with and there is no more sin? How easy it will be to follow the Man of Sin when there's a belief that there is no such thing as sin anymore. It would be best if we would return to the faith of our fathers and take another look at what has been so that we will have a clearer understanding of what will be.

The generation of the Exodus saw more signs and wonders than any other previous generation, yet it is forever labeled as a generation of no faith. The generation that lived during the time of Messiah saw more miracles, signs, and wonders than any generation since, and yet they, too, are forever labeled as a generation of no faith. In the Gospels, Yeshua questions whether He will find faith on earth when He returns (see Luke 18:8). The generation that sees the return of the Messiah will again witness many miracles, signs, and wonders, yet we now realize that they never produce true faith. Miracles do not produce faith. *Faith produces miracles.* Amazingly, in these last days, too many people are chasing after miracles, signs, and wonders. They gullibly follow anyone or anything that seems supernatural—be it the Blessed Virgin in a grilled-cheese sandwich or false prophets wanting to control and manipulate everybody.

There are basically three monotheistic religions: Islam, Judaism, and Christianity. Islam and Judaism adherents do not cast out demons in Jesus' name. They do not prophesy or do many wonderful works in His name. These acts are only carried out within Christianity. Yet, read Jesus' own words from the book of Matthew:

> Many will say to me in that day, Lord, Lord, have we not prophesied in thy name? And in thy name have cast out devils? And in thy name done many wonderful works? And then will I profess unto them, I never knew you: depart from me, ye that work iniquity. (Matthew 7:22–23)

This is why so many will be deceived: They believe in a false gospel. They believe they are in a relationship with the Lord, and He doesn't even know them! It's only a one-way relationship. The Man of Sin is about to arrive, and we see the spirit of lawlessness and the spirit of anti-Semitism again reaching a fever pitch. We need to repent and return to the foundation of the Torah if we do not want to be deceived.

4

Wars and Rumors of Wars
The Brink of World War III

By Carl Gallups

I know not with what weapons World War III will be fought,
but World War IV will be fought with sticks and stones.
—ALBERT EINSTEIN[55]

T wenty-six-year-old Hiroki drew back the curtains of his bedroom window and looked at a cloudless August morning sky.
His wife, Yuri, lay asleep in their bed. She would soon rise and
prepare breakfast—the typical Monday morning ritual of the Tanaka
household.

Just down the hall, their two children had already begun to stir,
their awakened state telegraphed by occasional muffled giggles. Their
five-year-old daughter, Kana, and three-year-old son, Naoki, would
soon join them for breakfast and morning hugs. Naoki's fourth birthday
was on Friday of this week. The family had planned a big celebration.

As Hiroki stood in front of the window, still clad in his bedclothes,
he thought about the routine of getting dressed for the day's activities.
Just as he turned to go to his closet, he noticed a faint twinkle of light
in the trees. A light breeze stirred, offering welcomed refreshment to
the warming day. *Perfect!* A child-like smile appeared on his face as he
contemplated the joy of plinking around in his garden. The garden was

[77]

his little turf of paradise, one that his own hands had caused to spring forth with soul-satisfying beauty. *Nothing,* he thought to himself, *could be more rewarding.* He turned again from the window to go about the simple routine of dressing…and that's when it happened—at that precise moment. He would never forget it.

— —

The first memory he had of the moment was the blinding burst of bright light. Right behind that explosion, there was another quick flash.

Hiroki rushed to the bedroom window. He gazed in disbelief upon the *toro,* the large stone oil-lantern in his garden; it had exploded into a spontaneous fiery life!

His wife stirred behind him…and then screamed as the house groaned and violently rumbled. The earth quaked beneath them. The electric light bulbs brightened and then died; every bulb in the house shattered and spewed missile-like shards of glass. What was this? How is this possible? Less than ten seconds had ticked on the clock since the first flash.

There was another shriek from his wife—and, at the same time, a terrifying silence from his children down the hall. What was happening? What should he do? What could he do? There was no place to take shelter! Why would his legs not move?

Within seconds the morning had turned back into the deepest of night. Great clouds of black dust filled the sky, replacing all natural light. The morning praise of the birds was silenced. Only darkness was present—and the darkness was growing blacker. Nothing in the yard was visible any longer. *Had the world come to an end?*

From the instant the first light flashed, the house buckled, and the roof sagged inwards. An indescribably violent rush of wind descended upon them only seconds later. Walls collapsed. Water pipes burst, spewing their contents full-bore into what was left of the home. Electric wires dangled from the rubble and sizzled like venomous snakes. The piercing noises of shattering glass and demonic groans of metal-on-metal took the place of what was, just moments ago, morning serenity.

Their children came shrieking towards the bedroom. Hiroki still stood near the window; his limbs rigid with terror. His feet felt as though they were cemented in place, refusing to move at his brain's panicked command.

Before they could reach the protecting arms of their father, his children vanished into the rubble as the roof and walls caved in upon them. In front of his disbelieving eyes, their lives were snuffed out. Black heavy soot enveloped him—filling his lungs with its poison. As he gasped for a clean breath of fresh air, there was little to be had. His throat and chest burned with each breath. There was no more "inside" of the house. There was no more Tanaka home.

Hiroki spun towards his wife, but in the same instant, she, too, was gone as the rest of their home imploded with a deafening roar, greedily swallowing his wife, children, home, and memories; everything that was his life no longer existed.

Hiroki stood beside the portion of wall that once held his bedroom window. He had never left the spot; he had been unable to do so. The battered, partially existent structure was all that remained of their house. The wall had saved his life during the collapse.

The window through which he had been peering exploded into his face only seconds ago—but he was not aware of the matter. It all happened, every bit of it, in a haze. From the light-burst of the first blast until this moment, barely twenty seconds had passed.

Hiroki looked down at his body. He was covered in black soot, moist with blood. He reached for his face and pulled away bloodied hands. His left ear was missing. In its place was a gaping hole, an incessant ringing, and a growing fiery pain. His lower lip had been severed and hung from his face by a thread of bloody skin. A shard of glass was lodged in his right arm. A huge splinter of wood had embedded itself in his left calf. The hair on his head was gone. He no longer had eyebrows. His parched tongue clung to the roof of his mouth. He clutched both the sliver of glass and the chunk of wood and jerked them from their nesting places within his flesh. He felt no pain from this impulsive action—not *yet*.

Hiroki looked down again in shocked disbelief. He was naked! *When had he removed his clothing?* His nostrils were aflame with a nasty sulfuric odor. *Why is there the overwhelming stench of burning flesh in the air? Is my family really gone? Did they actually just perish before my eyes—in an instant?*

Loneliness enveloped him. He couldn't speak. No intelligible words came to his mind. He fell to his knees and began to sob—long, heaving sobs. But no tears fell. His body was devoid of moisture. Hiroki opened his mouth to scream, but he was incapable of making a sound. He *heard* his scream, but only in his mind. Haunting sounds of tormented human misery drew closer.

It was in that moment that Hiroki first saw them: the grayish ghosts emerged from the cloud of soot and ash that covered his home and enveloped his neighborhood. A line of the ghost-people, big ones and small ones, ambled along, not recognizable to Hiroki as anyone he knew, for they, too, were bleeding, and torn. They were hairless and burned, some of them with great strips of charred flesh dangling from their bodies. The little entourage of pitiful humanity was in shock—going nowhere in particular and seemingly unaware of or uncaring about their stark nudity as they ambled through his yard. In morbid fascination, he watched them disappear into the dark clouds from the hell that enveloped his world.

He could not know it at the time, but even more terror was still to come to Japan—just three days from now.[56]

Hiroki's Nightmare—Our Current Obsession

At 8:15 a.m. on August 6, 1945, a hellish fireball with a temperature of over ten thousand degrees Fahrenheit had formed the shape of a gigantic mushroom in the sky above Hiroshima, Japan. The fiery cloud rose to well over thirty thousand feet in height—taller than the highest mountains on earth. From a distance, the ominous site appeared as if it were a giant mountain all ablaze.[57] On the ground, the temperature at the hypocenter rose to fifty-four hundred—far hotter than the melting point of iron.

A United States B-29 Superfortress bomber, the Enola Gay, named after the pilot's mother, had dropped the world's first atomic bomb over Hiroshima. The bomb was nicknamed "Little Boy"; it took forty-three seconds to fall to the earth. On that forty-third second, the world was forever changed.

Three days later, the Bockscar, named after its commander Captain Frederick C. Bock, would drop another nuclear bomb upon Nagasaki. That bomb was nicknamed "Fat Man."

In both Hiroshima and Nagasaki, half of all those within three-quarters of a mile of Ground Zero died on the day of the explosion. More than 80 percent eventually died from wounds and/or radiation effects inflicted by the bombs. By the end of 1945, the atomic bombs had claimed the lives of 140,000 in Hiroshima and 70,000 in Nagasaki.

The main islands of Japan had been virtually untouched by the devastation of the vast war that engulfed large swaths of other parts of the world. The sanctity of that cherished Japanese security was first altered on the night of March 9, 1945, as the ferocity of the United States was unleashed on Tokyo in the beginning stages of retribution for Japan's earlier attack on Pearl Harbor.

The initial US attack began with a relentless firebombing mission, turning a fifteen-square-mile area of Tokyo into a blazing, hellish inferno. Witnesses described the area as containing streets that looked like "rivers of fire."

Everywhere one could see flaming pieces of furniture exploding in the heat, while the people themselves blazed like match sticks. Immense vortices rose in a number of places, swirling, flattening, sucking whole blocks of houses into their maelstrom of fire. 100,000 civilians died. More than one million homes were destroyed.[58]

However, just when Japan figured it could endure no more sorrow from the firebombing, only five months later, Little Boy and Fat Man were dropped on Hiroshima and Nagasaki. The nuclear age had begun.

The resulting desolation of the nuclear detonations over Japan was apocalyptic. The world quickly awakened to the newly revealed fact that a lone nation now possessed an almost supernatural power—unlike any the world had ever imagined. It appeared to the other nations of the world that a singular "kingdom," the United States of America, could now rule the world if it so desired…unless they, the less fortunate nations, could also get "the bomb."

What Japan and the rest of the world did not know at the time was that the United States was prepared to drop a third and even more powerful bomb than the first two if Tokyo had not surrendered unconditionally. If the third bomb still had not done the trick, the US was geared up to unleash a veritable nuclear holocaust upon the Asian island. They were ready to drop up to a dozen more.[59]

Seven decades have passed since those doleful days over the skies of Japan. As of today, nine nations together—the United States, Russia, the United Kingdom, France, China, India, Pakistan, Israel, and North Korea—possess approximately 16,300 nuclear weapons.[60]

At the height of the Cold War, the US and USSR jointly possessed more than twenty-one thousand nuclear warheads, enough to wipe out human civilization several times over.[61] Today, the United States and Russia account for 93 percent of all known operational nuclear weapons. It is rumored that other nations, including Iran, also have nuclear weapons or are garnering the technology to produce them.

Accordingly, much of the world waits in morbid anticipation of…
World War III.

Did Jesus Say Anything about a Possible WWIII?

Numerous prophecy watchers believe that our Lord was fairly clear that a world war atmosphere would be a defining characteristic of the very last days before His return. Most believe that Jesus laid out a descriptive understanding of the dynamics of those "times."

Of course, it is no secret to serious students of the Bible that Jesus spoke directly to His disciples' original question concerning the "signs" of the end times. They asked Him, "What will be the sign of your coming, and of the end of the world?" Based upon the context of their words, many scholars believe the disciples assumed Jesus' "coming" would be directly tied to the end of the age of man's rule and the beginning of the age of the rule of Christ.

Christians around the world still ask the question, and they continually search out the supposed mysteries associated with Jesus' answer. Let us examine the way in which Jesus began His reply on that day, as recorded in the book of Matthew:

> And ye shall hear of wars and rumors of wars: see that ye be not troubled: for all these things must come to pass, but the end is not yet. For nation shall rise against nation, and kingdom against kingdom: and there shall be famines, and pestilences, and earthquakes, in divers places.
>
> All these are the beginning of sorrows. Then shall they deliver you up to be afflicted, and shall kill you: and ye shall be hated of all nations for my name's sake. And then shall many

be offended, and shall betray one another, and shall hate one another. (Matthew 24:6–10)

As with most prophetic utterances, in both the Old and New Testaments, there are usually several veins of fulfillment associated with such a profound prophecy. That fact can be clearly observed, for example, in the prophecies of Psalm 22 and Isaiah 53. Both of these prophecies are comprised of elements that first speak to the day in which they were written, followed by the vivid foretelling of the passion of the coming Christ. Yet, in the very same prophecy, the words flow straight into the days of the Church Age and perhaps right up until the time of the end. They are "compound" prophecies. Many other biblical prophecies follow comparable patterns.

Similarly, some of the things Jesus spoke about in Matthew 24 actually came to pass before the close of the first century—specifically, Jesus' earlier prophecy concerning the destruction of the Temple.

However, it was *after* Jesus uttered the "destruction of the Temple" portion of the prophecy when the disciples asked the questions about the timing of *His return* and the *end of the world*. They most likely assumed the destruction of the Temple would accompany the "time of the end."

Jesus apparently did not address the specific timing of the destruction of the Temple. Perhaps He did not address this question at that time because the Temple would have still been standing in downtown Jerusalem when the vast majority of the New Testament documents would later be written. Accordingly, many Bible scholars believe that Jesus skipped right to the most prominent feature of the question, namely, "What are the signs of your coming, and the end of the world"?

Terrorism Will Be a Feature of the Last Days

Notice the emphasis Jesus placed on the turbulent, war-torn, terror-obsessed days of the end-times generation. Yes, you read that correctly—

"terror-obsessed." If we're not careful, it is possible to miss this striking emphasis by reading only the English translations.

The King James Version, for example, renders the interpretation in verse 6 as "be not *troubled.*" Yet the Greek word used in that verse for the English word "troubled" is Strong's #2360—*throeó*. The word *throeó* is used to speak of a case of *extreme anxiety.* It means to be "highly unsettled" and "wanting to scream." It is also interpreted in some texts to mean "to cry aloud because one is *terrified*—and ultimately thrown into an emotional uproar." In other words, *overcome with terror.*[62]

As a matter of fact, Jesus specifically emphasized the feature of the "terror" of the last days (perhaps related to global *terrorism* fears?) in His words recorded in Luke 21:26. In this passage, Jesus deals with the same discourse recorded in Matthew 24. Jesus proclaimed that men's hearts would fail them because of the "terror" (Greek: *phobos;* Strong's #5401) associated with those days. This Greek word is the one from which we derive our English word "phobia," defined as "an obsessive fear, dread, horror, and *terror.*"[63]

In addition, Jesus quite frequently references the "Tribulation" (Greek: *thlipsis*) of those same days. This word translates to "an overwhelming, inescapable pressure—or intense persecution." A number of biblical scholars also draw the parallel to this particular Greek word with that of "sheer terror" and/or the possibility of the prevailing atmosphere of "terrorism" being directly associated with the persecution that naturally follows such terrorism.

The totality of this understanding certainly sheds a brighter light on the emotional condition and the prevailing atmosphere of the "nations" during the times about which Jesus prophesied. Somehow the simplistic English words "be not troubled" take on a whole new meaning in light of the literal Greek interpretation.

We have discovered that the words of Jesus could then be, quite accurately, translated as something along the lines of, "Do not be overcome with anxiety and emotional upheaval. Do not scream out because of the *terror* (or terrorism) of those times." The element of the "terrorism" of the very last days, as defined by Jesus Himself, simply cannot be denied.

A Distinct Generation? A Specific Generation?

A closer look at this passage reveals still more tidbits of information that beg for serious consideration, and might point to a specific generation of fulfillment.

Jesus told His disciples that in the last days (just before His return), wars and the relentless pouring out of the threat of wars (such as the world had never before seen) would dramatically mark the time of the end. He also said this prophetic era would eventually result in nations and kingdoms being at war with one another—perhaps, by implication, at *one time*. Some also make the inference that the resulting cataclysmic strife would be one of a global scale—possibly a *world war*.

Those who object to this interpretation will usually cite the fact that Jesus made it clear that these "wars and rumors of wars" are "not the end," but rather "just the beginning." They would also argue that *wars and rumors of wars* have been a characteristic of practically every age of man's history since the time of Jesus—right up until the present.

While this may be so, let us not lose sight of the fact that in over six thousand years of recorded human history, there have been only two world wars, and both have occurred exclusively in our generation of history! We are the first generation to enter the literal time of "nations [many nations] *rising* [rearing up for war] against other nations" on a global scale. Clearly, we are history's only generation that could rightly be labeled as the generation of *world wars!*

The first of the world wars took place just a little over one hundred years ago, and the second one burst forth barely over seventy years ago. Both of those world wars have been copiously documented to be historically and politically linked to each other in myriad ways. World

War II literally grew out of World War I. So, if Jesus were speaking of a literal global war scenario (and it certainly is plausible that He was)—He would *have* to have been referencing *our* historical lifetime.

And if a Third World War does occur, numerous experts agree that it will most likely be linked to the Middle East and to the meteoric rise of Islamic terrorism, two undeniably prophetic factors of consideration that are hugely relevant to our time.

Still a Long Way Off?

There are further contextual contemplations we must observe in the matter of Jesus' words and their potential meanings. When Jesus said, "These things must come to pass, but the end is *not yet*," He was answering the question about *the specific time of the very end and His coming.* Accordingly, His words are in view of the context of the *very end.*

Jesus is not saying, "When you see these things happening, *don't worry*—everything is still a long way off." No! Rather, He is answering their question about the *very last days.*

Jesus, in effect, says to that last-days' generation: Understand that these things *must* come. They are *going* to happen. They have been decreed. But God is in control. God's people must not be terror stricken and anxiety ridden, for there is more to come. You will know that it has begun when the initial days of terror begin.

And, the very next proclamation that Jesus utters is that those days would eventually culminate in the ultimate and unprecedented "nations against nations" war, and that those times would also be accompanied by famines and pestilence in various places (the result of World War III?) as well as earthquakes.

Those who still object to this line of reasoning might then point to Jesus' very next words, "All these are the *beginning* of sorrows." They might argue that Jesus was simply saying these things would go on "as usual." They would claim that these things are just the beginning of a very long process. In light of these protestations, let us do another revealing word study.

The word translated by the King James Version as "sorrows" is the Greek word Strong's #5604: *odin* (pronounced o-deen'). According to the Greek lexicon, this word is used to speak of *birth pangs*…and specifically the time in which the pain is so great the mother knows the baby is *very near its arrival*.[64]

Now this certainly is a different take altogether than, "Jesus simply meant there was more to come." In fact, several of the modern translations actually use the more accurate translation "these are the beginnings of birth pangs" rather than the word "sorrows."

Are We That Generation?

So, if you want further confirmation concerning what Jesus *must* have meant by using the word *odin*, just ask any expectant mother what she thinks about all this! When the birth pangs (labor pains) begin, she knows it is the *end* of the nine months and the baby is signaling, "It's time!" And when the *severe* birth pangs (*odin*) ensue, it is the *very, very end;* the baby is almost here! There is not some additional and lengthy process yet to unfold, especially in light of the nine-month period that has already passed. The understanding of *odin* is no small matter in determining the most accurate interpretation of these prophetic utterances of our Lord.

Jesus said when you see "all these things" (wars and rumors of wars and the times when terror rules the day, eventually resulting in a "nations against nations" war), you know you are at the time of the *very, very end,* just before the return of the Lord! And, as we have seen, we are the first generation in two thousand years to see a literal fulfillment of these words in two world wars and a possible third one looming on the horizon. When the original languages of the Scripture are examined, Jesus' words could not be any clearer.

What about the Rapture?

Of course, the overwhelming majority of Christian scholars believe the Rapture of the Church is somewhere in the mix of all these end-time happenings. And, most assuredly, theologians of every ilk hold to their favorite interpretations of the Rapture. However, the topic of the specific *timing* of the Rapture (pre-Tribulation, mid-Tribulation, post-Tribulation, pre-wrath, etc.) is not within the concern of this chapter.

Some theologians point to a World War III scenario as occurring *after* the Rapture. Others claim it will happen *before* that event.

A large number of prophecy watchers claim that World War III will precede the Battle of Armageddon.[65] An equally fervent school of eschatological pondering insists that World War III and the Battle of Armageddon are the same event.[66]

> Since it was customary for the king to consult experts in matters of law and justice, he spoke with the wise men that understood the times. (Esther 1:13)

However, in this chapter, we are simply examining the biblical evidence that might point to the certainty of an end-time World War III development. In so doing, our purpose is to discern the "season" in which we are now living by observing the geopolitical occurrences of our day and how certain historical, as well as current, events might align with Bible prophecy. And, as we will soon discover, the marked anticipation of a potentially imminent World War III is an astoundingly prevalent "spirit" of our day—and not simply a concern that is expressed by prophecy watchers alone.

You Will Be "Afflicted"

The striking relevance of Jesus' last-days prophetic utterances in Matthew 24, in possible relation to our time in history, do not end with the study we have thus far completed. There are additional important considerations to examine within this text. Notice Jesus' next words concerning the times of the "nations and kingdoms rising against one another":

> Then [during the time of nations at war with nations] shall they deliver you up to be afflicted, and shall kill you: and ye shall be hated of all nations for my name's sake.
>
> And **then** [during the time of nations at war with nations] shall many be offended, and shall betray one another, and shall hate one another. (Matthew 24:9–10, emphasis added)

The English word "afflicted" is, once again, the Greek word *thlipsis*. You will remember that this Greek word speaks of intense persecution associated with terror. Jesus is saying, "You will be *terror-stricken* or *terrorized*" in those dreadful days.

The word used for "hate" in the Greek language speaks specifically of a hatred that leads to direct persecution. This word is Strong's #3404 (*miseo*).

Notice again Jesus' use of the words "all nations." This fact is significant. Jesus was speaking of a last-days lashing out towards anything "Christian" that would eventually encompass the entire last-days world (prophetically beginning with the Middle East)—*all nations.*

We can also take from this understanding that, quite naturally, there would be an associated hatred for all things "Jewish" or "Israeli," and that the nations of the world would turn against Israel and leave her to defend herself against the rise of the last-days' international (and even ecclesiastical) spirit of anti-Semitism.

Surely, Jesus would have known of a *returned Israel* in the last days when He uttered this prophecy. Surely He would have been aware of the intense hatred towards Jews, Israel, and born-again believers in Christ that would break out (particularly in the Middle East) in the last days. Unquestionably, Jesus would have known about the rise of ISIS and the wholesale slaughter of Christians and the extinction of entire Christian communities, villages, and cities during the same time that evil sights were focused on the destruction of a prophetically returned Israel... would He not?

Certainly, Jesus would have known of the days of terror and terrorism in which the world is currently immersed. Wouldn't He have known of the abject evil and barbaric butchery leveled upon His people by Islamic terrorism, starting in the Holy Lands? Yes, without doubt. He would have known *all* these things! Accordingly, a large number of Bible scholars believe we could be in at least the edges of the fulfillment of Jesus' words in this prophetic passage recorded in Matthew 24.

Many Will Be "Offended"

Jesus continued the prophecy by declaring (in the English translation), "And then shall many be *offended*, and shall *betray* one another." These words are also very telling, especially when the Greek language of the New Testament is examined.

The word rendered "offended" is Strong's #4624 (*skandalizo*). The term means "to be entrapped." It can also mean to be "set up" or "made to commit apostasy." Considering the demonic spirit of *political correctness* that is so insidious in today's American culture, and spreading throughout the world, we can see how Jesus' description of the *purposed entrapment* and *setting up* of Christians in the last days speaks directly to our current predicament. This phenomenon is becoming more pervasive as it applies to the radical homosexual movement and the legal redefining of a normal and natural marriage relationship.

Now, even in America, Christian business owners, government employees, elected officials, preachers, and churches are continually being *entrapped* and set up—many believe for the targeted purpose of undermining Christianity, God's Word, and the people of God specifically. And, probably without coincidence, the catchword of today's politically correct society is frequently heard uttered as, "I am *offended!*"

And You Will Be "Betrayed"

Jesus said that people "betraying" one another would also characterize those days. The specific word used in the text is *paradidomi* (Strong's #3860). The word means to be "delivered up to custody, and often with a sense of close personal involvement" (as the word is used in Matthew 10:21 and Matthew 26:15). In other words, in those days of which Jesus spoke—even friends, family, and close acquaintances—will be involved in turning each other over to the authorities in the name of enforcing the political correctness of the day. Does any of this sound familiar?

Paraphrasing What We Have Learned

Translating to a *dynamic equivalence* from Greek to English is often a difficult task, especially considering the continual word-meaning and word-usage changes within the English language alone.

However, it is sometimes a helpful exercise to take the verses upon which we have conducted a scholarly word study and restate them (or paraphrase them) in a more conversational manner. In so doing, we might come up with something like the following that Jesus *may have meant* in the Matthew 24 discourse:

In the time that is very near to my return, and the setting up of my earthly Kingdom, here is what will happen: The world will be in turmoil like never before. The nations around the globe will be distressed and continually speaking of, and engaging in, horrendous wars and acts of brutal terror. International wars will follow more international wars. The spirit of world war will hang heavy in the air around the planet.

Eventually, a final and devastating world war will mark those days; many nations and kingdoms will rise up against other nations and kingdoms. Famines, plagues, and pestilence will result. The earth will quake in expectation. It will then be very, very near to my return, as in the final hours of labor, just before the child is born.

In those same days, terrorism and treachery will be the order of the day. My people will be persecuted, imprisoned, and even executed—and some of this will be affected at the hands of friends and family. Some will turn from their claimed belief in God's Word. Others will be set-up, entrapped, falsely accused and betrayed.

Being called a "believer in Christ," or a Jew, or an Israeli, will mark you, the world over, as an object of hate.

Based upon the word-by-word study of Jesus' utterances in Matthew 24, it is quite possible that Jesus spoke something like this more collo-quial way of expressing the words in English. If so, perhaps the reader will observe that our historical generation could very well be the one of which Jesus spoke.

The "Technology" of Biblical Prophecies

Additionally, do not discount the important prophetic fact that our gen-eration is the only one since Jesus spoke those words to possess and to daily depend upon the communication, information, and transportation technology systems to make His words a literal possibility. For now—and only now—it is possible for *the entire world* to express "hatred" for a certain people group, or for the *entire world* to insist upon a particular "truth" of politically correct acceptability.

It is only our generation that has been able to instantly communicate, unhindered by language barriers (employing internet translation abilities), with nation-to-nation and person-to-person communications capability. The Tower of Babel has been reconstructed. The biblical reality of a literal one-world communication process is here.

The instantaneous exchanging of information and cultural ideas (both good and evil) are the norm. Even our children walk around with immediate connection to the entire globe at their disposal—they carry their global connection in their hands or in their back pockets.

In the Matthew 24 passage we have been examining, Jesus proclaimed that the gospel of the Kingdom would be preached in the whole world and "then the end would come" (Matthew 24:14). We are the first generation since He spoke those words not only to see the technology in place for the prophecy's fulfillment, but to actually see, and to participate in, the prophecy being rapidly fulfilled.

The technology to "mark" every human on the face of the earth with an identification system is a reality. This could be done with a literal marking process or the now relatively simple ability to biometrically identify and catalogue every human on the planet. The ability to track, spy upon, and even control entire people groups is already in our grasp and being used every moment of every day by certain factions and organizations.

In 2015, Pope Francis boldly called for a *global government system* to combat man-made global warming. For the first time in history, a world-renowned religious leader actually suggested that the world should usher in a one-world governance mechanism. And, for the first time in history, we have the technology and the politically correct global atmosphere to pull it off.[67]

All of this, and so much more, has converged into an everyday reality, and all of these things have come to pass in the last thirty years or less.

Also, when one considers the Middle-Eastern-centric interpretation of end-time prophecy (which is the contextual way to first approach biblical prophecy), the signs of our time become an even starker reality. According to the Word of God, everything began in that corner of the world, and the beginning of the *end* will originate there as well. Many believe we are now watching that commencement process unfold. Regardless of how one interprets Jesus' words in Matthew 24 and related passages, we are indeed a uniquely prophetic generation.[68]

The Widespread World War III Spirit of Our Time

In April 2015, WND ran a headline article titled, "Is World War III Coming Soon?"[69] The diverse list of the world's movers and shakers who assert that this war is on the near horizon, by actually using the words "World War III," is fascinating.

The article's quoted roll call includes: Pope Francis, former Congresswoman Michelle Bachman, former Soviet leader Mikhail Gorbachev, former Ukrainian ambassador Yuri Shcherbak, news mogul Glenn Beck, syndicated radio host Mark Levin, the king of Jordan, Brig. Gen. Masoud Jazayeri (Iran's deputy chief of staff), and various internationally known authors.

Since that time, many other influential people have joined the list and/or are reporting on the possibility that they, too, believe World War III may be just around the corner. That inventory includes various major global media sources, Jack Ma (founder and executive chairman of Alibaba Group), a variety of international financial experts, and Sirajul Haq (a renowned Pakistani Muslim cleric). A quick Internet search reveals that many other recognized people and entities are also expressing the same concern.

Even China has weighed in on the matter by threatening "World

War III is inevitable" if the United States doesn't capitulate to specific geopolitical demands.[70]

Billy Graham, Franklin Graham, and Anne Graham Lotz have each made public statements as to their belief that we are living in noticeably prophetic times. They all note the escalation of the spirit of global *war talk* and the need for Christians, even in America, to prepare for a possible coming period of intense persecution.

In September of 2015, China and Russia both appeared in Syria with naval ships, fighter jets, and other machines of war. ISIS is wreaking havoc in the Middle East, particularly along the Euphrates River area from Syria through Iraq, as well as directly threatening the United States and Israel. Consequently, an ever-growing number of media pundits are eyeing the situation as the groundwork for a potential World War III.[71]

The point is that those speaking of a possible looming World War III are not just prophecy buffs and doomsday preachers or loony conspiracy theorists. The whole world seems to be talking about, in one fashion or another, the possibility of an imminent global conflict. Is this not the last-days spirit of which Jesus was speaking in Matthew 24—based upon the word study we just observed?

Other Potential World War III Scriptural References

Consider the following truths: Israel is prophetically back in the land of the Middle East and is currently a formidable nuclear power and international player. Its presence has been a political bone of contention since inception. Jerusalem is now, also, prophetically, under the control of the returned Israel.

Israel is surrounded by enemies on every side. Several of those adversaries consistently call for Israel's total destruction. Many believe that even the United States is now pulling away from its once strong support of Israel.

In addition to these factors, we are witnessing the unprecedented rise of brutal Islamic terrorism in the Middle East and North Africa, with continual threats of its purposed spreading around the globe. ISIS has called for a holy jihad against Israel, as well as against the United States and its Western allies.

The FBI reports an ISIS presence in all fifty of the United States, at the same time that Islamic jihadists openly beckon for a World War III scenario especially targeted at Israel and the West. ISIS' warped theology *demands* the apocalyptic war. They believe that their *Mahdi* (Islamic savior and world ruler) will not come until the earth has been cleansed through a world war born of Islamic dreams of global dominance.

Moreover, Iran has made clear its intentions of, very soon, possessing nuclear weapons. On many occasions Iran has threatened to use nuclear weapons on the United States and Israel. In addition, Iran funds proxy terrorist groups like Hezbollah and Hamas for the specific purpose of engaging in targeted acts of terrorism. Iran and Russia are presently in close alliance, especially in the area of nuclear proliferation.

On top of these developments, we currently watch China's and Russia's growing aggression—especially against the Western powers, most of which are, or have been, allies of Israel. Numerous experts predict the possibility of global economic collapses on the horizon.

Additionally, the pope, at the same time he is calling for a *one-world government system*, is insisting on the official establishment of a legitimate state of Palestine. And the *wars and rumors of wars* spirit continues to ooze around the world—while worldwide anxiety increases.

All the while, much of the globe is hoping for a strong, world-impacting leader to arise to *save us all* from certain destruction. Thus, without realizing it, many are longing for the rise of the biblically prophesied Antichrist, who will promise just such a supernatural deliverance. He will effect a *covenant with many*, bringing peace to the world—but only temporarily.

Not surprisingly, each of the aforementioned elements, from the return of Israel to the rise of Antichrist, is mentioned (often quite directly) in the pages of biblical end-time prophecy. We are the first generation to see all these things converging, starting less than one hundred years ago. And the convergence continues to advance at a rapid pace.

Ezekiel 38–39

In light of the foregoing truths, let us consider the prophecies found in Ezekiel chapters 38 and 39. Again, some students of the Bible put these particular prophecies as occurring after the days of the Rapture and the Great Tribulation. Others see the events as unfolding before the days of Tribulation.

Regardless of eschatological preferences, it is in these chapters of Ezekiel where we discover that after a literal geographical and politically viable Israel is "resurrected" to a new life in the very last days, there would eventually arise a coalition of nations whose desired purpose will be to wipe the *returned Israel* from the face of the map. Nothing short of Israel's total annihilation will satisfy them.

The terms used to identify these coalition nations are found in Ezekiel 38. In the King James Version, they are listed as: Gog, Magog, Rosh, Meshech, Tubal, Persia, Ethiopia, Libya, Gomer, and Togarmah.

We, of course, immediately recognize the names of the modern nations of Libya and Ethiopia. The other names in the Ezekiel list are ancient tribal names originating from the Genesis chapter 10 table of nations. Scholars are not unified as to the exact identification of these tribal names as they correspond to the national designations of our day. However, most schools of interpretation agree that at least the following modern nations are represented in the Ezekiel 38 listing: Iran, Russia, Turkey, Libya, Ethiopia, Sudan, Syria, Lebanon, Jordan, and Iraq.

The point is that Ezekiel declares that these nations will form an alliance for the purpose of attacking the nation of Israel sometime in the last days. Strikingly, our historical generation is the first to witness Israel's return and the first to witness the coalition beginning to form right before our eyes.

Another prominent feature of the nations of Ezekiel 38 is that most are thoroughly Islamic. Although Russia is not an Islamic nation, it is in strong alliance with Iran and is currently building alliances with other Islamic nations in this list.

Islam would not be born until the AD 600s. So, when Ezekiel was given this end-times list of nations, he could not have known of Mohammed and Islam and the resulting vitriolic hatred of Israel and modern-day Western powers. Yet, Islam is now an authoritative, unifying, and spiritually motivated force in bringing together these nations for the expressed purpose of destroying Israel.

Additionally, we are currently witnessing the modern resurrection of the ancient Ottoman Empire. This portentous rebirth focuses upon the relatively recent re-Islamization of the nation now called Turkey. Turkey currently boasts a 99 percent Islamic population. To many students of the Word of God, this turn of events is seen as a certain, and ominous, predictive marker.

A Prophetic Focus on Turkey

A growing number of Bible experts agree that we must keep an eye on Turkey in order to fully understand what is happening with end-time prophecy fulfillment. Why would observing Turkey be such a vitally important consideration to biblical prophecy understanding? Reflect on the following:

- Noah's ark came to rest in the mountains of northern Turkey (Mount Ararat). Thus, it would have been from the area of modern Turkey where the earth was eventually repopulated and thus "reborn."

- The geographical locations of the seven churches, to which the seven letters of the book of Revelation were written, are all located in modern-day Turkey (Revelation 1:4).

- The book of Revelation states that the earthly seat, or throne, of Satan is located in modern-day Turkey, in the region of the ancient city of Pergamum (Revelation 2:12–13). Thus, it makes sense to many that the last-days outpouring of evil against Israel might emanate from the place biblically designated as Satan's earthly headquarters and domain.

- The Scriptures speak of Israel being attacked in the last days—from the "north." While many prophecy experts believe this to be a likely reference to Russia, others have noted that Turkey is due north of Israel and may be the more likely candidate from where an attack of that nature might emanate.

- The Euphrates River originates in the mountains of northern Turkey and runs through Syria and Iraq, eventually emptying into the Persian Gulf. The Euphrates River figures prominently into end-time Bible prophecy. As we will observe in a moment, the Euphrates is the featured landmark location of a possible World War III event foretold in the book of Revelation. Additionally, the vast majority of the current barbaric terrorism strongholds of ISIS are *currently* located along the Euphrates River.

- Some prophecy experts believe that Ezekiel's Gog and Magog references speak directly to Turkey and not to Russia. Simply put, this assertion is based upon the fact that the ancient Scythians (as the Greeks called the Magogites) were known to have originated in the area of modern-day Turkey. This would have been familiar information to Ezekiel. The Scythians did not move into the more recent Russian areas until hundreds of years after Ezekiel's time.[72]

- All of the seven "stan" countries of modern Asia (Afghanistan, Kazakhstan, Kyrgyzstan, Pakistan, Tajikistan, Turkmenistan, and Uzbekistan) originated from Turkey. This is also true of modern Russia.
- Islam, the driving force of the majority of the world's hatred for Israel and Christians, still looks to Turkey as the central leading caliphate of the Muslim world. Turkey was home to the fourth and last caliphate, which was abolished in 1924.[73]

Thus, keeping a careful eye on Turkey and its geopolitical and Islamic wrangling may very well serve as important signposts as to the prophetic times into which the world is currently moving.

Revelation 9 and Trumpet Six

Regardless of one's eschatological view regarding the placement of the trumpet prophecies of Revelation as being fulfilled *before* the Rapture or *after* the Rapture, there is little denying the fact that trumpet number six appears to point to a monumental world war event. Additionally, it can hardly be missed that the last-days' global war scenario of trumpet six plays out on the central stage of the heart of the Middle East…along the *Euphrates River.*

Again, we are struck by the Euphrates River region as being named as the scene for what certainly appears as a likely candidate for World War III. And once more, we observe that we are the first historical generation to perhaps see that specific war, in that precise location, formulating its beginnings—just as prophesied.

When we read the sixth trumpet prophecy, we are often overwhelmed by the vastness of the war its words predict. We are told that there will be two hundred million people fighting in that region. Over the centuries, there have been many speculations among Christian scholars as to how this unprecedented number of troops could actually appear for battle in that relatively small area of the world. Some have theorized that perhaps China would play a role in this war, since it might be the only nation capable of fielding such a vast army.

Yet, we now have a new factor of consideration. There are currently 1.6 billion Muslims living around the world—23 percent of the world's entire population. There are almost 320 million Muslims living in the Middle East and Northern Africa alone.[74] As we are now painfully aware, we know that even Muslim women and children will pick up an AK-47 or strap bombs to their bodies to fight in a holy jihad. So there could easily be two hundred million Muslims fighting in this war.

However, we know there will not be only Muslims involved. The war will most likely be levied against Israel. If this is so, then that war could involve many nations, including the United States, Great Britain, Russia, and even China. Given the current geopolitical climate and alignment of nations (including the presence of Russia and China in Syria), it is no longer inconceivable to imagine such a vast number of fighting forces in a world war that starts in the Middle East, along the Euphrates River.

Add to this mix the fact that the trumpet six prophecies speak of the obvious spiritual nature of this war. The prophecy speaks of four angels bound in that area, ready to be released for that day of war. Thus, it is easy see the Islamic/Jewish/Christian/demonic atmosphere upon which such a war might hinge.

It's in the "Little" Things

History has yet to give us a global war in one single, overnight, and monumental occurrence. Rather, there has always been a lengthy "build-up" process. Of course, the world has only experienced two world wars from which we can draw these conclusions, but they are, nonetheless, important considerations. It appears a similar pattern may be developing right under our collective noses.

How World Wars Begin

Do you know how many times we've come close to [WWIII] over a flock of geese on a computer screen?[75]

World War I did not begin with an overnight explosion of conflict. The war actually escalated over *four decades* out of a protracted series of conflicts in the Balkans. The international matters of heated discord were political, economic, military influenced, and territorial.

The conflict culminated in late July 1914 with the assassination of Archduke Franz Ferdinand and his wife Sophie. Gavrilo Princip, who was an ethnic Serb and Yogslav nationalist from the group Young Bosnia, carried out the assassination attack. This was the unforeseen spark that finally ignited the fire of the world's first global war.[76]

World War II, the deadliest and largest international conflict in history, was birthed out of a long process of "wars and rumors of wars" involving many nations and complex geopolitical issues. However, practically every historian agrees that World War II actually grew out of World War I. The end of the First World War and the beginning of the second were only about twenty-one years apart.

World War I had vastly altered the map of Europe, and proved to be devastating, especially to Germany. Under the Treaty of Versailles, Germany lost a sizable percentage (about 13 percent) of its home territory and forfeited all of its overseas colonies as well. German annexation of other territory was prohibited, massive reparations were forced upon them, and limits were placed on the size and capacity of the country's military forces.[77]

A charismatic revolutionary by the name of Adolf Hitler became the chancellor of Germany in 1933. He abolished Germany's democracy and demanded a radically and racially motivated *new world order*. Hitler instituted an immense campaign of Germany's rearmament. Leading political scientists of the day predicted that a second Great War was on the brink of commencement.

Through several more years of complex geopolitical maneuverings by a number of world powers of the day, as well as other *aspiring* world powers, Hitler invaded Poland, sparking the greatest world war humankind has ever known…to date.

And now, many historians, military analysts, major media outlets, and Bible scholars believe they see an analogous process in the works. They believe the world might be witnessing a similar buildup of the "little things" that could very well lead to a dreaded World War III scenario.

Will World War III Be Traced Back to Saddam Hussein?

We cannot have another world war. War is the wrong word. We should ban the term "World War III" and say instead apocalypse or holocaust.
—GOLO MANN, popular German-born historian,
   essayist and writer

A number of experts see the beginnings of a possible Third World War as having opened with the invasion of Kuwait by Saddam Hussein in August 1990. Detailed analytical reports have been published demonstrating how the first Gulf War had a direct causational connection to the rise of ISIS in the Middle East. Even *The New York Times* chronicled the theory in a comprehensive manner.[78]

Now, we are beginning to understand that if another world war were to develop in our time, it could certainly be linked to the political and military power struggle associated with the current Middle Eastern turmoil. Not surprisingly, this would bring us right back to the proposition that the Bible undoubtedly points to a world-war event in the Middle East in the very last days—situated upon the Euphrates River, the current stronghold of ISIS, and the laser focus of current world attention.

Ultimo Verbo

Here is the final word in the matter: It appears that it is not a matter of if—but of when—an end-time World War III will occur. It also appears that a geopolitical/prophetic scenario that could lead to such a conflict may be in the process of building in our lifetime. The Word of God admonishes God's people to pay attention, to be discerning of the times in which we are living, and to be ready.

However, as born-again believers, we should not be anxiety-ridden about this possibility; rather, we must trust in the Lord to fulfill His Word according to His intention and believe that He will preserve and/ or use us for His Kingdom purpose in the midst of His unfolding plan. This promise is found throughout the New Testament and brought to a glorious crescendo in 2 Peter 2:

> And [God] spared not the old world, but saved Noah the eighth person, a preacher of righteousness, bringing in the flood upon the world of the ungodly; And turning the cities of Sodom and Gomorrah into ashes condemned them with an overthrow, making them an example unto those that after should live ungodly; And delivered just Lot, vexed with the filthy conversation of the wicked:
>
> (For that righteous man dwelling among them, in seeing and hearing, vexed his righteous soul from day to day with their unlawful deeds;) The Lord knoweth how to deliver the godly out of temptations, and to reserve the unjust unto the day of judgment to be punished. (2 Peter 2:5–9)

Think of it! Peter uses Noah and Lot, and the wicked days in which they lived, as an example of the promise to God's people that the Lord would protect His ambassadors in those days just before the return of Christ! The point of Peter's writing is that both Noah and Lot (and their families) lived through some of the most wicked, turbulent, and terror-filled days recorded in the Bible. Yet, they were not only used of God and protected by God, but they also were delivered (raptured) before God poured out His wrath and destruction upon the wicked world.

And where did Peter get his understanding of the last days as they relate to the days of Noah and to the days of Lot? He got them directly from Jesus Himself:

> And as it was in the days of Noah, so shall it be also in the days of the Son of man. They did eat, they drank, they married wives, they were given in marriage, until the day that Noah entered into the ark, and the flood came, and destroyed them all.
>
> Likewise also as it was in the days of Lot; they did eat, they drank, they bought, they sold, they planted, they builded; But the same day that Lot went out of Sodom it rained fire and brimstone from heaven, and destroyed them all. **Even thus shall it be in the day when the Son of man is revealed.** (Luke 17:26–30, emphasis added)

Some of the more modern translations state the bold words above as: *It will be just like this.* In other words, Jesus told us, in very clear terminology, how it would *be* just before His return. He said, "Look at the days of Noah and Lot, and then you shall know how it will be in the end. I am giving the church a blueprint it can follow. You have not been left in the dark."

Certainly, we have *not* been left in the shadows of prophetic utterances concerning these matters. Surely, we are able to discern the times into which this world is headed.

> But of the times and the seasons, brethren, ye have no need that I write unto you. For yourselves know perfectly that the day of the Lord so cometh as a thief in the night. For when they shall say,

Peace and safety; then sudden destruction cometh upon them, as travail upon a woman with child; and they shall not escape.

But ye, brethren, are not in darkness, that day should overtake you as a thief. Ye are all the children of light, and the children of the day: we are not of the night, nor of darkness. Therefore let us not sleep, as do others; but let us watch and be sober. (1 Thessalonians 5:1–6)

No other generation in history comes close to the prophetic last-days implications of our day—especially those detailed insights given by Jesus Himself. Let us then live in the light of God's revealed Word to His Church.

It could very well be that we are the generation to see the coming of our Lord. Let us always be prepared. Let us have ample oil in our lamps. But most importantly, let us remember that we have been raised up…

"…for such a time as this."

5

Collapse of the Global Economy

By Josh Tolley

When we look to the economic future of the Western world or the future of any area of life (war, politics, new world order, etc.) we need to understand how predictions can be made.

I have been predicting future situations for years now, and I want to make one thing very clear: I am NOT a prophet, I do not "see" the future, and God is not "telling me of things to come." When I predict the future, I don't actually refer to it as "predicting," but, more accurately, I refer to it as "forecasting." Just like a weatherperson forecasts the weather climate with remarkably good accuracy, so, too, can we look at life on planet earth and forecast the economic, political, and social climate, and so on.

When I teach people to forecast, I tell them it is all based on dance steps. I have never been called a good dancer, but I do know the general idea: music is played, and that music denotes the speed at which the dance will take place. If the music speeds up, the dance speeds up. If the music slows down, so too does the dance. The world is dancing, and the music it is dancing to is the geopolitical rhythm of politics in the Westernized nations.

Once the music is identified and the speed of the dance is determined, the next step is figuring out the moves. The moves in world events are markers or major events that denote the next "step" in the world's path to the end of the dance. Just like a standard waltz where you might make a couple hundred steps based three moves, so, too, does God's dance plan for earth have a set number of steps carried out in predetermined (and somewhat predictable) moves. It is not that God is predictable as much as it is that the people living on God's planet are. If we identify where we are in the dance and the speed at which the music is being played, and we look at the dance steps that have already happened, it then becomes fairly easy to predict where the next step in a dance is going to happen.

Let me say it this way: If you and your spouse were dancing at a wedding, we could use the information of the dance as follows:

- Your previous move was husband's left leg straight forward towards the wife in a long stride, extending his back leg in a stretching motion.
- The wife has her right leg lifted as the husband steps forward, and as the husband completes his step forward, the wife completes her step over the husband's leg with her back arched.
- The husband's right hand is behind his wife's back, holding her up and providing her balance.

So what do we know?

We know that the dancers only have two arms and two feet. The husband has his right hand behind his wife's back, so we can rule out the next move being a move with that hand; otherwise, she would fall. We know that the husband's left leg is forward in a lung fashion, meaning that he cannot step forward with that leg—nor can he move it until he transitions weight to the back leg.

What can we predict then?

The husband's next move will be his right leg coming to a point equal to his center of balance, his right hand and leg will stay where they are, and his left hand will come down in motion or stay at the level that it currently is, because if it were to go higher, it would further place his wife off balance. This means that we know the next move (where his leg and hand are going). If we could hit the "pause" button and tell the room what would come next, we would appear as if we could tell the future.

Of course, we couldn't tell the future in some sort of magical or spiritual way, but it would be pretty cool nonetheless.

I give that rudimentary explanation just to clear up the perception that the reader may think I believe myself to have some special gifting. I do not; I just know the dance, hear the music, and can forecast the next move.

Looking at global issues, I first need to identify the body parts of the dancer, aka humanity.

- The Head—Knowledge
- The Heart—Justice & Social Equality
- The Gut—Health
- The Sexual Organs—Sexuality and Population Control
- Right Leg—Economy
- Left Leg—Property and Assets
- Left Hand—Food and Provision
- Right Hand—Force
- Mouth—Technology (as tech is the expression of knowledge)

As far as the speed of the dance, I have elected to break the prediction/forecast into three main sections: 1–4 years, 5–9 years, 10+ years.

1–4 years:

Politically speaking, at the time of this writing, the US will soon have a new president. Based on who the likely winner is looking to be, there will be a period of economic excitement returning to America. This will not be a long term or even substantial increase in people's personal income and disposable income, but it will be reflected in commercial construction increases, heavy equipment sales, and diversification of increased investments across a number of financial sectors.

Because the appearance of economic increase is only that, an appearance, there will be a continued growth in the wealth gap. As a matter of fact, in the next four years, I would say that the wealthy will see their wealth increase 7–12 percent while the purchase power of the rest of the people will continue to decline, gently at first. So gently in the beginning, in fact, there will be reports that the decline in the purchase power of the middle class will be said to be slowing, and there may even be reports that the declining take-home pay for the middle class is about to level off.

In addition, I predict that there will be a catastrophe (i.e., war, massive terrorist attack, natural disaster) that will cause the declining energy prices to go back up. What late 2015 witnessed with declining oil prices will be revealed as an OPEC effort to cripple US energy production.

If the US decides to separate from OPEC (which will largely be determined by Russia/China relationship in the Middle East), then the catastrophe will be one that pits the US against OPEC nations. If, however, the OPEC nations retain their relationship with US, EU and TPP partners, then the catastrophe will be heralded as a time for the world to unite and pull itself up from the bootstraps. Either way, energy prices will go up under the guise of emergency.

There will be continued increases in food costs, housing costs, and healthcare costs. This, of course, is due to the over-leveraged positions that dominate those three industries. Because of that, we will see continued increase in obesity, homelessness, multigenerational homes, and untreated chronic diseases.

This leads us to one of the top three sectors I suggest investing in: anti-aging.

I predict that there will be human trials starting on drugs and gene therapies that will extend life—not just drugs to treat conditions, but drugs and therapies that will be solely purposed to stopping and reversing the aging process. As such, this industry will be a hotbed for investing. As a matter of fact, the idea of longevity and immortality will be such a booming industry that it will make the invention of the Internet look like a tiny blip on the radar when the thirty-year initial run of investment into this industry is looked back on.

This booming industry will actually offset some of the economic decline…for some.

During this one-to-four-year period, we will also start to see mainstream exposure of artificial intelligence. Television, movies, and gaming will see pop-culture inclusion of artificial intelligence/robotics. What was theoretical in sci-fi in the 2000–2015 time span will start popping up in sitcoms, crime dramas, and morning shows. There will be growing excitement for all the cool "toys" that are coming to make life better.

"Better" will be the key word. But, better for whom? How will it be better?

The opposite of better will be experienced by most. We will start to see manufacturing change. No longer will large manufacturers in the US and Europe be supplementing with robots like they have been doing for decades while having cheap, mass-produced consumables (phones, cups, baseball gloves, etc.) made by cheaper manual labor in emerging markets. We will witness the decline of emerging markets in terms of those nations lifting up their middle class. We will see robots replacing even the cheapest of workers in places like China, Vietnam, and India. As the technology to replace those cheap workers with even cheaper automated systems becomes accessible, there will be a rapid increase of disproportional wealth in those countries.

This decline in wages earned in the countries where most of the world's products are made now will be a big story in the financial world, but only a minor blip on the attention span of most people in North

America and Europe. Instead of worry, there will be an excited expectation for the coming technology in the minds of those who are not realizing what will soon follow.

In addition to automation in the labor-intensive sectors like mining, manufacturing, and construction, there will be a growing replacement of service jobs. We are already seeing this with bank tellers becoming fewer and farther between and cashiers at a twenty- checkout-lane grocery store only staffing five lanes, with the rest being supplemented by self-checkout. This replacement of service jobs will, however, even become more prevalent. What many would consider middle-class service industry workers in the airline, rental car, fast-food, hotel, banking, and insurance industries, along with a number of other industries will have their jobs replaced. The pace at which this is happening, though, will not alert the masses. The mainstream media and the hundreds of millions who follow the mainstream will just think that there are less jobs to be had for some reason, not realizing that everywhere they turn, the average American will use two to three automated services every day, those services not being completed by what would have been humans only ten years prior.

We will see the return of foolish lending as well. Cars, houses, business, and education loans will be getting bigger in value and weaker in secured debt. The excuse will be that because interest rates finally went up (yeah, that will happen in this time period), lending is once again making sense.

However, with the "practical poverty level" still being in excess of $70,000, and the take-home pay of most households going down, the risky lending practices of the 2000s will be making a comeback.

On a positive note, I think that because of the college-loan bubble about to burst in this period, there will be a shift back towards a responsible look at college education. People will begin realizing that the money spent is not making up for money lost and certainly no longer guarantees money earned.

We will see an even more increased rate of global shifting of population. Immigration, migration, invasion, whatever people want to call it: The shifting of the population will only increase as the world's economic powers volley for population. All of Europe, North America, and Asia are trying to figure out a way to increase their working, aged populations as all of those areas continue to face population decline based on fertility rates.

Church foreclosures and debt will break new records, and tithing will break new lows as poor financial practices continue to infect houses of worship.

At the same time, we will see a rapid growth in the financial position of mosques around the Western world. Muslims will increase the number of small businesses they own, and banks will begin offering more Sharia-compliant financial products.

I see Turkey making a major play to increase its financial power during this time as well, whether that will be through energy distribution or, more likely, through the creation of an Arab economic exchange. While the Arab and Muslim nations in the Middle East region will experience a decline in the "build it and they will come" phenomenon that Dubai experienced in the late 1990s and early 2000s, and while the energy sector will be still strong yet not as bullet proof, I really see Turkey making a move to become an enterprise hub. New focus on regional stock exchange, lending, investing, and diversified civilian level financial products will be coming out of that nation.

The global entertainment space will continue to shift as well. By the end of this period, you are going to want to be invested not only in anti-aging and artificial intelligence, but also in virtual reality (VR).

Going from concept and geek toy to mainstream consumer product, VR is going to be the TV of the next generation. Movies, television, gaming, and even teleconferencing will be making major plays in the VR space during this time. An interesting aspect of this period, too, is that we will see the decline of Christian entrepreneurs, and while that may seem insignificant, I argue that this decline is the reason we will be suffering what will come in the future. Overall, this time will not be a massive economic crash, nor will it be a major economic boom, but it will be more of a repositioning of the chess pieces on the global financial game board.

5–9 Years

This is when things start to get interesting.

By this point, Iran will be a larger player in the international economic world. It would not surprise me if they want recognition with a global organization, perhaps a seat at the G20. With Mexico and Argentina feeling the crunch of TPP by this point, it would not be unrealistic to see them ask for a seat. They have the population and the GDP, and by this point, they will have had years free from the financial restrictions lifted from them in their 2015 agreement with Western powers.

Speaking of TPP, this nasty nation killer of an economic agreement will really start getting ugly at this point. The bottom third of participating nations will start to see an increasingly declining per-capita income amongst their citizens, and the top two-thirds will start negotiating for power…and not just economic power. It will be inevitable that legal cases, magistrates, and court rules will start being affected by TPP, and there will be a loss of sovereignty for every nation involved. There may even be discussion of setting up an EU-style government body to manage the changing legal landscape that TPP and its sister agreements begin implementing. The devastating aspect of this is how large companies will use this legal system to trump civilian populations and interests in pursuit of eased access to resources and/or funneling of funds to avoid financial losses.

The formation of TPP to the exclusion of countries like Russia, China, and Iran will lead to the financial world splitting in two.

Russia and China both have shrinking populations but massive amounts of untapped resources empowering them to form their own monetary exchange, getting off the dollar as a trading currency. The excuse of not being involved in TPP will be seen as valid to their internal financial experts, and the then-escalating decline of North Korea will lead to an economic inclusion of that rogue nation as well.

From the artificial intelligence standpoint, things will really be heating up. We will start seeing massive layoffs around the world and in every sector: white collar, blue collar, and service. The experts will try to reassure the growing number of unemployed that this change in technology will lead to more opportunities in new industries. There will be an emphasis on "job training," but this will largely fail to produce any lasting improvements. The reason is simple. For the first time in human history, an advancement in technology will not lead to offsetting opportunities. In other words, traditionally, when humanity moved from one system to the next, the new system provided a new set of careers. For example, when the horse-and-buggy days were over, the blacksmith went out of business, but he then became an automobile mechanic, so the loss was equally replaced.

However, this will not be the case in the future. With a dozen people being replaced by one machine in ALL employment sectors, individuals will not be able to recover by changing career fields. Some might point out that the machines will need to be built, programmed, maintained, and repaired. Wouldn't this create more jobs? The answer is no, it won't. We will have automated systems that will build their own replacements, program their own creations needed for expansion, and teach themselves the necessary skills. Gone will be the days of machines doing only what they are programmed to do. Instead, we will be giving machines tasks to accomplish, and they will determine what they need to know in order to do that. Even in the case of repairing machines, one human can oversee dozens, if not hundreds, of machines.

This may seem like science-fiction mumbo-jumbo, but we need

look no further than trash collecting to prove this point. Years ago, when trash was collected, trucks were driven by a driver. Two additional workers would be riding on the back of the truck. When the truck stopped to pick up the trash, the two in the back would jump off, grab the trash cans, empty them into the back of the truck, process the newly deposited refuse into the holding compartment, replace the trash cans at the curb, and then move on to the next home. That whole process was replaced in the 1990s when the trucks were outfitted with robotic arms that could grab a trash can, empty its contents into the truck, and replace it on the curb in a matter of seconds. Almost overnight, two-thirds of all sanitation workers lost their jobs, and that new technology didn't create any new jobs to fill the void.

By the time we get to this period, this type of job-loss problem will hit record levels. Millions of people will replaced by automated systems. We will reach a tipping point during this time because of it; more households will be getting government assistance than those not receiving any.

I project that one-third or more of all jobs around the world will be lost to automation. There will be a new revelation at this time that many overlooked in the lead-up to an automated world: Automated workers may be cheaper, and they may work 24/7 without taking a break, but they do not pay taxes, nor do they earn a wage.

Initially, this will be seen as a good thing for businesses and a bad thing for governments. The businesses will be profitable; the governments will be losing revenue, so the governments will create new tax laws to tax automated systems somehow or increase corporate tax in other ways to offset the loss.

In the beginning, the companies will complain about the tax, but will be able to afford it because of the increased profitability the automated systems bring into play. However, because the automated systems do not earn a wage and the majority of humans on the planet will be seeing their income go down, sales will begin to decline across the board.

We will also continue to experience a hardening of the hearts of people.

When we look back at the Great Depression, people cared about one another. Families pooled their resources, shared meals, and helped raise one another's kids while what work was available was being done. In today's world, people care less. We do not know our neighbors and we do not stay connected with our families. For goodness sake, even high schools are canceling dances and sports teams because people just don't care anymore.

In 2015, we live in a world that has seen someone die in line at a McDonald's. Instead of trying to save the victim's life, other customers actually stepped over the man's dying body to get their burgers. In another instance, a mother crashed her car into a tree. Citizens ran to the scene—but not to help save her live and the lives of her children. Rather, they wanted to steal what she had in the vehicle.

If events like that are happening now, what will life be like in 2022? There will be less interaction and less use of public common areas like parks and such. While a reader may wonder what that has to do with economics, the reality is it has everything to do with economics. At the end of the day, economics is monetary interaction between humans. Even with Internet sales dipping due to falling incomes, the interactions made will also decline.

In the past, a decrease in monetary holdings didn't always equate to a decrease in economic involvement. For example, during the Great Depression, many families didn't have dollars, but they did have services to trade for gain. In the future, we will see less of that activity, as we will become more of a cocooned society.

During this time, we will see a couple of bubbles popping as well. The existing housing sales will decline, subprime mortgages will explode, college debt will explode, and new housing starts will only be kept alive by government-led financial incentives. Nations will also begin blowing hot air into new economic bubbles like new housing starts, first-time construction loans, and in-state college loans.

We have seen subsidizing in areas of life before, and it has typically destroyed those industries for generations. For example, farming had become a subsidized industry, initially to support an industry that employed a large portion of the nation's population. But because subsidizing is just another form of creating a bubble, we also witnessed the destruction of the family farm.

Nations will really start experiencing the results of their declining working-age populations at this point. Because of that, we will probably see China become more militarily aggressive, and Russia will probably go through its own version of financial restructuring. Europe will be largely using Muslim workers to fill what positions are left. And in the Americas, we will be seeing more people doing odd jobs just to make ends meet, with fewer people being able to retire.

Gold and silver at this point will have some value left, but will start to become harder for average people to acquire through international regulations on precious metals. Alternative currencies will be more popular than ever, as the people scramble for a financial lifeboat in a hurricane of international monetary manipulation. Governments will appear to embrace these alternative currencies, like Bitcoin, but they will also set up systems to monitor purchases made with these currencies. We will continue to experience a decline in small business start-ups and an increase in regulations on businesses, as well as a continued societal attack on free enterprise.

The mindset of the people and their hearts will continue to blame free enterprise for the decline in livelihood. There will be a growing call for a socialist-run system the world over. The idea that the world's large corporations are playing the political system to increase the bottom line will be viewed as capitalism instead of what it is: fascist socialism.

There will emerge a new movement, one that calls for a unified global financial system of shared resources. The pitch this movement will make is that for far too long, the world has been divided by lines on a map, different currencies in our wallets, and varying political systems around the globe. In light of the global employment crunch, growing hunger and health crises, and a never-ending war on terror, this movement will call for a one-world currency.

This one-world currency will appear to be the solution the world needs. By switching to a one-world currency, we could raise everyone out of poverty. Initially, it will lift the poorest nation to a median level while pulling down effective wages in the richest nations to that median. When a worker in a third-world nation used to get $50 a week because he was paid in his nation's currency in his nation's economy, the new currency would place a value of an hour of labor in his nation at the same rate as an hour of labor in any nation. Who wouldn't like this?

Realizing, though, that because one-third of the population is not employed, the idea of raising the wage via the global currency still wouldn't work. This will usher in the call not only for a new currency but for a new economic system as well. The system of being paid what you earn has been around for millennia, but because technology is basically making human labor obsolete at this point, there will be a new system proposed, one in which money is not really money at all. In this new movement, no longer will there be the idea of accumulating piles of resources; instead, there will be a global standard of resource allotment that will be equally shared amongst all peoples. The movement may even use *Star Trek* as an example of an allotment system that works without using money in the way we know it now. As hard as it may be now to believe there will be a movement of people wanting this, it won't just stop there. In today's world, most people would laugh at such a movement; sounds like some sort of hippie-commune idea that would have been tried in the 1960s. However, when technology is being sold as a way to make the world go 'round, the focus on what a man can accomplish when he doesn't need to earn a living but instead can focus on bettering his fellow man by cultural, artistic, or societal pursuits will be the new idea of the American and global dream.

This new movement will not be implemented yet, but it will be gaining major popularity. A reformed version of socialism, a technologically based version…techno-socialism will be envisioned.

During this time, too, we will see increases in homelessness, chronic diseases, and hunger. We will also see though a new shift in aging. Products and therapies being tested in the last period will now start making their way onto store shelves. The new products and therapies being sold will not just be anti-aging skin care, but they will be actual anti-aging. There will even be evidence of reverse aging—and not in some sort of science-fiction way in which an adult goes back to being a child—in a way that optimizes the design of the human cell. For example, let's say twenty-five is the optimal age; the therapies developed will be moving people's cellular structure to that of a twenty-five-year old.

You may be thinking that sounds cool, but shouldn't the future of transhumanism be in a different chapter of this book? Perhaps it is, but transhumanism will have profound economic effects, too.

What happens when someone's pension plan is designed to have him live to the age of 90, but he is living to 120? What happens when the workforce doesn't retire and move on, thus opening those limited number of jobs to the following generation?

We will also be reeling from a global housing collapse at this point, as most people have their wealth in their homes. Millions of older people selling to a smaller population of younger people will bring declining housing prices. The fact that these homes will be leveraged to the rafters as people try to use that equity to survive will have reverse mortgages up 30 percent from where they are today. Combine that with the fact that the smaller purchasing base of people available to occupy these homes will not be earning anywhere near what will be required to have a "comfortable" life will create a housing market decline that makes the great recession of 2008 look like a speed bump.

It should be said that in this period, too, we will see the strongest regulations ever when it comes to business. The masses will still believe that the regulation has something to do with protecting workers and customers, but more of the people who are awake and paying attention will see that this is just the continuation of a war against entrepreneurship. The forces that be know that entrepreneurship is the only way for the people to regain their freedom, and being this close to globalization victory, these powers will not want the people having the opportunity to fight back.

10+ Years

Hold on to your hats, because the ride humanity is on will really get crazy at this point. International trade regulation will have essentially killed national sovereignty.

We will see a global war again at this time. That may not take the shape of one group of nations holding a line across the battlefield from another group of nations in what would consider a "traditional" war, but it more than likely would be a war that is 40 percent cyber and 40 percent military action that is hidden from the people. The remaining 20 percent would be waged under the guise of taking on global evil.

The globe will be dominated by four groups of people:

1. Group A of a globalist agenda
2. Group B of a globalist agenda
3. Radical and moderate Islam
4. Everyone else

Globalist groups A and B are the two parties that are largely responsible for designing the decline of nations and economies. These two groups will basically be fighting for who gets to be king of the hill of this newly destroyed geopolitical world in order to usher in their totalitarian design. Even within these two globalist groups, we will begin to see infighting in those groups, a jockeying for power as they start to realize their global power play is working.

Radical Islam will have its own global domination agenda, and it will still fail to see that its entire religion was a creation by groups A and B centuries earlier, when those two groups needed to create a false religion in order to create an enemy. The purpose of creating that false religion enemy was to unite the rest of the world, which was starting to break in unity against a common threat. People were looking at their faith and disagreeing with the humanist and the Catholic branches of globalism, and were deciding instead to use logic and reason to determine their life's trajectory. Not wanting that to happen, they created the false religion of Islam as a mix of sun/moon worship practices that have been around for centuries.

Regardless of the fact that radical/moderate Islam is funded by groups A and B, radical/moderate Islam still is a force in and of itself. This force will not only continue to carry out the invasion of the world that we started experiencing in the early 2000s (when everyone thought it was about refugees and immigration), but they will continue to use the weapon of business that they are so good at using.

By this point, the Ottoman Empire, an Islam empire, will really begin to become formalized, and I still believe that Turkey will be the main organizing body. The rulers in Turkey will continue their push from elected official to Allah-appointed ruler.

Artificial intelligence (AI) will be commonplace, with the majority of homes having a system of AI in their homes by this point. The promise that AI will usher in a utopia of humans will still be keeping most people blinded to the death of humanity that technology is ushering in.

We will start seeing the justice system implementing AI at this point—and not just drones that patrol the skies to issue traffic tickets while using predictive crime software. I think we will see it in the judicial branch as well. The law will become more black and white, so why have a human judge when an artificial-intelligence judge can make a ruling while being able to instantly examine every example of precedence and case law in human history? We will also start seeing technology used in gathering mental evidence from the accused and witnesses.

Not only will reverse aging be the hottest topic, but we will also be in the foothills of singularity. Again, so many of the topics in this book overlap, and this is one of them. We will start seeing mind/computer interfaces in human trials—not just skull caps with wires, but some form of in-body tech that connects us to other devices. The transition may start simply, like a heart valve that feeds information directly to an external smart device.

Healthcare has always been a major sector of America's economy; as a matter of fact, that one industry alone in America has been larger than entire economies of our other G20 nation members! The impact to the economy of technology and healthcare will be massive, ushering in a decline of traditional doctors and a larger portion of medical engineers. Three-dimensional, printed organs that match your DNA, devices to supplement the senses, diagnostics based on DNA and frequencies rather than monitoring symptoms to determine treatment will be examples of engineering health instead of treating health.

Because of the decline of the economy and the less relevance humanity will be seen as having in the world, more decisions about treatment will be based on one's economic contribution to society and less on issues concerning the value of life.

Medicare/Medicaid will be in economic shreds.

We will see an interesting phenomenon happening at this point, too, in response to all the technology and AI: a movement of organic living. Companies and even communities will make decisions to reject artificial intelligence. For example, posh vacation destinations will advertise themselves as "AI free" for the wholesome and human vacation experience. Businesses will market their products as having been "human made," and that moniker will be likened to the "Made in the USA" marketing push in the generation prior.

Driverless cars will be taking us not only to and from airport terminals like we witnessed in the prior two time periods, but we will also be seeing major increases in the number of driverless vehicles on the roadways. These cars not only will be used to transport their occupants, but also, because of GPS accuracy, they will be used to be sent, occupant-less, to pick up the kids from school or the pizza from the pizzeria.

We will see a significant rise in suicide at this point, as the meaning of being alive will be challenged in the hearts of many. After failing to realize their purpose, many people will choose to end their lives. Financial stress and lower standards of living will be contributing factors.

We will start seeing the decline of many major corporations at this point, too. The utopia dreamed of—with fewer workers and more automation—will instead become a living nightmare as declining purchasing power will cripple many companies.

I see a greatest depression happening in this period, and this depression will be the one that ushers in true globalism. In order to pull itself out of this global depression, the idea that was floated in the previous time frame of a global currency will become a reality. The argument will be that there is no way for any one nation to pull itself out of the depression alone, and it was all of these countries having independent economic systems that created the problem in the first place (that's not true, but it's what they will say), so the only option is to unite. They will cite the fact that the world is already just a handful of trade agreements anyway, so "let us unite the currency."

Initially, the masses will believe that this is the solution, but the currency will soon be followed by a global government—because if everyone is using the same money, we need to be using the same rules, right?

I believe that in this period we will also see America divided into regions—not through political maneuvers, but more along the lines of unofficial recognition that will be brought about by mass pockets of poverty, resource depletion, and violence. Just like "the South" isn't legally a definition but we all know it is that area from Tennessee down to Georgia and over to Louisiana, I think we will have smaller but similar designations. For example, poverty will be so prevalent in areas, they will become like Detroit in the 2010s—but these areas will be multiple counties wide. We will also have Muslim counties that become "no-go" zones for those who want to live in peace.

Can Anything Be Done?

As I pointed out in the beginning of this chapter, I am NOT a prophet. This is just my forecast, and just like a weatherman, I can be wrong. To be honest, I kind of hope I am. But also just like the weatherman, while I might not get it exactly right, I will bet you dollars to doughnuts that I'm right within a degree or two.

The great thing is that this doesn't have to be all doom and gloom.

If people want to prepare for this coming storm, I suggest getting involved in entrepreneurship today. I also suggest that they start building community and culture again.

This doesn't mean the economic storm will not come; it will. Sadly, we did have an opportunity to stop this, but the people failed to respond. Now, I believe we cannot stop the economic storm from happening. All we can do is prepare for its arrival.

[6]

The Ark of the Covenant and the Third Temple

By Derek Gilbert

The arc of human history orbits around an uneven rocky plateau thirty-three miles from the eastern shore of the Mediterranean Sea. The faith of Abraham, the dynasty of David, and the divinity of Jesus were established there. At the heart of this plateau is a hill on which Yahweh, the Creator of the universe, established His "Mount of Assembly," Zion. The temples of Solomon and Zerubbabel were built there, and a prophesied Third Temple will someday occupy that place. The eternal significance of the site was accurately described by the title of David Flynn's 2008 book, *Temple at the Center of Time.*

While setting dates with any kind of precision is foolish, since no man knows the day or the hour of Christ's return, a day is fast approaching when Jerusalem's Temple Mount will be at the very center of the most important event in human history—the final conflict, a supernatural showdown between good and evil at the place the apostle John called Armageddon.

Americans have a difficult time understanding the intensity of the emotions behind the conflict over Jerusalem's Temple Mount. Nationalism, religious fervor, and racism are focused like a laser on an area of only about thirty-five acres. The irrationality spawned by these emotions—for example, the grand mufti of Jerusalem recently declared that the Al-Aqsa Mosque has occupied the Temple Mount "since the creation of the world"[79]—argues for their supernatural origin.

This speck of land, roughly 0.00000003 percent of the earth's land mass, is the focus of constant confrontation between Muslims, Jews, and Christians. And one day, it will be the site of the very climax of human history, Armageddon. The passions and aspirations that swirl about the Temple Mount will play an ever-increasing role in global geopolitics as the world draws closer to that day.

The Temple Mount is the holiest site in Judaism, the place where Solomon built the Temple to Yahweh. The Second Temple was constructed by Zerubbabel after the decree of the Persian emperor Cyrus, between 538 and 516 BC, and was rebuilt with expansions by Herod the Great beginning in 19 BC.

The Temple is the center of Jewish life, at least for conservative and orthodox Jews. The Holy of Holies, the inner sanctuary within the tabernacle, was the most sacred site in Judaism, screened from the outer sanctuary by the veil of the covering. The Holy of Holies was the home of the Ark of the Covenant, or Ark of the Testimony, a gold-clad wooden chest that contained Aaron's rod, a pot of manna, and the stone tablets on which Yahweh had written the Ten Commandments. Only the high priest was allowed to enter the Holy of Holies and approach the Ark, and then only once a year on the Day of Atonement (Yom Kippur). Contrary to its description in the blockbuster film *Raiders of the Lost Ark*, it was not "a transmitter...a radio for speaking to God." The Ark of the Covenant was far more important than a simple communicating device; it was literally Yahweh's seat when He appeared among His people.[80]

However, both the Ark of the Testimony and the Temple have seemingly been lost to the ages. After the Jewish revolt in AD 70, Roman soldiers destroyed and looted Jerusalem, leaving most of Herod's Temple in rubble. The menorah was depicted among the spoils of from the Temple on the Arch of Titus in Rome, commemorating his victory over the Jewish rebels.

The Ark disappeared long before. The last sure mention of it in the Bible is 2 Chronicles 35:3, where King Josiah of Judah, who reigned from 640 to 609 BC, ordered that the Ark be returned to the Temple as it had apparently been removed by one of his predecessors. At some point after that, for all intents and purposes, it vanished. Jeremiah prophesied a time when the Ark will no longer be discussed or used,[81] and indeed, it was never in the Temple from the time of Zerubbabel until the Temple's destruction. A raised area on the floor of the Holy of Holies indicated where the Ark should have been.

And yet we are entering a period of history in which the Ark and the Temple will play central roles—possibly within seven years of this writing (2023). A spiritual conflict is developing that will pit Christians, Jews, and Muslims (and subsets within those groups) against one another. Some seek control of the Mount for political reasons while others may believe they can literally trigger the Apocalypse. The Temple Mount and the Ark of the Covenant will be right at the center of the oncoming storm.

Arab Muslims have controlled the Temple Mount since the conquest of Jerusalem in AD 638, with brief exceptions during the eleventh and twelfth centuries when European crusaders occupied the city. The Al-Aqsa Mosque, the third holiest site in Islam, and the Dome of the Rock, which sits on the spot from which Muslims believe Muhammad ascended to heaven, were constructed in the late seventh century.

The geopolitical consequences of taking full control of the Temple Mount were considered so dangerous that the first action of Israel's Defense Minister Moshe Dayan on securing the area during the Six-Day War in 1967 was to take down the Israeli flag that paratroopers had raised over the Mount.

The Temple Mount today is administered by the Waqf, an Islamic religious trust that has overseen the area since 1187. The government of Jordan acts as custodian of the Islamic religious sites on the Mount, although security is provided by Israeli police. This mutually dissatisfying arrangement is a constant source of irritation and provocation to Jews and Muslims alike.

Christians, as spiritual descendants of Judaism, also attach special significance to the Temple Mount. In addition to the Old Testament history linked to the site, which is believed to be Mount Moriah, where Yahweh tested Abraham's faith by asking him to sacrifice Isaac, some of the major events of Jesus' life took place on the Temple Mount.

As an infant, Jesus was presented at the Temple in accordance with the Law, where Simeon, a man who had been told he would live to see the Messiah, and Anna, an eighty-four-year-old prophetess, were led to Jesus by the Holy Spirit. When Jesus was twelve, He remained behind in the Temple after His parents began the journey back to Nazareth following the Passover celebration in Jerusalem. It was a full day before Mary and Joseph discovered that Jesus was missing, and it was at least three more days before they found Him in the Temple talking with the rabbis.

Early in His ministry, Jesus visited Jerusalem during Passover, as must have been His custom, and with a zealous anger He drove the moneychangers and animal merchants out of the Temple. Later, probably during the second Passover during His ministry, Jesus healed the lame man at the Pool of Bethesda at the north end of the Temple complex. Shortly before the crucifixion, Jesus drove out the moneychangers a second time, and Matthew records that He healed many lame and blind people who came to Him at the Temple.

Ultimately, the prophesied final battle between good and evil, Armageddon, will be fought for the Temple Mount, the historical Mount Zion. (The Western Hill that bears the name "Zion" today is outside the Old City of Jerusalem. Apparently, being taller than the Temple Mount, it seemed a more fitting location for the by-then lost palace of David to Jews of the first century.)

Still, its importance to Christians, especially in the increasingly secular West, pales in comparison to the significance of the Temple Mount to Jews. One example that might give American Gentiles a sense of the frustration that religious Jews feel over the status of the Mount, where visits by non-Muslims are restricted and only Muslims are allowed to pray, would be to imagine the site of the World Trade Center occupied by mosques and access to the 9/11 Memorial and Museum limited—except to Muslims. That is a poor example, of course, but it conveys the sense.

Moshe Dayan and Israel's secular leadership in 1967 apparently believed that the Mount was a holy site only for Muslims and nothing more than "a historical site of commemoration of the past" for Jews. By granting them access to the site, Dayan thought Jewish demands for worship and sovereignty there would be satisfied. By allowing Muslims to retain religious control of the Temple Mount, he sought to remove the site as a source of inspiration of Palestinian nationalism.[82]

It was the ultimate no-win situation, as the recent wave of Palestinian violence reminds us. Western observers have difficulty grasping the historic and eschatological significance that Arab Muslims attach to the Holy Land.

Syria was the first area outside the Arabian peninsula to be conquered, and not only was it taken from the superpower al-Rum (the Byzantine Christian Empire), but al-Sham, "Greater Syria" centered on Damascus, included Jerusalem, the capture of which "proved" Islamic superiority to the other, corrupted monotheistic religions: Judaism and Christianity.

This fervent triumphalism only intensified after the hated Crusaders were expelled from their 88-year occupation by the Syrian Kurd Salah al-Din in 1187, and the "Zionist occupation" of al-Quds ("The Holy"=Jerusalem) since 1948 is seen by many Arab (and other) Muslims are merely a temporary setback, which the Mahdi and Jesus will rectify.

Thus many hadiths predict eschatological events transpiring in what the French and Brits used to call "the Levant," the most important among them including: *al-Sufyani*, (a "type" of the Muslim antichrist, *al-Dajjal*, "the Deceiver") will emerge from Syria; Christians will (re)conquer Syria; the Mahdi will reveal himself; the Dajjal himself appears; Jesus will return by descending into Damascus; the armies of the Mahdi and the Sufyani will battle; and Jesus will kill the Dajjal in or near Jerusalem.

After all this the Mahdi and Jesus will jointly rule over a Muslim planet, and eventually both will pass away.[83]

The Jewish State is under near-constant pressure from the global community to give up land to the Palestinians in exchange for peace. Although the United States has not formally recognized Palestine, it is among a minority of nations. On November 22, 1974, the United Nations General Assembly passed a resolution recognizing the right of the Palestinian people to self-determination and independence, and the Palestine Liberation Organization was recognized as the sole legitimate representative of the Palestinian people.

The Palestinian National Council declared independence on November 15, 1988, which was acknowledged by eighty nations by the end of that year. As of late 2015, 136 of the world's 195 nations recognize Palestine as an independent state. Israel does not, maintaining that such status can only be conferred by direct negotiations between Israel and the Palestinian National Authority. To date, Israel still maintains *de facto* military control over the Palestinian territories.

But even in the United States, which has arguably been Israel's strongest supporter since 1948, calls have been heard even from Republican presidential administrations for the establishment of an independent Palestine. In October of 2007, Condoleezza Rice, secretary of state for George W. Bush, said at a news conference with Palestinian President Mahmoud Abbas:

Frankly, it's time for the establishment of a Palestinian state. The United States sees the establishment of a Palestinian state and a two-state solution as absolutely essential for the future, not just of Palestinians and Israelis but also for the Middle East and indeed to American interests.[84]

Interestingly, a majority of both Israelis and Palestinians support a two-state solution in opinion polls. However, when the compromises required to reach such a solution—drawing permanent borders, the status of settlements, and dividing Jerusalem—are spelled out, support collapses.[85]

The Roman Catholic Church recently waded back into these contentious waters. On June 26, 2015, the Vatican signed a treaty with the "state of Palestine," essentially acknowledging the independence of a sovereign Palestine. The Israeli Foreign Ministry immediately expressed its disappointment and declared that this move would not benefit the peace process. If the Palestinian Authority can achieve independence through outside influence on Israel, why should it negotiate with the Israeli government?

News of this agreement stirred old suspicions among some Jews that the Vatican is conspiring with Palestinian leaders, and possibly with Israeli elites, to take control of the Old City and/or the Temple Mount. Stories have circulated on the Internet for years that the Vatican is working with Jewish elites on a secret deal to turn over administration of the Old City to the Roman Catholic Church.

This is not entirely conspiracy theory. The 1947 United Nations Partition Plan for Palestine included a proposal to designate Jerusalem *corpus separatum* (Latin for "separated body"), a zone under international control because of the city's shared religious importance. That proposal was included in the plan largely because of a powerful diplomatic effort by the Vatican, which had been concerned about the status of Christian holy sites in the Holy Land since the nineteenth century.

However, the partition plan failed when war broke out almost immediately after Israel declared its independence. Months of intense fighting left Israeli forces in control of western Jerusalem, and Israel held on to that territory when the armistice was signed ending the 1948–49 war.

Today, at least one Middle East think tank, the Jerusalem Old City Initiative, formed by Canadian diplomats after the failure of the Camp David talks in 2000, has "concluded that an effective and empowered third party presence was imperative in the Old City."[86] A similar proposal was reportedly made by the Obama administration in late 2013. US Secretary of State John Kerry, in Israel trying to broker a deal to establish a Palestinian state by April of 2014, was said by sources to have proposed a "third-party solution" for administering eastern Jerusalem, with the Vatican controlling holy sites in partnership with a coalition of Muslim countries such as Turkey and Saudi Arabia. Sources close to the talks said Israeli leaders were unreceptive, especially to the idea of Turkey's participation.[87]

A suggestion that Jordan might replace Turkey in the international coalition was met with a lukewarm response in Amman. King Abdullah was reportedly less than eager to involve his nation in a delicate and potentially explosive political situation while the Syrian civil war intensified on his northern border.

Relations between Israel and Turkey have soured in recent years, and this is likely due to the regional ambitions of Turkey's President Recep Tayyip Erdogan. Turkey supported the so-called Gaza Freedom Flotilla, a 2010 mission to deliver construction materials and humanitarian aid to the Gaza Strip coordinated by the Free Gaza Movement and the Turkish Foundation for Human Rights and Freedoms and Humanitarian Relief. However, since Israel and Egypt have blockaded access to the Gaza Strip since 2007, aid is normally delivered to Israel and then transferred to Palestinian authorities. The flotilla attempted to deliver the aid directly to Gaza by running the blockade.

When Israeli forces intercepted the flotilla on May 31, 2010, nine people were killed in the ensuing confrontation on the Turkish ship MV Mavi Marmara. Although President Erdogan said in 2013 that relations with Israel could be normalized if certain conditions were met, in May, 2015, he called for Sunni and Shia Muslims to set aside their differences and resume efforts to assert dominance over Jerusalem, and specifically over the Temple Mount.[88]

Turkey's deteriorating relationship with Russia after two of its F-16s shot down a Russian SU-24 fighter-bomber over Syria on November 24, 2015, have given Erdogan an unexpected incentive to improve relations with Israel. Russia supplies more than half of Turkey's natural gas, and Vladimir Putin has demonstrated in the past that he is willing to use Russia's energy resources as a geopolitical weapon. Israel, meanwhile, is developing a potentially huge reserve of natural gas in the eastern Mediterranean. That said, as of this writing, Turkey is still making unrestricted access to Gaza a condition of any formal restoration of diplomatic ties.[89]

Under current political conditions, it appears that Israel will grow increasingly resistant to pressure to relinquish control of the Temple Mount. The Netanyahu administration, which has governed Israel since 2009, has been quietly investing in efforts to prepare for the construction of the Third Temple. Those efforts include education to teach young Israelis about the importance of the Temple to the state and to Judaism, and practical efforts, mainly by a private organization called the Temple Institute, to prepare the plans, utensils, and even sacrificial animals needed to make the Temple a reality.

The Israeli newspaper *Haaretz* disclosed in a recent investigative report that close supporters of Prime Minister Benjamin Netanyahu—specifically a deputy defense minister and a key US fundraiser—have made significant financial contributions to advance the cause of the Third Temple's construction.[90]

This is fueling a developing confrontation of literally biblical proportions. While modern Israel is mainly a secular society, eschatological proclamations by respected Israeli rabbis are becoming more common.

At the same time, a growing majority of Muslims, especially in the nations closest to Israel, expect the imminent arrival of the Mahdi, or "rightly-guided one," a figure in Muslim prophecy who is analogous to the Messiah.

In recent years, several prominent figures in the Orthodox Jewish community have publically stated that the Messiah's appearance is very near. Rabbi Chaim Kanievsky, considered a leading authority in mainstream Haredi (ultra-Orthodox) Judaism, and not previously given to messianic predictions, has reportedly been advising Jews since 2014 to make *aliyah* (relocate to Israel) as soon as possible to prepare for Messiah's arrival.[91] (It should be noted that Rav Kanievsky predicted the Messiah's arrival by the end of the Shemitah year, which fell on the 29th of Elul—September 12, 2015.)

Rabbi Moshe Sternbuch, vice president of the Rabbinical Court, said in early December 2015 that the political conflict between Turkey and Russia means that Jews should anticipate the coming of the Messiah.

> "We have received a direct teaching, passed down from one to another, from the Gaon of Vilna, that when Russia goes and conquers Istanbul...it is time to quickly put on your Shabbat clothes and expect the Messiah," he said.
>
> "Here we have Russia and Turkey in a conflict with each other. We hear sounds of war. All of the nations seem so surprised that Turkey began a fight with Russia," Rabbi Sternbuch explained.
>
> "But we see in this the realization of the teachings of the sages, that when the Messiah needs to come, God will incite nations against each other, until, against their will, there will be a war. Therefore, as the Shmittah goes out, we should have great inspiration to wake up and repent."[92]

The *Vilna Gaon* ("Genius of Vilnius"), Elijah ben Shlomo Zalman, was an eighteenth-century rabbi and kabbalist who is considered one of the most influential rabbinical scholars since the Middle Ages. Rabbi Sternbuch is a great-grandson of the Vilna Gaon. The "direct teaching" to which he refers is a prophecy passed down within the family, revealed for the first time by American-born Hasidic Rabbi Lazer Brody in March of 2014:

> When you hear that the Russians have captured the city of Crimea, you should know that the times of the Messiah have started, that his steps are being heard. And when you hear that the Russians have reached the city of Constantinople, you should put on your Shabbat (Sabbath) clothes and don't take them off, because it means that the Messiah is about to come any minute.[93]

Rabbi Brody was moved to reveal the prophecy by Russia's annexation of Crimea in March 2014 as part of the civil war in Ukraine. Apparently, Rabbi Sternbuch and others believe this fulfilled the first part of the Vilna Gaon's prophecy. (Constantinople is the former name of Istanbul.) As for the second part: At this writing, the political situation between Turkey and Russia remains tense. A spokesman for the Russian Ministry of Defense claimed the attack on its war plane was a premeditated act by Turkey—one that may have been planned with information shared by Russia with the United States.[94]

While we give credence only to those prophecies recorded in the Bible, it is difficult to come up with an explanation for Turkey's provocative act that makes more sense than the one offered by Rabbi Sternbuch: "It is impossible to understand how a country like Turkey can start a war and refuse to apologize. They are crazy! God is confusing them, therefore we need to strengthen ourselves in repentance so we will merit a true redemption very soon."[95]

In other words, when political leaders behave in irrational and self-destructive ways, supernatural forces may be guiding their decisions—as when Yahweh hardened the heart of Pharaoh in spite of the plagues that laid waste to Egypt.

Whether the Vilna Gaon's prophecy was inspired is irrelevant. What matters is that there are people in Israel who believe it. One's actions are determined by what one believes. And there are other religious leaders in Israel who apparently believe the end of history is fast approaching.

World events prompted Rabbi Yosef Berger, one of the rabbis in charge of King David's Tomb, to initiate a project to create a Torah scroll to unify all of Israel—which he hopes to present to the Messiah upon his arrival. In an interview, Rabbi Berger told a reporter that he was inspired by a prophecy in chapter 3 of the book of Hosea:

> For the children of Israel shall abide many days without a king, and without a prince, and without a sacrifice, and without an image, and without an ephod, and without teraphim:
>
> Afterward shall the children of Israel return, and seek the Lord their God, and David their king; and shall fear the Lord and his goodness in the latter days. (Hosea 3:4–5)

Rabbi Berger said he believes that bringing Israel together with a single Torah scroll housed on Mount Zion, the site of David's Tomb and adjacent to the Temple Mount, will fulfill the prophetic goals of seeking the Lord, seeking the dynasty of David, and the construction of the Third Temple.[96]

Perhaps the most well-known recent rabbinical prediction of the Messiah is the claim by the late Rabbi Yitzhak Kaduri, a renowned kabbalist and Haredi rabbi, who claimed he actually met the Messiah on November 4, 2003.[97] Rabbi Kaduri sealed a note containing the name of the Messiah that was not to be opened until a year after his death on January 28, 2006.

Needless to say, the revelation that the name in Rabbi Kaduri's note was Yehoshua—Jesus—touched off a bit of controversy.[98]

Meanwhile, Israel's Muslim neighbors are likewise experiencing a surge in apocalyptic beliefs. Contrary to the publicly expressed opinions of Western political leaders and progressive pundits, groups such as Jabhat al-Nusra and ISIS do not represent the lunatic fringe of Islamic thought. Their expectation of the Mahdi's imminent arrival is actually shared by the vast majority of Sunni Muslims. In contrast to American Christians, some 80 percent of whom do not expect the literal return of Jesus anytime soon,[99] upwards of three-quarters of Muslims in the Middle East and South Asia expect to see the Mahdi before they die.

> Looking at specific countries, the highest percentage of the population expecting the Mahdi's near-term appearance is found in Afghanistan (83 percent), followed by Iraq (72 percent), Turkey (68 percent) and Tunisia (67 percent). Sixty percent of Pakistanis, 51 percent of Moroccans, 46 percent of Palestinians and 40 percent of Egyptians are looking for the Mahdi in their lifetimes. The conventional wisdom in recent decades among many journalists, and not a few area "experts," has been that Mahdism is an eccentric outlier belief held mainly by (Twelver) Shi`is and the uneducated on the fringes of the Sunni world. This Pew data, among other things, shows the intellectual vacuity of such biases. The average for the 23 countries Pew surveyed on this issue of Mahdism comes out to 42 percent, and extrapolating from that to the entire Muslim world means there are over 670 million Muslims who believe the Mahdi will return here in the first half of the twenty-first century.

> What does this Pew information on Mahdism mean? First and foremost, Mahdism must be taken seriously as an intellectual, sociological and even political strain within the entire Islamic world – not dismissed as archaic, mystical nonsense.[100]

In other words, the Islamic state hasn't hijacked Islam, *it is a purer form of Islam*—and it has a hands-on approach to jump-starting the Apocalypse.

It may not be a coincidence the nations with the highest percentage of Muslims expecting the Mahdi's imminent arrival are the ones that have been occupied by American soldiers for the last twelve to fourteen years.

While many Muslims do not support the methods and/or aims of ISIS,[101] "Islamic history is rife with violent jihads led by self-styled Muslim messiahs and waged by their followers."[102] ISIS caliph Abu Bakr al-Baghdadi and the Islamic state certainly fit the description of such a movement. And if only 1 percent of the world's Muslims rally to its cause, nearly seven million jihadists could be available to serve the emerging caliphate.

In the near term, the danger posed by ISIS to the Christian communities of Syria and Iraq is shared by other Muslims in the area. Islam is splintered into a number of subgroups under the general definitions "Sunni" and "Shia," and the Islamic State views other Muslims as a more immediate enemy (because they are heretics) than Jews, Christians, and practitioners of other religions.

> Like his predecessors in [Al Qaedi in Iraq], Baghdadi favors first purifying the Islamic community by attacking Shia and other religious minorities as well as rival jihadist groups. The Islamic State's long list of enemies includes the Iraqi Shia, Hezbollah, the Yazidis (a Kurdish ethnoreligious minority located predominantly in Iraq), the wider Kurdish community in Iraq, the Kurds in Syria and rival opposition groups in Syria (including Jabhat al-Nusra).[103]

It may surprise the reader to learn that ISIS carried out attacks against Hamas and Islamic Jihad in the Gaza Strip in 2015.[104] ISIS publicly condemned Hamas for being too narrowly focused on the Palestinian cause, working with Shias (Hezbollah and Iran), and not promoting a rigid enough interpretation of Islamic Law.[105] After ISIS announced its intention to conquer Saudi Arabia in December of 2014, the Saudis considered the threat serious enough to begin building a six hundred-mile, high-tech fence along the border with Iraq, where ISIS has a strong presence in Anbar province. Bringing the holy sites of Mecca and Medina under ISIS control would grant the caliphate a greater degree of legitimacy with the world's 672 million Muslims, and some analysts believe that is, in fact, the group's objective.[106]

Now, the ability of ISIS to hold the territory it has overrun has been questioned. As of this writing, however, eighteen months declaring its caliphate, the only military force in the region that has held its own against the Islamic State is the Kurdish *peshmerga*. The Kurdish resistance, however, is hampered by opposition from the Turkish government, which wants to prevent the emergence of an independent Kurdish state that would likely annex a portion of southeastern Turkey.

Turkey's support of the Islamic State may be the worst-kept secret of the Syrian civil war. The Turks view their southern neighbor, Syria, as a rival, and relations between the two countries have been tense for decades. The leadership of the Kurdistan Workers Party (PKK), a group considered a terrorist organization by Turkey and the United States, operated out of the Syrian capital, Damascus, from 1978 to 1998. Syria only ended support for the PKK after Turkey threatened to invade. It is possible that the government of Turkey's President Recep Tayyip Erdogan considers its support for ISIS justifiable payback for PKK terror attacks carried out against Turkish targets.

It may also be that Erdogan is using the Islamic State as a cat's paw in his long game to revive the Ottoman Empire. The rise of Erdogan's Justice and Development Party (AKP) has given Erdogan the clout to roll back some of the secular reforms of Mustafa Kemal Ataturk, who modernized Turkey and aligned it with the West after the collapse of the empire in 1923. Ottoman Turkish and Arabic script will again be taught in government schools, and the number of students enrolled in state-run Islamic seminaries has grown from sixty-two thousand in 2002, when

Erdogan first came to power, to over one million.[107] Considering Erdogan's public call for Muslims to work toward wresting control of Jerusalem away from Israel, it is no surprise that some Middle East observers are asking in so many words: Is Turkey attempting to resurrect the Ottoman Empire on the back of the Islamic State?[108]

In the interest of giving equal time, it should be noted that while the leading authorities of Shia Islam, the ayatollahs who rule the Islamic Republic of Iran, are openly hostile toward Israel and the West, there are good reasons to believe that they are not as eager for the arrival of the Mahdi as Sunnis.

First, unlike Sunni Muslims, Shias believe (as do Christians) that there is nothing they can do to immanentize the eschaton. In other words, the Mahdi will arrive when Allah wills it and not one heartbeat sooner. And Twelver Shia views of jihad require that "victorious holy war" be prohibited until the return of their Mahdi, the Twelfth Imam— not employed to force him to appear.[109]

Second, and perhaps more significantly, Shiite religious authorities in Iran wield ultimate political power, not unlike the Sanhedrin in Jesus' day. And like the Jewish religious establishment when confronted with the Messiah, "The ruling ayatollahs are probably the most vociferous opponents of a true Mahdist claim on the planet—because acknowledging anyone as such would end their rule of Iran, and with it their wealth, power and privilege."[110]

However it happens, the focus of conflict in the Middle East will ultimately return to Israel, and to the Temple Mount in particular. While the Islamic State may not be involved directly, there are hints that ISIS and Hamas have begun moving toward a more cooperative arrangement, especially in the Sinai Peninsula,[111] and al-Baghdadi in recent days issued his first public threat against the state of Israel.[112]

Regardless of the identity of the human actors who take part, one thing is certain: The final battle between God and the angels who rebelled against His authority (and their human dupes, of course) will be fought for control of the "Mount of Assembly," the Temple Mount—the historic Mount Zion.

The struggle for Yahweh's holy mountain is a narrative thread woven through the entire Bible. From Eden to Armageddon, the conflict between God and the rebellious *bene elohim* centers on the Mount of Assembly, which, since the time of David, is the hill called the Temple Mount.

Entire books have been devoted to this topic, so we will just summarize here: It was understood in the ancient world that mountains were the domain of the gods. They were inaccessible and remote, far removed from the mundane plane of existence that is the lot of mortal men. Olympus is the most famous, but there were others: Mount Othrys in central Greece was the base of Cronus and the Titans, Mount Ida on Crete was home to the Titaness Rhea, mother of the Olympians, and Mount Zaphon (today's Mount Aqra in northwestern Syria) was the location of the palace of Ba'al.

The *original* holy mountain, however, was Eden. Yes, it was a garden, but a garden on a mountain. Ezekiel's lament over the king of Tyre, considered by most commentators to be an indictment of the rebellious cherub we know as Lucifer, describes the setting:

> Son of man, say unto the prince of Tyrus, Thus saith the Lord God; Because thine heart is lifted up, and thou hast said, I am a God, I sit in the seat of God, in the midst of the seas; yet thou art a man, and not God, though thou set thine heart as the heart of God:...
>
> Thou hast been in **Eden the garden of God**; every precious stone was thy covering, the sardius, topaz, and the diamond, the beryl, the onyx, and the jasper, the sapphire, the emerald, and the carbuncle, and gold: the workmanship of thy tabrets and of thy pipes Thou art the anointed cherub that covereth; and I have set thee so: thou wast upon **the holy mountain of**

God; thou hast walked up and down in the midst of the stones of fire.

Thou wast perfect in thy ways from the day that thou wast created, till iniquity was found in thee. (Ezekiel 28:2, 13–15, emphasis added)

"The seat of God" (or "seat of the gods," depending on the translation) is the home of the Divine Council, a sort of supernatural task force that assists Yahweh in carrying out His will. Again, an entire book can be devoted to this topic,[113] but it is clear enough from Scripture that a long war for this holy mountain, the Mount of Assembly, has been waged since Lucifer's deception led to humanity's banishment from Eden.

This idea illuminates an aspect of one of the most famous miracles in the Bible, the parting of the Red Sea. Just before the fateful confrontation with the Egyptian army, Yahweh told Moses where the crossing would take place:

And the Lord spake unto Moses, saying, Speak unto the children of Israel, that **they turn and encamp before Pihahiroth**, between Migdol and the sea, **over against Baalzephon**: before it shall ye encamp by the sea. (Exodus 14:1–2, emphasis added)

No one is sure just where Pi-hahiroth is located, but this we know: Somewhere along the west coast of the Red Sea, God commanded Moses to *turn around* (most English translations use the words "turn back") and make camp at a specific place—"over against" (or "in front of") a place called Ba'al-Zephon.

That begs the question: What was so important about Ba'al-Zephon?

Apparently it was sacred to Ba'al of Zephon—Ba'al, whose "holy mountain" was Mount Zaphon. While it may seem odd that Ba'al, the supreme Canaanite deity, was venerated in Egypt, the temple of Ba'al at Ugarit, an ancient port city less than twenty miles south of Mount Zaphon, contained a sandstone relief dedicated to the god by a royal scribe from Egypt.

[146]

According to Ugaritic records, Ba'al was a god of storms, with particular power over the fertility of the soil and the cultivation of crops. The Ba'al Cycle describes the victory of Ba'al over Yam, the god of river and sea, the deity representing primordial chaos. This Bible, of course, ascribes the victory over chaos, represented by Leviathan, to Yahweh.[114]

The worship of Ba'al was a snare for the people of Israel that the prophets and priests of Yahweh contended with for centuries. From the time the Israelites crossed into Canaan, the worship of Ba'al seems to have been the most persistent threat to draw them away from Yahweh.[115] And there in Egypt, before Israel had even escaped from the army of Pharaoh, God directed Moses to fire a warning shot, crossing the Red Sea right in front of Ba'al-Zephon—essentially disrespecting the holy mountain of Ba'al by demonstrating the authority of Yahweh over the power of the sea that Ba'al had supposedly mastered.

Ba'al was on notice: Canaan belonged to Yahweh, and it would be there that Yahweh would establish His *harmo'ed*—His Mount of Assembly or "Mount of the Congregation."

This theme is echoed elsewhere in the Old Testament. In one of the Psalms, God's holy mountain, Zion, is equated with Mount Zaphon for literary effect:

> Great is the Lord, and greatly to be praised in the city of our God, in the mountain of his holiness.
>
> Beautiful for situation, the joy of the whole earth, is Mount Zion, on the sides of the north, the city of the great King. (Psalm 48:1–2)

Since Zion isn't much of a mountain—it isn't even the tallest peak in Jerusalem—and it certainly isn't "on the sides of the north" (located in the far north, the location of Zaphon, a word that actually means "north" in Hebrew), a deeper meaning is implied. What is intended is a comparison, appropriating the imagery of Ba'al's mount of assembly, his *har-mo'ed*, to show the superiority of Yahweh.

Ultimately, this conflict for Zion will be played out in the natural realm at the final battle between the forces of God and Satan. While it is popularly believed that the Hebrew words transliterated into English as "Armageddon" refer to the "Mount of Megiddo," a closer study reveals the flaws in that interpretation.

On the surface, the identification of Megiddo makes sense. It sits in a strategic pass on an important trade route between the Levant and Mesopotamia. Megiddo was the site of several historic battles; notably, between Egypt and rebellious Canaanite vassals in the fifteenth century BC, Egypt and Judah in 609 BC (at which King Josiah fell), and during World War I between Allied troops and the Ottoman Empire. Thus most prophecy scholars have assumed that the Battle of Armageddon prophesied in the book of Revelation would be fought at Megiddo.

> And the sixth angel poured out his vial upon the great river Euphrates; and the water thereof was dried up, that the way of the kings of the east might be prepared.
>
> And I saw three unclean spirits like frogs come out of the mouth of the dragon, and out of the mouth of the beast, and out of the mouth of the false prophet.
>
> For they are the spirits of devils, working miracles, which go forth unto the kings of the earth and of the whole world, to gather them to the battle of that great day of God Almighty.
>
> Behold, I come as a thief. Blessed is he that watcheth, and keepeth his garments, lest he walk naked, and they see his shame.
>
> And he gathered them together into a place called in the Hebrew tongue Armageddon. (Revelation 16:12–16)

However, there are two insurmountable problems with this interpretation. First and foremost, Megiddo is a valley. There is no mountain at Megiddo.

Second, it is common in Greek translations for the letter *gamma* to represent the Hebrew *ayin*, so that the original *harmo'ed* was trans-formed into *harmagiddô*. But given that most Old Testament apocalyptic prophecy centers on Jerusalem and Mount Zion (for example, Joel 3 and Zechariah 14), placing Armageddon at Megiddo is both linguistically and geographically inconsistent.

Armageddon will not be at Megiddo. It will be fought at Jerusalem for Yahweh's *harmo'ed*, His holy mountain, Zion—the Temple Mount.

Whether this conflict occurs soon or in the distant future, there is no doubt that it will happen. And geopolitical events are moving elements into place, setting up conditions for a war that seemed unlikely just a few years ago. Discoveries of potentially huge reserves of natural gas in the Mediterranean and oil in the Golan Heights are transforming Israel into a player in world energy markets, adding another incentive for conflict in a region that already has more reasons to hate than it needs.

This leads to the question hanging over any analysis of the future of the Temple Mount: How can the prophesied Third Temple be con-structed when the site is already occupied by the Dome of the Rock and the Al-Aqsa Mosque?

As Christians who believe in the inerrancy of Bible prophecy, we accept that a Temple *will* occupy the mount someday. Daniel was told by the angel Gabriel of a day when the Man of Sin, the Antichrist, will put a stop to the sacrifices and the offerings. For sacrifices and offerings to be stopped, there must be a place for them to resume. The question of a Third Temple is not *if*, but *when*.

Admittedly, at this point in history, it is difficult to imagine an answer to that question. Just exercising sovereignty over the Mount has been rejected by Israeli governments since 1967 as too dangerous. How could a mosque, built on the spot where Muhammad allegedly ascended into heaven, be demolished for the Temple without triggering a regional war—one that could unite Muslim factions that have been fighting each other for fourteen hundred years? Sheik Azzam al-Khatib, director of the Waqf, warned, "If they try to take over the mosque, this will be the end of time. This will create rage and anger not only in the West Bank but all over the Islamic world—and only God knows what will happen."[116]

Still, there are several ways this might be accomplished. Most simply, an earthquake could clear the Temple Mount without the need for human intervention. Israel is geologically active; experts say the area gets hit with a major earthquake of magnitude 7 or greater every thousand years or so, and smaller ones, such as a 6.2M quake that killed four hundred people in 1927, about every eighty to one hundred years. Seismologists say the likelihood and the probable intensity of the next earthquake increases with each passing year.[117]

Another (admittedly less plausible) option would be to construct the Third Temple on the Temple Mount without disturbing either the Dome of the Rock or the Al-Aqsa Mosque. A Jewish interfaith initiative launched in 2009, "God's Holy Mountain," argues that *halakha* (Jewish law) allows for a prophet to rule on the location of the Third Temple.[118] Appropriate divine revelation could result in the Temple being built alongside the Muslim sites on the Temple Mount.

However, this alternative has found little enthusiasm among Muslim authorities, as one might expect. Even rabbinical leaders reject the idea, as many believe that the Temple should not be constructed until the Messiah arrives. In fact, the Chief Rabbinate of Israel has posted signs outside the Temple Mount in English and Hebrew that read:

ANNOUNCEMENT AND WARNING: According to the Torah it is forbidden for any person to enter the area of the Temple Mount due to its sacredness.[119]

Rabbis are concerned that visitors may walk across the spot formerly occupied by the Holy of Holies unknowingly, and there is no purification system currently in place to make them ritually clean.

The final option for constructing the Third Temple is, of course, the path of greatest resistance—simply demolishing the Dome of the Rock and the Al-Aqsa Mosque to make room. It does not seem likely that any Israeli government will find the political will or popular support, even among most Jews, to go that route.

However, until the path to constructing the Third Temple is revealed, preparations for the Temple are being made. The Temple Institute, a group organized in 1987 by Rabbi Yisrael Ariel, has reportedly spent more than $30 million assembling the garments, utensils, and other items needed for Temple service.[120] And, as noted above, the Temple Institute is supported at least tacitly by the Netanyahu government, and people with close connections to Netanyahu and his political allies have been contributing financially to the Institute's work.

One of the more unusual prerequisites for the Temple's construction is a perfect red heifer. It is believed, based on Numbers 19:1–10, that a red heifer without spot or blemish that has never been yoked must be sacrificed before the Temple can be built.

> [I]n truth, the fate of the entire world depends on the red heifer. For G-d has ordained that its ashes alone are the single missing ingredient for the reinstatement of Biblical purity—and thereafter, the rebuilding of the Holy Temple.[121]

In 2015, the Temple Institute addressed that need by launching a crowd funding campaign to raise the money needed to begin breeding red cattle in Israel.

From the time of Moses through the destruction of the Second Temple in AD 70, ashes were prepared from only nine red heifers. The influential medieval physician and Torah scholar Maimonides, whose teachings are considered authoritative by many Jews, including the leadership of the Temple Institute, believed that the tenth would be prepared by Messiah Himself.

The search for a perfect red heifer has intensified in recent years as public interest in the Third Temple has increased. A candidate attracted tens of thousands of visitors to New Jersey in the spring of 2015 eager to see the animal that might welcome the Messiah. Its owner rejected an offer of $1 million for the heifer, saying he would donate the animal when the Messiah arrived.

Sadly for all interested parties, the heifer gave birth to a black calf a few months later, disqualifying it from service—and surprising its owner, who told a reporter it must have become pregnant at an unusually young age.[122] (A heifer becomes a cow after it has a calf.)

Another key element in making the Temple a reality is, of course, actual blueprints for the construction. On Tisha B'Av, or the 9th of Av (July 25/26), 2015, architectural drawings and a video featuring a three-dimensional representation of the proposed Temple were released via the Internet.[123] The design is a fascinating blend of tradition and high technology (WiFi in the Temple!), and the video tour includes the menorah, incense altar, and shewbread table, all of which have already been prepared by the Temple Institute.

The 9th of Av was a significant date on which to unveil the blueprints. Tisha B'Av is a day of fasting and mourning to commemorate the anniversary of a number of disasters in Jewish history, especially the destruction of both the First and Second Temples in Jerusalem.

Perhaps significant by its absence in the preparations by the Temple Institute is the Ark of the Covenant. There is no doubt that the Ark played a central role in the early years of the Jewish state. It moved with the Tabernacle during the Israelites' forty years in the wilderness. It resided at Shiloh and Gibeon before finding a permanent home in the Holy of Holies within Solomon's Temple. During the time of Samuel, the Philistines learned to their dismay (and great discomfort) that capturing the Ark brought a curse instead of victory.[124]

The Ark disappeared from history around the time of Nebuchadnezzar's invasion of Judah in 597 BC. There are a number of theories on the location of the Ark: One, based on 2 Maccabees 2:4–5, is that the prophet Jeremiah hid the ark in a cave on Mount Nebo in present-day

Jordan. Another, an inspiration for the plot of *Raiders of the Lost Ark*, contends that the pharaoh Shishak took the ark back to Egypt when he plundered Jerusalem in the days of Rehoboam, the son of Solomon.

Other theories hold that the Ark is being kept in Ethiopia, transported there by Menelik, the offspring of Solomon and Queen Sheba, or by Necho II, the pharaoh who killed King Josiah at the Battle of Megiddo. One archeologist even claims that the Ark was carried to southern Africa twenty-five hundred years ago by a tribe called the Lemba—which, oddly enough, has a higher occurrence of a genetic marker particular to Jews among males of one leadership clan than the general Jewish population.[125]

But hunting the Ark, or reconstructing it, doesn't seem to be a priority for the Temple Institute. According to Rabbi Chaim Richman, director of the Institute's International Department, it's because Jews already know where it is. Richman said in an interview that the Ark is buried under the Temple Mount, a belief held by many Orthodox Jews, hidden in a secret tunnel constructed by Solomon on the orders of King Josiah as a precaution against a Babylonian invasion. Richman says, "Jews have an unbroken chain of recorded information, passed down from generation to generation, which indicates its exact location."[126]

Of course, excavating under the Temple Mount is forbidden by the Waqf—at least to Jews. So getting to the Ark would be problematic, at least until the political calculus is changed by the arrival of the Messiah.

But even if it should turn out that the Ark is not under the Temple Mount, or at any of the other locations put forward, it would not necessarily prevent a new Temple from being built and used. The Ark was never housed in the Temple constructed by Zerubbabel, and Jesus still referred to it as His Father's house.

The next seven years may be the beginning of the end game of history. Forces with very different agendas are on a collision course over their mutually exclusive visions for the future of the Temple Mount. Analysts have noted that Islamists often look to anniversary dates of significant historical events as catalysts for action,[127] and an important historical marker is just ahead: The 2023–24 time frame marks one hundred years since the collapse and formal dissolution of the Ottoman Empire.

There are a number of reasons to watch the next several years very carefully:

- The Muslim Brotherhood, which briefly tasted power in Egypt before being deposed by the Egyptian military, was formed in response to the fall of the caliphate. It may try to return to power on or about the anniversary of that date.
- The Islamic State, which has declared its own caliphate, may seek to extend its legitimacy by extending control over the Temple Mount and/or the Muslim holy sites in Saudi Arabia.
- President Recep Tayyip Erdogan has publicly declared that his goal for Turkey is to achieve the status of "a great nation, a great power" by 2023.[128] (He also said Turkey would "reach the level of our Ottoman and Seljuk ancestors by the year 2071." That would be one thousand years since the Seljuk Turks defeated the Byzantine Empire at the Battle of Mazikert, a decisive victory that led to the transformation of Anatolia into Turkey. Note that at their peak, the Seljuks controlled Asia from the Aegean Sea to China, including the Levant—most of modern-day Syria, Jordan, Lebanon, and Israel.) Erdogan and his supporters may try to use one or both of the groups mentioned above as tools to advance his Neo-Ottoman agenda.
- In Israel, the government quietly supports initiatives to prepare for constructing the Third Temple, and educational programs to teach youth its importance, while prominent Orthodox and Ultra-Orthodox Jewish rabbis publicly proclaim that the Messiah's appearance is imminent.

Again, we credit only those prophecies contained between the covers of the Bible. Other prophecies, predictions, and anniversary dates are important only insofar as they shed light on the motives for the actions of others.

Considering the Muslim penchant for finding significance in round-number anniversary years, the apocalyptic beliefs of a majority of Middle Eastern Sunni Muslims, *hadiths* that prophesy a showdown between Jesus and the Dajjal (the Muslim Antichrist) at Jerusalem, and a growing belief in the Messiah's imminent arrival among Jewish religious leaders, it is safe to say that the near future for the Temple Mount—God's holy mountain, Zion—will be turbulent indeed.

[7]

Angels Everywhere

By Josh Peck

Will angelic manifestations increase in the near future? For quite some time, it has been my belief that the world will see an exponential increase of angelic activity prior to the Lord's return. Exactly what that activity may look like will be the focus of this chapter. The best proof text we have available to us is the Holy Bible. We can look to ancient accounts of angelic activities to deduce whether or not we will be seeing something similar in the near future. We can also compare ancient eyewitness accounts with experiences reported today to see if they line up.

There is a biblical principle we can use in this study to help learn from the past. Ecclesiastes 1:9–10 states:

> The thing that hath been, it is that which shall be; and that which is done is that which shall be done: and there is no new thing under the sun.
>
> Is there anything whereof it may be said, See, this is new? it hath been already of old time, which was before us.

It is my belief that this is telling us that history has a way of repeating itself. We also learn about prophetic types and shadows in the Bible.[129]

God has blessed us by providing historical accounts throughout Scripture that can give us clues to what we will see in the future.

When considering angelic manifestations, we must be clear about which angels we are considering. Culturally, when the word "angel" is used, the immediate image that comes to mind is either a small, chubby toddler with wings or a winged, adult female. These, and really all angels, are considered to be the "good guys" in our culture. Biblically speaking, these images of angels are far from accurate.

Setting aside the obvious fallacies in physical description for a moment, there is a larger problem to consider. One of the most overlooked facts in our culture concerning angels is that they are not all benevolent. There also exist fallen angels: malevolent rebels obsessed with the destruction of humanity. The reason this is so important is because the Bible seems to predict a physical return of these fallen beings. To understand how this will occur and what it may look like, it is of great benefit to explore the ancient past. Angels, both malevolent and benevolent, manifested to humans in antiquity. These accounts may provide us with clues of what we can expect to see today and in the near future.

The most obvious place to start would be chapter 6 of the book of Genesis. This is where we read the account of the sons of God mating with human women to produce their evil Nephilim offspring. After that, the Nephilim take control of the world and God sends the Flood. The chronology of this account is what is most important to us today. The angels physically manifested themselves to humanity *prior* to the worldwide Flood.

The reason this is important goes back to the idea of types and shadows. Many, as well as I, believe the global Flood of Genesis can be looked at as an example, or shadow, of the coming Rapture of the Church.[130] Just prior to God's judgment on the inhabitants of the earth, He made sure Noah and his family were safe in the ark. The separation of Noah and his family from the rest of the world is a shadow of the Rapture. Before God's future judgment on the world, the Church will be removed.[131] If the Flood can be viewed as a shadow of the Rapture, we should expect other details to coincide as well. It would stand to reason, since the world saw angelic manifestations prior to the Flood, we should expect to see them before the Rapture.

Of course, the Flood account gives us an example of the manifestations of malevolent angels. Is there another example that might show manifestations of benevolent angels? In the account of the destruction of Sodom and Gomorrah, we read that Lot was visited by two angels.[132] These angels warned Lot about the coming destruction and instructed him to leave with his family.[133] Once again, parallels can be drawn between God's judgment against Sodom and Gomorrah and the coming judgment against the world. As we can see, angels were sent to ensure the safety of Lot and his family. The escape of Lot and his family from the coming destruction can be looked at as another shadow of the coming Rapture. Benevolent angels manifested themselves physically just prior to God's judgment against Sodom and Gomorrah; thus, it stands to reason we will see the same thing prior to the Rapture of the Church.

These are only two of many examples that can be drawn from Scripture. As we dig deeper into this study, we will be able to piece together how exactly these angelic manifestations will take place. We will also learn how we can tell the difference between malevolent and benevolent angels should we ever encounter one ourselves. Of course, I cannot accurately determine the probability of any given person actually witnessing an angelic manifestation; however, I do believe it is wise to be prepared. After all, Hebrews 13:2 states:

> Be not forgetful to entertain strangers: for thereby some have entertained angels unawares.

Notice that this verse is not specific as to what kind of angels some have unknowingly come across. An argument could be made toward the possibility of this verse referring to both benevolent and malevolent angels.

UFOs

When we think of UFOs, typically we think of alien spacecraft. Of course, this isn't exactly what the term "UFO" means. If we are being technical, "UFO" stands for "Unidentified Flying Object." The term itself only implies it is an object in the sky that is lacking identification. This could be anything mechanical, biological, or even spiritual. However, it has become commonplace in our culture to use the term "UFO" when referring to suspected alien spacecraft. Consider the term "flying saucer." If we are being technical, I could take a plate or bowl out of my kitchen cupboard, throw it in the air, and call it a flying saucer. However, in our culture, if someone claims to have seen a flying saucer, this is probably not what he or she is talking about. When we really get down to it, it all depends on context. Context is key.

This is so important because context can help us understand, among other things, eyewitness accounts of UFOs. This is especially true when reading ancient texts concerning UFO encounters. For example, when it comes to Ezekiel's vision in chapter 1 of his biblical book, people most often fall into two camps. One camp will say that it was merely a vision and nothing more. In my opinion, this view is partially correct, but not fully. The other camp, which is growing exponentially, will say Ezekiel is describing a UFO: an actual alien spacecraft. In my opinion, this view is even less accurate, yet there is a hint of truth.

Many who subscribe to the ancient astronaut theory, made popular by television shows such as *Ancient Aliens*, will claim that Ezekiel was describing something purely mechanical. There are problems with this, however, as what Ezekiel describes is vastly different than any UFO commonly reported today. To get around this, the ancient astronaut camp will claim that Ezekiel was so overwhelmed by what he was seeing, he was having trouble communicating it properly and only used words that were available to him in his time. One example of this is Ezekiel 1:15–18, which states:

Now as I beheld the living creatures, behold one wheel upon the earth by the living creatures, with his four faces.

The appearance of the wheels and their work was like unto the colour of a beryl: and they four had one likeness: and their appearance and their work was as it were a wheel in the middle of a wheel.

When they went, they went upon their four sides: and they turned not when they went.

As for their rings, they were so high that they were dreadful; and their rings were full of eyes round about them four.

There are those who will claim that these verses must be describing something purely mechanical. After all, Ezekiel uses the word "wheels," which could have a flying saucer shape. He also uses the word "eyes," which could be windows or portholes in the craft.

The problem with this view is it is not consistent with the text. If Ezekiel was trying to describe a window, he could have easily used the Hebrew word *challown*, which literally translates to the English word "window."[134] Instead, he used the Hebrew word *ayin*, which translates to "eyes" in English.[135] Basically, when Ezekiel wrote he saw eyes, he meant that he saw eyes.

The really interesting thing about this account is the wheels themselves. Ezekiel used the Hebrew word *owphan*, which translates to the English word "wheel."[136] When this word is plural, it is *ophanim*. By itself, *ophanim* merely means "wheel" in the most traditional sense.[137] However, when Ezekiel uses it to describe his vision, he is actually referring to a class of angels. What we have is something similar to the "flying saucer" problem we looked at earlier. It's all about context.

There are ancient texts that actually refer to the *ophanim* as a specific class of angel.[138] This is not a new idea. The Sephardic Jewish philosopher and astronomer Maimonides wrote that the *ophanim* are the second class in the hierarchy of angels.[139] Pseudo-Dionysius, in the fourth or fifth century, wrote that the *ophanim* were among the first sphere of angelic hierarchy.[140] There are even other Bible passages that speak of the *ophanim*.[141] We also know there exist fallen angels, which are described throughout Scripture. What we're not always told, however, are the specific classes to which each fallen angel belongs. It is entirely possible that certain *ophanim* may have rebelled against God.[142] In any event, Ezekiel was not describing something purely mechanical. In fact, he was describing something extradimensional.[143]

This, among other evidence my research has turned up throughout the years, has led me to believe there are basically three types of UFOs. The first type includes the UFOs that the governments of the world manufacture. These are completely human-made and are kept relatively secret from the rest of the population. Possibly the reported UFOs that do not seem to do anything to break the laws of physics, they are clearly more technologically advanced than what we are told is available today. The second type of crafts are built with physical materials, but aren't manufactured by humans. Constructed of materials that can be found on earth or elsewhere, they are far more advanced than what humans can design. These crafts are able to travel at incredible speeds, yet make right-angle turns without slowing down. Any normal human pilot would be instantly killed by the g-forces, yet these crafts can perform such feats seemingly with ease. Most commonly described in alien abduction reports, these crafts are piloted by beings who claim to be extraterrestrial in nature, but are actually extradimensional entities: what we would call fallen angels and possibly demons.

The third type of crafts are by far the strangest, because they are completely extradimensional in nature. They are not built by natural materials and possibly may have never been "built" at all. If there are fallen *ophanim* masquerading as alien craft, they would fall into this category, which completely breaks the known laws of three-dimensional physics.[144] For example, they can change shape and color, be in more than one place at one time, and converge into a single craft. These accomplishments would be physically impossible if the crafts were limited to three spatial dimensions. However, given the existence of four or more spatial dimensions, these feats are completely possible.

Probably the best method I have come across in helping me understand higher spatial dimensions is used in fictitious literature. One popular example of this among physicists is a novella entitled *Flatland*.[145] The basic idea of the story is to consider what it would be like, as a being of three spatial dimensions, to interact with a being of only two spatial dimensions. These beings, known as *Flatlanders*, would have no up or down. They would only have access to the x and y axes: right, left, forward, and backward.

Imagine if you were able to breach Flatland as a three-dimensional being. Let's say you were able to stick your finger through the Flatlanders' two-dimensional space. How would that look to the Flatlanders? They would see a very small line segment appear out of nowhere.[146] As your finger would pass through the two-dimensional plane, they would see the line segment grow in size. When you took your finger out again, they would see the line segment shrink in size, then disappear again, seeming to vanish in thin air.

Similarly, you could stick your whole hand through their two-dimensional space. They would first see a small line segment appear as the tip of your middle finger breached the two-dimensional plane. Next, your index and ring fingers would break through. The Flatlanders would see two more segments appear at either side of the first one as the first one grew in size. Then, as your pinky and thumb would break through, they would see two more segments appear. What they see next would be truly surprising. As the rest of your hand went through, they would see all five segments combine into one large segment. Then, as your wrist went through, they would see the large segment shrink in size. When you pulled your hand out, they would see the entire spectacle again, only this time in reverse; until all of the segments disappeared completely.

We can use the example of Flatland to help understand what a four-dimensional interaction would look like in our three-dimensional world. If a four-dimensional sphere (often referred to as a "hypersphere") were to move through our three spatial dimensions, we would only be able to perceive it through our three-dimensional eyes. We would see a very tiny sphere suddenly appear as it breached our dimension. We would see the sphere grow in size as it moved through our dimension, shrink in size as it moved out, then disappeared completely. Similarly, if different parts of the same extradimensional object were to travel through our three dimensions of space, we could see multiple objects come together and converge into one. This is the same type of phenomenon many reports of UFO sightings describe. The only way these things are possible is if these crafts are extradimensional in nature.

As I have shown in my earlier works, the terms "extradimensional" and "spiritual" are synonymous when both ideas are understood correctly.[147] Reports of human encounters with extradimensional crafts and/or life forms are rising exponentially.[148] What this really means, in biblical terms, is that angelic sightings and encounters are on the rise. As we will see, the UFO phenomenon is only one piece of a much larger puzzle. It would seem that the veil between here and the place of spiritual/extradimensional existence is thinning, thereby allowing these things to breach our space. If we truly are living in the last of the last days, we should expect this to happen, as we will see further in this chapter.

Human-type

We are probably all familiar with stories of possible encounters with angels who look perfectly human. One example of this is a typical story of a family driving down a long and lonely road. The family is in the long stretch of their trip, with no cars, gas stations, or any other signs of civilization for miles in either direction. All of a sudden, the car stops working as they realize they have run out of gas. A kindly stranger appears, seemingly out of nowhere, with a can full of gas. This stranger sometimes engages the family in polite conversation while offering to help, then he puts gas in the tank of the car and leaves. The family doesn't think anything about it right away, but later deduces it may have been an angel, though he looked completely human.

Whether or not the above scenario ever actually occurred, I cannot say for certain. However, the Bible does seem to corroborate the human-type aspect of stories such as these. Many times when angels are described in the Bible, they look human, even to the point that others don't realize they are angels. Most often they are described as men. For example, Genesis 19:1–5 states:

> And there came two angels to Sodom at even; and Lot sat in the gate of Sodom: and Lot seeing them rose up to meet them; and he bowed himself with his face toward the ground;
>
> And he said, Behold now, my lords, turn in, I pray you, into your servant's house, and tarry all night, and wash your feet, and ye shall rise up early, and go on your ways. And they said, Nay; but we will abide in the street all night.
>
> And he pressed upon them greatly; and they turned in unto him, and entered into his house; and he made them a feast, and did bake unleavened bread, and they did eat.
>
> But before they lay down, the men of the city, even the men of Sodom, compassed the house round, both old and young, all the people from every quarter:
>
> And they called unto Lot, and said unto him, Where are the men which came in to thee this night? bring them out unto us, that we may know them.

This passage describes angels, yet verse 5 tells us the men of the city mistook them for ordinary men. Genesis 18:1–2 states:

And the Lord appeared unto him in the plains of Mamre: and he sat in the tent door in the heat of the day;

And he lift up his eyes and looked, and, lo, three men stood by him: and when he saw them, he ran to meet them from the tent door, and bowed himself toward the ground.

This is another example that describes angels as men. In fact, in this account, one of the "men" is the Lord Himself. These are two of many examples throughout Scripture where angels appear as ordinary humans. This provides more fullness to what we looked at earlier in Hebrews 13:2, which again states:

Be not forgetful to entertain strangers: for thereby some have entertained angels unawares.

If angels are indeed appearing more frequently as we draw closer to the Tribulation and end of days, we should expect these types of encounters to increase as well. Interestingly enough, as researchers of angelic visitations have pointed out, these occurrences happen across all cultures and religious beliefs.[149] We are living in a time when even atheists are having angelic encounters.

Miraculous Visitors

In August of 2013, various outlets released a story of a mystery priest who blessed, and allegedly healed with anointing oil, a car-crash victim before disappearing unnoticed.[150] This priest was referred to by many as an angel. As it turned out, the mystery priest was identified as Father Patrick Dowling of the Diocese of Jefferson City, Missouri. Before the identity of the priest was revealed, the victim's mother, Carla Churchill Lentz, went on record to say she believed it had been an angel who had helped her daughter. The *Huffington Post* reported:

She told *USA Today* that emergency workers said there is no way her daughter should have lived through the crash. She believes the man may have been "an angel dressed in priest's attire because the Bible tells us there are angels among us."[151]

There are many reports such as this, yet not as many end up with the mysterious helper being identified. The frequency of these types of accounts, however, does speak to the general public's willingness to believe in angels when a sighting such as this is made. At times, this willingness comes with compromise. Many times in reports such as these, there will be a detail or two that doesn't line up biblically. Those details are often passed off as inconsequential and are not considered in determining whether the sighting was actually heavenly or angelic. In the story about Father Dowling, no one was reported as having questioned why an angel would appear as a Catholic priest. Also not addressed was why an angel would need anointing oil to heal anyone. However, disbelief was suspended and many were convinced it was an angel. Thus, a compromise was made.

Another such account happened in Joplin, Missouri. On May 22, 2011, a deadly tornado ripped through the town, killing 161 people.[152] After the devastation, stories started to surface about angelic "butterfly people" who miraculously saved some of the residents from the tornado's destruction. Most of the accounts were reported by children of the affected area. The story was so impactful that it can still be found in the online blog of *MissouriLife*, Missouri's state magazine. Abby Holman reported:

In the wake of the destruction, after the wind had settled, children who endured the storm began telling those family, friends, and relatives the stories of what they saw. Some said that the butterfly people protected them during the storm.... As the accounts circulated, more and more children came forward, saying that they too saw the butterfly people. Some say they believe

that the butterfly people were angels; others called them an inde-
scribable presence.[153]

Mural artist Dave Loewenstein even painted a giant mural to commemorate the angelic butterfly people. The mural is a large depiction of
children and beautiful, giant butterflies. What neither the mural nor the
story in *MissouriLife* reports, however, are some of the stranger details
concerning this encounter.

On March 18, 2015, the television show *Monsters and Mysteries
in America* dedicated a segment to the butterfly people sightings.[154] In
the show, these beings are said to have been big—much larger than a
human being—with extraordinary capabilities. One was reported by
a child as looking like a lady dressed in white with large wings. This
particular being was also reported as being able to communicate to the
child, seemingly by telepathic means. A nurse on the scene, after the
tornado passed, reported seeing a phantom-like being. She described
this being as tall, wearing a robe, and appearing completely gray like a
statue.

Interestingly enough, according to the show, the children who witnessed these beings never described them as angels, even though the
majority of people in the area are religious. Time and time again, the
children described the entities as beings of light with butterfly wings. It
wasn't until later that some of the adults started believing these beings
were angels.

Again, these descriptions bring up interesting questions that have
gone unasked: Why did the beings help some people and not others?
Why did the children call them butterfly people instead of angels? Why
are the physical descriptions of the beings so odd compared to other
reports of angelic visitors?

I ask these questions not to discourage a belief that these beings may
have been angels. The fact is, I have no idea whether these were angels
sent by God or something else entirely. I ask these questions because I

believe we should never make assumptions concerning the supernatural. We should ask questions. We should be sensitive to possible deceptions. We live in a world that is inhabited by a spiritual enemy of darkness who can appear as an angel of light.[155] Just because something appears to be an angel, or even says it is an angel, doesn't mean it actually is. The enemy is set out to deceive, and as Christians, we have a responsibility to be sensitive to that fact.

Angelic Gospels

Certain angels, not sharing the best interest of God, are set out to deceive mankind. Galatians 1:8 states:

> But though we, or an angel from heaven, preach any other gospel unto you than that which we have preached unto you, let him be accursed.

Along these lines, 2 Corinthians 11:4 states:

> For if he that cometh preacheth another Jesus, whom we have not preached, or if ye receive another spirit, which ye have not received, or another gospel, which ye have not accepted, ye might well bear with him.

A true angel of God will preach the true gospel of Jesus Christ and direct all worship to Him. When the prophet John was with the angel in the book of Revelation, he began to worship him. Yet the angel, being an angel of God, corrected this behavior. Revelation 19:10 states:

> And I fell at his feet to worship him. And he said unto me, See thou do it not: I am thy fellowservant, and of thy brethren that

have the testimony of Jesus: worship God: for the testimony of Jesus is the spirit of prophecy.

A fallen angel, on the other hand, will preach other gospels. A fallen angel will try to deter someone from Jesus Christ. There have been multiple reports of supposed alien beings telling contactees things contrary to Jesus' teaching and the Bible. They will even go as far as to try to influence the contactees' entire worldview to one that better suits the aliens' purposes. Leo Sprinkle, who holds a PhD in counseling from Wyoming University, summarizes the experiences by stating:

> UFO contactees have been chosen…no UFO contact is accidental…and that the manifestations are designed to influence the worldview of contactees…. What follows is a summary of these claims about UFO experiences and related conditions:

1. UFO contactees have been chosen; no UFO contact is accidental.
2. Contactees are ordinary people, who exhibit a caring or a loving concern for all humankind.…
4. UFO experiences include paraphysical, parapsychological, and spiritual manifestations which are designed to influence the "world view" of contactees.…
8. Contactees are programmed for a variety of "future" activities, including awareness of their own contacts and desire to share their messages and knowledge with other contactees.
9. The lives of contactees move in the direction of greater self-awareness, greater concern for the welfare of planet Earth, and a greater sense of Cosmic Citizenship with other beings in the universe.
10. The personal metamorphosis of UFO contactees is the forerunner of a social transformation in human consciousness,

which now is leading to changes in the economic, educational, military, political, and religious institutions of nations of the Earth: the "New Age" of true science and spirituality.[156]

The last point is of special importance when considering the plan of the enemy as described in the book of Revelation. We are told of a coming one-world religion and government that will rule the world. Revelation 13:7–8 states:

And it was given unto him to make war with the saints, and to overcome them: and power was given him over all kindreds, and tongues, and nations. And all that dwell upon the earth shall worship him, whose names are not written in the book of life of the Lamb slain from the foundation of the world.

There are also many reports from people of the New Age movement who claim to be in contact with spiritual beings. These beings go by different titles, such as *ascended master* and *spirit guide*, but the messages are usually similar. The message is usually focused on the individual instead of Jesus. Usually, contactees of ascended masters are told they can attain salvation or "enlightenment" without need of the Jesus of the Bible. In fact, some ascended masters even go as far as to claim they *are* Jesus Christ. One such website, the Ascension Research Center, shows on the "Jesus" page a picture of Jesus with the title "Ascended Master Jesus Christ." Under the title and picture is a long collection of nonsensical and unbiblical teachings that compare more with gnosticism than anything Jesus Christ taught. Among these is written:

Flowing through your chakras are the Electrons of Light that come forth from your own God Presence. These Electrons are fashioned, Beloved, according to your co-creation.... You have not come merely for your own salvation through the Ascension in the Light. You have come to raise the vibration of the entire Earth! Mastery, yes—attainment, yes—but in so doing, you will have exacted the conscious awareness of your own God Presence, changing all about you into the highest vibration which can be brought forth.[157]

Not only is this scientifically inaccurate (photons are the particles of light, not electrons); it is outright heresy by biblical standards. Notice that this preaches a message of self-salvation by means of realizing your own "God Presence," which again, is a gnostic teaching.

To be clear, I do not bring up this specific website and teaching to ridicule it maliciously. I bring it up because it is a classic example of what is being taught in the world, especially in New Age theology. It is important to see how some can use very similar words we use as Christians, and even take texts directly from the Bible and subtly twist them to mean something completely different.[158] The closer the world comes to the Tribulation, the more these false teachings and deceptions will increase. This is why we need a solid foundation in the true gospel of Jesus Christ, lest we fall into deception ourselves.

Testing the Spirits

Thankfully, God has provided us a way to tell if a message we may receive, a being we may see, or a doctrine that may be taught is truly of God. We already looked at how to tell different gospels and teachings apart from the examples given in the Bible, but what about actual entities? The Bible teaches that we need to test the spirits. 1 John 4:1–3 states:

> Beloved, believe not every spirit, but try the spirits whether they are of God: because many false prophets are gone out into the

world. Hereby know ye the Spirit of God: Every spirit that confesseth that Jesus Christ is come in the flesh is of God:

And every spirit that confesseth not that Jesus Christ is come in the flesh is not of God: and this is that spirit of antichrist, whereof ye have heard that it should come; and even now already is it in the world.

We are required by biblical teaching to test every spirit. I wholeheartedly believe the closer we come to the end, the more people will have experiences with angelic beings, both benevolent and malevolent.

We are told specifically not to believe every spirit. I believe this can refer to humans as well as spiritual beings. The passage tells us that there are many false prophets in the world, which can be human or angelic. There is no way to tell how many of us will ever have to confront a spiritual being of any kind prior to the Rapture, but it is a good idea to be well versed in proper teachings just in case. This passage teaches us how to test the spirits: it all revolves around Jesus Christ. If a person or spirit denies Jesus in any way, such as the examples we looked at earlier, then we know they do not speak the truth.

Given the amount of deception and delusion that is said to come in the end times (and I believe we are starting to see that now), we need to know how to test the spirits and refuse to partake in deception. Second Thessalonians 2:10–11 states:

And with all deceivableness of unrighteousness in them that perish; because they received not the love of the truth, that they might be saved. And for this cause God shall send them strong delusion, that they should believe a lie: That they all might be damned who believed not the truth, but had pleasure in unrighteousness.

Regardless of where we may fall in eschatological beliefs, this is a warning we should all take very seriously.

Revelation Angels

The book of Revelation alone shows us that we can't judge an angel based solely on appearance. The benevolent angels at times can look just as strange as the malevolent ones. Revelation 4:6–8 states:

> And before the throne there was a sea of glass like unto crystal: and in the midst of the throne, and round about the throne, were four beasts full of eyes before and behind.
>
> And the first beast was like a lion, and the second beast like a calf, and the third beast had a face as a man, and the fourth beast was like a flying eagle.
>
> And the four beasts had each of them six wings about him; and they were full of eyes within: and they rest not day and night, saying, Holy, holy, holy, Lord God Almighty, which was, and is, and is to come.

Being covered in eyes, resembling animals, and having wings certainly makes for an odd appearance. Also consider the angel described in Revelation 10:1, which states:

> And I saw another mighty angel come down from heaven, clothed with a cloud: and a rainbow was upon his head, and his face was as it were the sun, and his feet as pillars of fire.

The appearance of the angel isn't enough to determine where his allegiance is placed. It all depends on his message and/or purpose. A good example of this is the account of the four horses and riders of Revelation chapter 6. These obviously are malevolent beings. We can tell that not by how they appear, but by their purpose. They take peace from the earth. Conversely, in Zechariah chapter 6, we see similar horses, though these are benevolent. The text tells us they are spirits sent by God to bring peace to the earth.[159]

The book of Revelation is full of angelic beings, both benevolent and malevolent, giving the clear impression that the end times, specifically the Tribulation, will be very different than what we are used to in the world today. Revelation 12:9 states:

> And the great dragon was cast out, that old serpent, called the Devil, and Satan, which deceiveth the whole world: he was cast out into the earth, and his angels were cast out with him.

Revelation 12:12 states:

> Therefore rejoice, ye heavens, and ye that dwell in them. Woe to the inhabiters of the earth and of the sea! for the devil is come down unto you, having great wrath, because he knoweth that he hath but a short time.

The world will be confronted directly with these beings, and this will not always be a pleasant experience as it may sometimes be today. It will be a time when angelic visitations will be feared. Different terminology might be used for these beings, such as "alien," "extradimensional," or "hybrid," along with many others, but the result will be the same. Satan and his angels will know their time is short, and they will unleash hell upon the world.

The Great Hope

The marvelous thing is that no one in the world is required to go through this time of horror. Jesus Christ paid the ultimate price so that we can have salvation from the enemy. In fact, we can have salvation from death itself. This gift is available to everyone. 1 John 2:1–2 states:

My little children, these things write I unto you, that ye sin not. And if any man sin, we have an advocate with the Father, Jesus Christ the righteous:

And he is the propitiation for our sins: and not for ours only, but also for the sins of the whole world.

To be saved, all we need to do is admit we need saving. We admit to God that we have done wrong and cannot attain perfection on our own. We admit to Him that we believe Jesus died on the cross to take the punishment of sin in our stead, and that we believe He was resurrected, showing His power over death. We ask for forgiveness and His gift of eternal salvation. Then the real journey begins.

The Christian life only begins at acceptance of salvation. After that, it is all about cultivating a relationship with our Father. We talk to Him through prayer, learn about Him through His Word in the Bible, and live for Him by following His teachings. This will never be a perfect journey, at least not on this side of eternity, but is one of constant learning, growing, and maturing.

It is also acceptance of Jesus that can dispel all fear, even of death. 2 Timothy 1:7 states:

For God hath not given us the spirit of fear; but of power, and of love, and of a sound mind.

Through Jesus and His Holy Spirit, we can have access to authority over the enemy. With this authority, we never have to fear Satan or his angels. If we were left to our own authority, we would be without hope against these things. Whether demonic attack, UFO abduction, or even contending against false doctrines, the authority of Jesus Christ is our great hope. It's through this authority, based on His death on the cross, that we can be free from fear and have eternal security.

My hope is this chapter has provoked you to at least seek these things out through private study. It is good to ask questions, research, and compare things against Scripture to make sure they line up. We all have a personal responsibility to seek God and His truth from Him directly. If we seek God, He will meet us halfway, but it is up to us to make the first move. James 4:8 states:

> Draw nigh to God, and he will draw nigh to you. Cleanse your hands, ye sinners; and purify your hearts, ye double minded.

Wait no longer and begin your journey today.
Josh Peck
www.ministudyministry.com
joshpeckdisclosure@gmail.com

The Next Great Awakening

By Larry Spargimino

Wilt thou not revive us again:
that thy people may rejoice in thee?
—PSALMS 85:6

Imagine the following scene: churches filled with worshipping Christians humbled by their sin, but praising God; all-night home prayer meetings; new believers sharing their new-found faith with friends and family; and a determined resistance by an overwhelming majority of the population to godless policies mandated by the government.

What has happened?

Poison gas seeping from the earth? An invasion by UFOs? Group psychosis? A collective madness?

— · —

What do you do when you feel you have been dealt with in an unjust and unfair manner? It may be a court decision or a lawsuit; maybe it's government corruption or a situation that you have no possibility of changing. You appeal to a higher authority, one you believe can change your circumstances, one who understands and has the power to make the necessary changes, and who desires justice and mercy.

George Washington's first flag—a flag bearing a pine tree and the words, "An Appeal to Heaven,"—was flown by a squadron of six cruisers commissioned under Washington's authority as commander-in-chief of the Continental Army in October of 1775. The words, "An Appeal to Heaven," were an expression of the right to revolution used by the British philosopher John Locke in his *Second Treatise on Civil Government* (1690), in which he refutes the theory of the divine right of kings.

The tree on the flag is a white pine, a wood that was especially suitable for the masts of sailing vessels. The British restricted the colonists' use of the white pine, even on their own property. The flag and the white pine became a symbol of resistance to tyranny, but underscored the need for help from heaven: Britain was a formidable enemy for the fledgling nation.[160]

America and the rest of the world need help from heaven. Despite our early years, America has descended to a depth of perversity that is unprecedented in our short history. The legitimization of same-sex marriage, the recreational use of marijuana, and the radical ideas of the gender-equality proponents—i.e., the guys need to have free access to the girls' locker rooms—all indicate that we have lost way. Hamtramck, Michigan, now has an all-Muslim city council. All the conservative talk shows, radio pundits, rallies, and conservative candidates with great ideas are simply not slowing down what seems to be an irreversible drift into total anarchy, which, should it come to pass, will invariably be followed by tyranny. Something more is needed. We need revival. We need to appeal to heaven.

God, in His grace and mercy, has given us many warnings. He has put fences around certain behaviors, because He knows that such behaviors are harmful to individuals, groups, and whole societies. The fences around the expression of human sexuality have been erected in love. The "thou shalt nots" of Scripture were not given to make us miserable, but rather to give us lasting happiness. G. K. Chesterton's warning, however, is being ignored: "Don't ever take a fence down until you know why it was put up."[161]

Once we start taking the fence down, our wildest guesses cannot even imagine the mischief that will follow. How about "marrying yourself"?

> As for the woman who married herself, Nadine Schweigert, she explained to journalist Anderson Cooper after her "wedding" ceremony in May 2012, "I feel very empowered, very happy, very joyous.... I want to share that with people, and also the people that were in attendance, it's a form of accountability.... I was waiting for someone to come along and make me happy. At some point, a friend said, 'Why do you need someone to marry you to be happy? Marry yourself.'"
>
> Well, why not? If there can be same-sex "marriage," why can't there be self-"marriage"? As crazy as this sounds, it's happening. An audience member watching the Cooper interview decided that now she wanted to "marry" herself. A thirty-year-old Taiwanese woman "married" herself in 2010, and in 2014, a British woman did the same, with headlines announcing, "Woman Gets Fed Up with Being Single—and Marries Herself!" Why? Because "she didn't have enough time for a 'conventional' relationship."[162]

Appeals in Scripture

There are many appeals to a higher authority in Scripture. When Haman's plans for genocide against the Jewish people were discovered, Queen Esther made an appeal to king Ahasuerus. She asked for him to show mercy and justice (Esther 8:3–7). Similarly, when the apostle Paul was falsely charged, he made an appeal to Caesar (Acts 25:11). When the apostolic Church was threatened by the religious authorities and preaching and teaching in the name of Jesus was forbidden, the saints appealed to God, asking for boldness and for a demonstration of divine power:

> And now, Lord, behold their threatenings: and grant unto thy servants, that with all boldness they may speak thy words, By stretching forth thine hand to heal; and that signs and wonders may be done by the name of thy holy child Jesus. (Acts 4:29–30)

In legal parlance, "appeals" are an attempt to reverse what is perceived to be an unjust decision by a lower court by making an appeal to a higher court. Appeals, sometimes, must be made with great persistence. Our Lord's parable in Luke 18 gives us the sense:

> And shall not God avenge his own elect, which cry day and night unto him, though he bear long with them? I tell you that he will avenge them speedily. Nevertheless, when the Son of man cometh, shall he find faith on the earth? (vv. 7–8)

Those who pray for revival are making an appeal to heaven—and they must be persistent. They are admitting their need and their weakness. They are admitting that they are completely inadequate to deal with the present situation. It's an admission of humility.

> If my people, which are called by my name, shall humble themselves, and pray, and seek my face, and turn from their wicked ways; then will I hear from heaven, and will forgive their sin, and will heal their land. (2 Chronicles 7:14)

Israel's History

In the long and spiritually checkered history of Israel, there were periods of apostasy and calls for revival. During the time of temple worship, there was the erroneous view that Jerusalem was so special to God that He would somehow make exception for the sins of the city. He would simply wink at the evil and vice committed by Israel's kings and clergy. God, however, made it quite clear, through the words of Jeremiah the prophet, that judgment would be the penalty for Israel's sins (Jeremiah 4:1–7, 5:6, 24–25; 7:22–28). Godly king Josiah was deeply distressed when the Book of the Law was discovered and the certainty of judgment revealed (2 Kings 22:8–13).

The degree of perversity taking place in Jerusalem during those years was notorious. The sodomites lived by the Temple of the Lord and the women wove garments for the priests of Baal (2 Kings 23:7–8). Regarding Josiah, Scripture states:

> And like unto him was there no king before him, that turned to the Lord with all his heart, and with all his soul, and with all his might, according to all the law of Moses; neither after him arose there any like him. (2 Kings 23:25)

Yet, despite Josiah's sincerest efforts, "the Lord turned not from the fierceness of his great wrath, wherewith his anger was kindled against Judah, because of all the provocations that Manasseh had provoked him withal" (v. 26).

The Stages of Revival

Revivals are not all the same. History shows that there have been distinctive features (later we will enumerate), but there are also many similarities. They seem to progress through at least three stages, as explained by George Otis Jr., founder of the Sentinel Group.[163]

Stage One: Awakening. In this stage, one or a few individuals is impressed with the need for a change. There is an abiding sense that "all is not well." Josiah is a good example. He "rent his clothes" when the newly discovered Book of the Law was read in his presence. He realized how far out of step with God the nation and people were (2 Kings 22:11).

Stage Two: Visitation. God responds to the cries of His people and steps into their lives in a variety of ways. They come to realize that "this is the Lord's doing." Daily routines are often put on hold as God comes—somewhat like a heavenly chiropractor—and snaps all areas of dysfunction back into alignment.

It is at this stage that the revival can either fizzle out—as often happens—or move forward and affect an entire community, town, or city with transformation. Hence, the really important question is not just, "How do revivals begin?" but also, "Why do they often end prematurely?"

Why *do* they often end prematurely? Sometimes key players in the revival come to believe that the revival is *their* doing. They soon become proud and are no longer yielding to the Holy Spirit's influence.

Other times, there is division and disunity. As revivals grow, they begin to touch many lives and involve different churches, some of various doctrinal persuasions. Such is fertile ground for division, strife, and disunity. Petty bickering and a censorious spirit can cause a revival to grind to a halt. All Bible doctrine is important, but all Bible doctrine is not equally important, nor are all views on a certain point of doctrine equally true. Christians do not have to see eye-to-eye on every point of doctrine to move forward and see a community-wide transformation.

In Colonial America, the Wesleys held to a strong Armenian theology (Methodism, Pentecostalism) that emphasized man's response and free will; whereas others like George Whitefield, with his strong Calvinistic soteriology (Westminster Presbyterianism, Sovereign Grace teaching, and Reformed theology), was on the opposite end of the theological spectrum, yet the two groups never really let their theology get in the way of revival, though there was some limited disagreement.[164]

Stage Three: Transformation. This is the stage in which the revival continues and spreads and touches whole communities so that there is true transformation as God heeds the prayers of His people and their joint labors.

A good example is the First Great Awakening in America (beginning in the 1730s), which brought conviction and salvation to many, but which also marvelously transformed the fledgling colonial government. It helped give the United States its historical identity and impacted the educational system. The Second Great Awakening (beginning around 1800) led to mass evangelism and produced the rise of various groups and denominations. [165]

Is God Still Interested in Bringing Revival— Even in the Darkest Places?

Can God bring revival? Indeed, He can. He is doing it right now in some of the most anti-Christian places on the planet—Muslim-majority and Muslim-rim areas—and reaching out to a vast number of people who are sincerely seeking "something better." Not content with the violence, mayhem, and wanton destruction, God is responding to their heart cries in extraordinary ways to give some men and women, boys and girls not "something far better," but *Someone* far better than anything they have known up to this point. But what about the Middle East, and also North Africa and Central Asia? In his book, *Breakthrough: The Return of Hope to the Middle East,* Tom Doyle writes:

> The Middle East is the place where history, religion, and politics collide head-on. The lead news story of the day often emanates from this volatile region—and rightfully so, because of its instability. By watching the news on television, it would be easy to form an opinion about the people who live there. It would also be easy to form an opinion about the future of the region, and my guess is that your opinions would not be optimistic. How

could it be? Is there ever any good news from the Middle East? Yes, there is good news from the Middle East! In fact, there is great news from the Middle East.[166]

In a CBN interview, Doyle was asked: "How are young people in the Middle East responding to the demands of fundamental [radical] Islam?" He replied:

It is true that the militant Muslim leadership is directing some young people into the path of jihad. But in extensive interviews throughout the Middle East, we continually hear that over half of Muslims worldwide are not practicing their faith whatsoever. Muslims are born into their religion and do not choose it like born-again Christians do. Therefore a significant number of people within Islam have little investment in it. You can clearly see that in the young people in the Middle East today. In Syria the majority of young people dress in very modern clothes. In Iran, drugs are plentiful and parties are a nightly occurrence.... There is, in fact, a strong desire not to be isolated from the West. After 9/11, Muslims worldwide began to ask questions like, "Do I have to be a terrorist to be a good Muslim?"[167]

In their book, *Captive in Iran: A Remarkable True Story of Hope and Triumph Amid the Horror of Tehran's Brutal Evin Prison,* Maryam Rostampour and Marziyeh Amirizadeh describe the rebellion of young women in Iran against Islamic dress codes, as well as the honest searching for God. They both became Christians as young adults and met while studying theology and evangelism in Turkey in 2005. Deciding to work together, they returned to Iran and began sharing their faith. In 2009, Maryam and Marziyeh were arrested in Tehran for promoting Christianity—a capital crime in Iran. They had already given out thousands of tracts, Bibles and pieces of Christian literature, and had started two house churches.[168]

Dubai, United Arab Emirates, has become a favorite drawing card for many in the Middle East, including Saudi Arabia. The availability of wine, women, and dance, and the large numbers seeking such activities—while ultimately not in the best interest of individuals—is proof that there is a restlessness and rebellion against Islam. The Arab Spring, which started in January of 2011, was a pro-democracy movement spearheaded by youth. Unyielding Muslim leaders came to acknowledge the reality of rage, rap, and revolution.

Radical Islam is turning many people off. Even Muslim nations are at war with ISIS. The brutality of ISIS is well documented, and much of it has a religious basis. In a *New York Times* report titled "ISIS Enshrines a Theology of Rape," author Rukmini Callimachi writes:

> "Every time that he came to rape me, he would pray," said a 15-year old girl who was captured on the shoulder of Mount Sinjar one year ago and was sold to an Iraqi fighter in his 20s. Like some others interviewed by *The New York Times*, she wanted to be identified only by her first initial because of the shame associated with rape.
>
> "He kept telling me this is ibadah," she said, using a term from Islamic Scripture meaning worship.
>
> "He said that raping me is his prayer to God. I said to him, 'What you're doing to me is wrong, and it will not bring you closer to God.' And he said, 'No, it's allowed.' 'It's halal,'" said the teenager, who escaped in April with the help of smugglers after being enslaved for nearly nine months.[169]

This is horrendous human-rights abuse, yet it appears that it is preparing many hearts to look for the hope and joy that all humans crave. Can we believe that all Muslim parents are pleased with such abuse of their daughters? One of Muhammad's wives, Aisha, was married to the prophet when she was six. The marriage was consummated when she was nine. Can we believe that Muslim parents living in the twenty-first century approve of this behavior and want their prepubescent daughters to marry bearded old men? Hearts are being prepared by such horrors. God is also preparing hearts by appearing to many Muslims in dreams and visions. They are ready for the Answer.

Dreams and Visions: Do Things Like That Happen Today?

This author has received a variety of responses and comments from radio listeners and readers concerning the dreams and visions that some Muslims are experiencing. A proper care in investigating the report is proper, even a "holy skepticism" is warranted. We need to verify as best we can. However, when Muslims have a dramatic change in their belief system as well as in their lifestyle, that suggests at least a degree of authenticity.

Former Muslims no longer stumble over things that Muslims find offensive in biblical Christianity: The Trinity, the two natures of Jesus Christ, the death and resurrection of Jesus Christ, the reliability of the Judeo-Christian Scriptures over the Qur'an, and when they begin to have a love for all people—even Jews (!)—we marvel and must acknowledge that God is working supernaturally.

Just because there are reports of supernatural and extraordinary signs and manifestations does not automatically mean that the reports are fraudulent, or that those doing the reporting have a "low view of Scripture." The apostles of the first century had a very high view of Scripture, yet they reported many extraordinary signs and manifestations. Unfortunately, cessationists—those who believe that the manifestations recorded in the New Testament are no longer occurring today—see it as an either/or situation. Either you have a high view of Scripture and are a cessationist, or you have a low view of Scripture and believe in continuing manifestations. Such is a nonbiblical division. One can have a high view of Scripture and not be a cessationist.

To get into an extended discussion of cessationism versus continuationism is beyond the scope of this chapter. However, Acts chapter 10 does provide us with a biblical paradigm that provides a yardstick by which we can evaluate some of the present-day phenomena. Cornelius, a Gentile, a Roman centurion, is a seeker after truth. The Bible calls him "devout," a man who was obviously sincere. He "feared God with all his house, which gave much alms to the people, and prayed to God always" (v. 2).

As the story unfolds, he is told by "an angel of God" (v. 3) to send men to Joppa, to seek Simon Peter. In chapter 11:14, we are told that Peter would share with Cornelius "words, whereby thou and all thy house shall be saved." So, even though the story is somewhat unusual, it is really not that unusual: The Word of God is the means of salvation. Cornelius and his family were not saved on some kind of a dream, vision, or experience, but through the agency of the Word of God.

We need to remember that, at this point in the unfolding story of redemption given in the New Testament, something new is happening: The gospel is going out to Gentiles. So, as cessationists like to point out, there is something unique about the Cornelius account that will never again be repeated. As a result of what transpired here, believers everywhere know that God does not want to save just Jews, but people everywhere. Acts 10 is foundational to the mission and purpose of the Church. Once the foundation is laid, it need not be laid again.

Yet, this is only part of the story. The God of the Bible loves Muslims, too. However, many Muslims are not aware of that. Evangelizing Muslims is fraught with many challenges. Not only are there the physical dangers of going to Muslim-majority countries to preach the gospel, there are also the theological and philosophical challenges that the Christian meets. For centuries, Muslims have been told by their leaders that the Bible of the Jews and Christians has been woefully corrupted. Moreover, Muslims are taught that Christian theology is simply wrong. God has no son. The thought is, to them, totally blasphemous. A virgin-born Son of God? The thought is ludicrous. Further, they are taught to believe that Christians are idolatrous: They supposedly believe in three "gods." If God is going to reach Muslims, He is going to have to do something spectacular.

Many Muslims are very much like Cornelius. They are devout. They fear God. They are trying to raise their families to honor God. There is, as with Cornelius, a real heart-hunger for something truly meaningful. They hear about the barbarism of ISIS, and they don't want that. They are drawn to what they hear about Jesus. With longing hearts, they think, "If only Christianity were true." Do we really find it strange, and out of keeping with Scripture, that God would show Himself to them in some very dramatic ways?

Tom Doyle has spent some twenty years in the Middle East witnessing God's activity in the lives of many Muslims. He has also written extensively on the subject. In his book—*Dreams and Visions: Is Jesus Awakening the Muslim World?*—he gives "five dream principles" that he has observed:

1. The dreams do not suggest anything not supported by promises contained in the Word of God. If the dream portrays Jesus in a different light than what we see in Scripture, the dream is a false one.... Even though God uses dreams and visions, it's also true that most cults started with one, so it's crucial to measure whatever someone sees by Scripture.
2. Muslims who have dreams about Jesus remember the experience, complete with the concrete details. The specifics stay with the person....
3. Muslims who have dreams about Jesus realize their experience is purposeful and that it is not a stand-alone event.... the dream gives the spiritually thirsty a drink of water, but it doesn't quench their thirst. Only the Living Water provided by a salvation experience with Christ can do that.
4. When Muslims have dreams about Jesus, they realize a new order is in store. They grasp that Jesus loves them and welcomes them. This leads them on a search to know Jesus personally. Once they

find Him in all His glory, many Muslims have no trouble repenting of their sins and committing to follow Jesus for the rest of their lives....

5. A dream or a vision about Jesus brings definition to a Muslim's life. The dreamer cannot shake off the encounter. It becomes part of his or her personal testimony on the way to knowing Jesus.[170]

Bold Witnesses for Christ

In addition to the supernatural manifestations, Muslims who have accepted Christ are laying their lives on the line so that others will come to know Christ. In their book, Maryam Rostampour and Marziyeh Amirizadeh describe their activities prior to their arrest:

> While it was true Maryam and I had been raised in Muslim households and had Islamic names, we had not embraced Islam as children or young adults. In our minds, we had never "converted" from Islam because we'd never really believed in Islam to begin with. We had met each other at an evangelical conference in Turkey, had decided to work together, and had spent the last three years in Tehran quietly sharing the gospel with anyone who was interested. For two of those years, having divided the city into squares on a huge wall map, we had gone out at night between 8:00 PM and midnight, visiting one sector at a time. We handed out New Testaments in cafes, gave them to taxi drivers, and left them in cabs, coffee shops, and mailboxes. When we finished a section we marked it with a cross on our map. In three years altogether, we had given away about twenty thousand New Testaments.[171]

These two young women were incarcerated in Evin Prison, one of the most notorious prisons on the planet. They write:

The food in Evin prison was awful. One regular meal was a stew consisting mostly of water and fat with a few unpeeled carrots and potatoes. The vegetables hadn't been washed, so the water was always full of dirt. It was more like eating mud than stew… the food was also laced with formaldehyde, which was supposed to suppress the inmates' sex drive. This made the food smell and taste even worse, ran the risk of poisoning us, and is a hazard to a woman's reproductive system.[172]

Learning about Today's Revivals from the Revivals of the Past

God's Work in Early America

The Puritans—A binding commitment to the God of Scripture, and religious awakenings, have been a part of the American experience. America's original vision, though somewhat marred by an unbiblical view of church-state relations, has been expressed in the 1620 Mayflower Compact. The voyage to the new world was "for the glory of God, and the advancement of the Christian faith.…" So far, so good. Unfortunately, it also involved the advancement "of the honor of our King and country." It opens with these words: "In the name of God, Amen. We, whose names are underwritten, the loyal subjects of our dread Sovereign Lord King James, by the grace of God, of Great Britain, France, and Ireland, Kin, defender of the Faith, etc. (Wikipedia)

The Pilgrims who landed in Plymouth, Massachusetts, in 1620 were separatist Puritans. They wanted to reform the old churches of Europe and establish a new social order based on Scripture. The Puritans were dissatisfied with the limited extent of the English Reformation and felt that the practices of the Church of England were too closely aligned with those of the Roman Catholic Church.

The Downgrade

The Loss of Transforming Power—As the years passed, there was a creeping loss of spiritual vision and vitality. Succeeding generations could be characterized as "having a form of godliness, but denying the power thereof" (2 Timothy 3:5).

This loss was reflected in what was called "the halfway covenant" implemented in 1662. It offered partial (halfway) membership to individuals who did not have a testimony to being truly saved. On the basis of being "church members" through the concept of "the halfway covenant," members' babies and infants could somehow how be considered citizens in good standing. This was a clear indicator that many of the local churches had been seriously downgraded from New Testament fellowships to something far less.

The Loss of Brotherly Love—The Puritan experiment was a failure when it came to addressing those Christians with some different beliefs. When "outsiders" such as Baptists and Quakers migrated to their territory, the Puritans responded in a most uncharitable manner. They were soundly against the idea of "believer's baptism" and felt it was a threat to their covenantal views of church membership. The theological views of the Baptists, and especially the views of the Quakers, were perceived as a threat to "life and godliness." The Puritans banned these newcomers to their communities. In some cases, the newcomers were imprisoned and some were even executed by hanging.

This harsh reaction highlighted two things. First, it betrayed the loss of spiritual life. Secondly, it exposed the inherent weakness of a social order in which the civil government and a particular church are merged, using their cooperative power to coerce others in matters of faith.... In the end, the Puritans' treatment of outsiders made it clear that the Quaker/Baptist idea of the civil government not being aligned with any church was the better choice. In the Quaker/Baptist ideal, the civil government should diligently protect the free expression of faith for all sects and denominations, while taking sides with none of them. Just over 100 years later, all of this would play into the formulation of the First Amendment in which the Founders would state: "Congress shall make no law concerning the establishment of religion, nor hindering the free exercise thereof."[173]

This imperious attitude took an ugly turn with the Salem witchcraft trials (1692–93). Reports that some were practicing witchcraft brought a swift response from the Puritans—a response that sounds definitely rooted in the Mosaic Covenant. Hyatt gives a balanced approached when he writes:

> In defense of the Puritans, however, mark Noll has pointed out that, compared with what was happening in Europe at the time, the actions of the Puritans were quite guarded. In fact, in Europe during this same period, hundreds of alleged witches were executed at the behest of both Catholics and Protestants.
>
> Others have pointed out that witchcraft was, in fact, being practiced. This being the case, when unexplained accidents began to occur, many New Englanders reacted in fear by going after those whom they believed to be responsible...In defense of the Puritans—without exonerating them—Attorney William H. Cooke, in his excellent book, *Justice at Salem: Reexamining the Witchcraft Trials,* shows the importance of judging their actions within the context of their own worldview rather than the context of a secularized, 21st Century worldview.[174]

The witchcraft trials have been considered "the hammer that shattered the theocratic faith of America." Applying the Old Testament theocratic law in seventeenth-century America was a dark shadow that did great harm to the cause of Christ. Can we learn from this? Is this not a lesson teaching us that God's work must be done in God's way?

God Shows Up in America

A Heart Cry for God—At the turn of the seventeenth century and moving into the early years of the eighteenth, a growing number of Americans were praying for God to quicken His work in the colonies. This was the "awakening stage" that we discussed earlier, when we discussed the stages of revival.

God wonderfully manifested a taste of glory in 1726 in a Dutch Reformed Church in New Jersey. It began as the fruits of the labors of Theodore Frelinghuysen (1691–1747), a Dutch Reformed pastor who began visiting his congregants in their homes and challenging them to live a more consistently Christian life. He brought the challenges to his pulpit ministry. Some became angry with "meddlesome preaching" and left the Church; but eventually his labors bore fruit and a powerful work of God spread among the churches of his area.

Frelinghuysen influenced a young Presbyterian pastor in the town of New Brunswick, New Jersey, by the name of Gilbert Tennent (1703–1764). Gilbert and his brothers were some of the more significant leaders in the initial stages of the First Great Awakening.

After graduating from the Log College (considered by many to be the forerunner of Princeton University), Gilbert was licensed to preach. Shortly after assuming the pastorate, he became deathly ill. Believing that he had accomplished so little in his short life, Gilbert promised God that if God would allow him just six more months of life, he would fully dedicate his life to the salvation of souls.

Jonathan Edwards and Revival in New England—As God was touching down in the middle colonies, there was a growing visitation in New England. A leader in the northern revival was Jonathan Edwards (1703–1758), pastor of the Congregational Church in Northampton, Massachusetts.

Edwards had a brilliant mind. He entered Yale College at thirteen years of age and graduated four years later as class valedictorian. A careful student of Scripture, Edwards became proficient in the ancient languages of the Bible and prepared himself for service to his Lord. During the summer of 1735, a sense of the divine presence was felt. Without any sort of planned evangelistic outreach, Edwards wrote that "souls did as it were come by flocks to Jesus Christ." Instead of going to the tavern, people flocked to Edwards' home. "A loose and careless person could scarcely be found," wrote Edwards.[175]

The Awakening Impacts Women—The place of women in ministry has been a topic of discussion, and sometimes of heated debate. On the mission field, some women take a lead role. Even in the modern American church, the women are the ones who host prayer meetings, faithfully attend the services of the church, sponsor church camps, prepare food, and remind their husbands that they are to be the spiritual pace-setters in the home.

In the First Great Awakening in colonial America, critics of the revival movement took offense at what they claimed were excesses of emotion, and were even more heated in their condemnation of the fact that "some white women, and African Americans, shed their subordinate social status long enough to exhort at religious gatherings." Edwards' wife, Sarah Pierpont Edwards (1710–1758), was noted to be a woman of prayer. She discussed theological themes with her husband and with visiting ministers, and exhorted others out of the overflow of her own experience.

Historians believe that, because Edwards' ministry was not confined to the strict gender roles evident in his day, he was committed to promoting "gender equity." In his comments on Genesis 3:20, where Eve is called "the mother of all living," some have even claimed that Edwards was a "proto feminist."[176]

The Awakening Impacts Native Americans—History shows that during this period of time, relationships between the colonists and Native Americans had become strained. Some of the chiefs and tribal leaders saw the colonists as competitors and as threats to their own influence. Several incidents developed in which the colonists seem to exhibit a lust for land. The cutting of timber, the harvesting of wild game, and the colonists' impact on the environment were viewed with growing suspicion.

Nevertheless, there were those individuals who realized that all are corrupted by sin—men, women, Europeans, and native Americans—and that Jesus Christ has rendered an efficacious atonement for those who believe on His name. One of those was David Brainerd (1718–1747) who ministered evangelistically to the Mohicans, Stockbridge and Susquehanna in Massachusetts, and the Delaware Indians in New Jersey.

Brainerd had enrolled in Yale, but was sent home because of his tuberculosis, which was causing him to spit blood. When he returned to Yale in 1740, tension was mounting between some of the students and faculty. The tension had arisen because of the spiritual enthusiasm of the students who, upon visits by preachers such as George Whitefield and Gilbert Tennent, started to say what was regarded as unkind words about faculty members. This led the college trustees to pass a decree in 1741 that "if any student of this College shall directly or indirectly say, that the Rector, either of the Trustees or tutors are hypocrites, carnal or unconverted men, he shall for the first offense make a public confession in the hall, and for the second offense be expelled." The faculty had invited Jonathan Edwards to preach the commencement address, hoping that he would support their position, but Edwards, instead, supported the students and called for a revival of religion amongst the faculty.[177]

Brainerd had a great love for the Native Americans and was used by the Holy Spirit to bring many to a saving knowledge of Jesus Christ. He lived under very arduous conditions, sometimes sleeping in wet forests, shivering in the cold and suffering from malnourishment and from the hardships of "the howling wilderness." In 1746 he became too ill to continue his ministry. He spent the rest of his life at the home of Jonathan Edwards and was nursed by Edwards' seventeen-year old daughter, Jerusha Edwards. The friendship grew. Some believe that there was a romantic attachment between the them.

The Awakening Impacts African Americans—Once again, a burden for the lost and the direction of the Holy Spirit drove evangelists to break with conventional distinctions. A number of evangelists in the First Great Awakening prayed for, and sought to win, African Americans, both slave and free. Hyatt writes: "The message of a personal 'new birth' experience with God resonated with these people. Also, they found specific parts of the Biblical narrative with which they could closely identify, such as Israel's time of slavery in Egypt and God's mighty deliverance of His people."[178]

Gilbert Tennent and Jonathan Edwards report on the "conversion of young people, children, and Negroes." George Whitefield recounts that after preaching his farewell message in Philadelphia and retiring to his lodging that "near 50 negroes came to give me thanks for what God had done for their souls." Whitefield considered this an answer to prayer, as he had a great burden of soul for African Americans. Again quoting Hyatt:

> The Awakening among the African Americans resulted in the emergence of black congregations, both slave and free. Later, it also opened the way for African Americans to serve in the Revolutionary War. In fact, David Barton notes that numbers of blacks were given honorable discharges and pensions, and some were honored with complete military funerals for their service in the Revolutionary War.[179]

What about the Extrabiblical Manifestations?

Whenever the topic of revival comes up, people often ask questions about the jerks, twitches, moaning, falling over, and other such occurrences. Jonathan Edwards did see some unusual manifestations in the First Great Awakening. He comments on them in his *A Faithful Narrative of the Surprising Work of God in the Conversion of Many Hundred Souls in Northampton.* Edwards says that they are not endorsed by Scripture, but neither are they condemned by Scripture. He did not believe that they were a necessary part of revival. On the other hand, he did not seem to consider them to be fraudulent, self-induced, or the result of dangerous demonic activity, either.[180] The following observations seem to be a balanced and sound view.

> We should note that strange and controversial phenomena are often associated with revivals: the "jerks," shouting, being "slain in the Spirit," speaking in tongues, barking, dancing in the Spirit, and more. Since none of these extraordinary manifestations have appeared in all revivals, we conclude that none of them are mandatory for a spiritual awakening. True revival can happen without them.
>
> Nevertheless, most of these unusual phenomena occur more than once in these accounts. What, then, do we think of such occurrences? We agree with those observers who have concluded simply that when the divine is poured into the human, we can expect the human to react in extraordinary ways.
>
> Some of these phenomena, we believe, are prompted by God. At other times they are just the exuberant expressions of those who are experiencing God's presence. For that reason we offer a few words of caution to those who read about the various displays of emotions while they pray for revival in our own day.

First, don't seek the extraordinary signs of revival, for these unusual expressions are not what revival is about. Second, don't measure the success of a revival by the number or intensity of extraordinary signs; if you do you'll miss the whole purpose of revival. Third, seek the Lord, because it is He who revives our hearts.[181]

Do You Have the Courage for Revival?

While there is no charge for salvation—"Jesus paid it all"—revival can be very costly. How costly depends on where we live and when we are living. Today, praying for revival might be asking for martyrdom.

Whenever the Holy Spirit begins to work and manifest Jesus in His saving glory, there are two groups that respond in widely different ways.

1. There are those who rejoice, and who say "Lord, may you continue to pour out your Spirit. Lord, use me. Empower me. This is wonderful!" As we approach the end of the age, there will be Christians from a variety of doctrinal persuasions, but the point of union will be the Lord Jesus Christ, as He is revealed in Scripture. They will be united on His deity, His Lordship, and His return. They will work together for revival.

2. There are those who are infuriated by the presence of God. Because they hate God, they will hate Him even more as His presence becomes more and more undeniable. Islam, atheism, secular humanism will all be in a rage. Since they cannot reach God, they will reach out to His messengers. The persecution will increase worldwide, even as the Body of Christ increases in strength and number. However, the Bible leads us to believe that as the rage increases, so will the extent of the Gospel's reach will increase. In Matthew 24 we read:

And ye shall hear of wars and rumors of wars: see that ye be not troubled: for all these things must come to pass, but the end is not yet. For nation shall rise against nation, and kingdom against kingdom: and there shall be famines, and pestilences, and earthquakes, in divers places. All these are the beginning of sorrows. Then shall they deliver you up to be afflicted, and shall kill you: and ye shall be hated of all nations for my name's sake. And then shall many be offended, and shall betray one another, and shall hate one another. And many false prophets shall rise, and shall deceive many. And because iniquity shall abound, the love of many shall wax cold. But he that shall endure unto the end, the same shall be saved. And this gospel of the kingdom shall be preached in all the world for a witness unto all nations; and then shall the end come. (Matthew 24:6–14)

In this passage, we see that there are two polarities, and both polarities are growing in intensity and scope. There is a rising tide of godlessness and persecution, yet there is also a growing company who proclaim the gospel of the Kingdom. The darkness will grow and grow, but the light will shine ever more brightly and a great number will come to the Savior.

We must also notice that in the increasingly difficult times we are reminded "but the end is not yet," and "all these are the beginning of sorrows." For those on the earth during that period of time, trials, suffering, and persecution should not be understood as signaling defeat. The saints will need to persevere in their outreach. Ultimately, the gospel of the Kingdom will be universally proclaimed.

Who Will Have the Courage to Persevere in Faithfulness?

Those who are facing martyrdom are usually given an opportunity to save their lives. All they need to do is to deny Christ. As the reality of a painful death becomes more obvious, some do. Some might say: "Jesus will forgive me for denying Him. He is longsuffering and knows that I am weak. After all, He gave Peter a second chance. He will surely give me a second chance."

Another might argue, "What good will I be if I die? I can do more for the cause of Christ if I stay alive. I will be like Peter and deny my association with Christ." Yet, as always, there will be those who refuse to deny Christ. From whence do they get their courage? Some possibilities:

- They've been to Bible college and seminary, and have read a lot of books.
- They have studied the scholastic proofs for the existence of God and are absolutely persuaded that God is real and that they will go to heaven after being beheaded.
- They've read the biographies of the great martyrs of the faith, and have memorized large sections of *Foxe's Book of Martyrs*.
- They are stubborn and will not give their persecutors the satisfaction of seeing them change their minds.

Of course, none of these adequately *answers the question*. Boldness and courage in our witness does not come from our academic degrees or depth and breadth of reading—nor does it come from our study of apologetics. There must be more to it than that, and there is.

A basic question is: "How far are you willing to go in your commitment to Christ?" I often meet Christians who have a pet theory or view on some point of doctrine, or some interpretation of Bible prophecy. They sometimes become quite argumentative about it and are willing to write everyone off who disagrees. My question to them is: "Are you willing to die for your belief?"

Isn't that really the question? How far are you willing to go in your commitment? How sure are you? What is your level of certainty?

Certainty and a Powerful Witness

Have you ever wondered how the prophet Elijah could say to King Ahab: "there shall not be dew nor rain these years, but according to my word"? (1 Kings 17:1).

Have you ever wondered what really happened to Peter? After cowering before a servant girl and denying that he ever knew Jesus, just a few weeks later he could boldly proclaim Christ in Jerusalem. What happened to him? Had he studied some theological textbooks and had a graduate seminar with some of the best Christian apologists the world had to offer?

If you are going to die for Christ, how do you know that Christianity is true? How do you know that YOU are a Christian and that the promise of eternal life belongs to YOU?

There are some who claim that we can have assurance of salvation by examining our lives to see how they measure up. If you've been a good Christian and have been living a godly life, then you can have assurance that you are a child of God and will be going to heaven when you die—right?

If that's the basis of our assurance, you are either deceived, are ignorant of your own sins and shortcomings, or you've lowered the stands of God to accommodate your own moral failures—which, by the way, is precisely what some people do.

The Witness of the Holy Spirit

The direct witness of the Holy Spirit is primary in bringing the soul certainty. "No man can say that Jesus is the Lord, but by the Holy Ghost" (1 Corinthians 12:3). God is the One who gives assurance and certainty. That's why "the natural man" remains in darkness:

> But the natural man receiveth not the things of the Spirit of God: for they are foolishness unto him: neither can he know

them, because they are spiritually discerned. (1 Corinthians 2:14)

God was obviously working in the hearts of the Thessalonians, revealing to them Jesus Christ and the divine source of the Word of God. Paul thanked God for that:

For this cause also thank we God without ceasing, because, when ye received the word of God which ye heard of us, ye received it not as the word of men, but as it is in truth, the Word of God, which effectually worketh also in you that believe. (1 Thessalonians 2:13)

This conviction was immediate and direct, and did not come through reflection and years of study.

The Holy Spirit uses the Word of God and gives certainty concerning its truths. But the Holy Spirit also acts independently of the Word of God in leading and directing in special situations. This is the way the first missionary journey began:

As they ministered to the Lord and fasted, the Holy Ghost said, Separate me Barnabas and Saul for the work whereunto I have called them. (Acts 13:2)

Peter couldn't understand the real meaning of his roof-top vision:

Now while Peter doubted in himself what this vision which he had seen should mean, behold, the men which were sent from Cornelius had made enquiry for Simon's house, and stood before the gate…While Peter thought on the vision, the Spirit said unto him, Behold three men seek thee. (Acts 10:17, 19)

Paul and Silas received instruction from the Holy Spirit not only regarding where to go, but where *not* to go:

> After they were come to Mysia, they assayed to go into Bithynia: but the Spirit suffered them not. (Acts 16:7)

Paul's Macedonian vision was instrumental in giving the apostolic team the certainty of the direction in which God wanted them to go:

> And after he had seen the vision, immediately we endeavored to go into Macedonia, assuredly gathering that the Lord had called us for to preach the gospel unto them. (Acts 16:10)

R. T. Kendall, the Oxford scholar and successor to Dr. Martin Lloyd-Jones at Westminster Chapel, writes:

> Many conservative evangelicals hold only to a soteriological [meaning salvation] doctrine of the Holy Spirit. This means that the Holy Spirit can only speak through the Bible and apply it when the gospel is preached. And yet they rightly believe that the Holy Spirit makes the Bible come alive and makes Jesus real. This is what we all believe! But according to them, the Holy Spirit would not speak directly today as he did to Philip—"Go to that chariot and stay near it" (Acts 8:29). In other words, most conservative evangelicals have on their radar screen the thought that the Holy Spirit will apply the Word when it is preached. They have no concept of an immediate and direct witness of the Holy Spirit Himself. The Spirit "applies" the Gospel to the mind and heart when it is preached. What is wrong with this? Nothing! This is the normal, necessary and needed witness of the Holy Spirit when the Bible is preached. The Holy Spirit reaching the hearts of men and women through the Word

is absolutely essential to the preservation of historic truth. It is what I lean on when I myself preach.

But there is more to be had. Either we believe that God the Holy Spirit is alive and well today—or our Trinity is merely God the Father, God the Son, and God the Holy Bible. It is this undoubted anointing of the Holy Spirit at work directly and immediately that is needed today![182]

God is still working today, giving certainty in unusual ways, even in times of tragedy. In his book *Killing Christians*, Tom Doyle tells of Shukri Hananiyah, his wife, Khadija, and their two little children, Sarah and Walid. Shukri and Khadija both had dreams and visions and came to put their faith in Christ. Shukri was a bold witness and even shared Christ at the Great Mosque in Mosul (ancient Nineveh), Iraq. Shukri was fearless, but was tortured and killed. His wife, Khadija, shares a message in the book and describes the certainty she has of God's will for her.

When the news of Shukri's torture and killing reached me, I was completely numb for about an hour. How could I fight against the will of God? He sent Shukri and me to Mosul to bring the fragrance of Christ to this dark and evil city. As we prayed, we reasoned that we would be martyred for our glorious Lord someday, and it would be an honor. But now that Shukri was really gone, it did not feel so honorable.

I share these words several months after I lost my beloved Shukri. I am not sure I would have been able to compose myself and voice my feelings before now. I ached for him. It's hard to put into words how much I miss my husband. He loved me with the love of Christ. And little Sarah and Walid were lost without their loving abu! But the Lord's grace is rebuilding their shattered hearts.

You must know this: We are not leaving. *God put us in Iraq, and here is where we will stay.* Perhaps you, too, have been called to persist at something God has called you to. I am convinced it is our duty as servants of the Most High to stay, go, or continue doing whatever He says until he tells us otherwise.[183] (emphasis added)

Dare We Believe That God Still Speaks and Gives Certainty?

The issue of God speaking today is bound to garner strong opinions and views from a variety of Christians. It is certainly beyond the scope of this chapter to answer every question and to broach every issue. Our context, however, limits the discussion. Does God still speak in the sense of giving certainty? Can we know His will? Can we face death in times when the spread of the gospel is raising anger and murderous rage, with boldness and confidence knowing that we are in the will of God?

Revelation is a communication from God. It is a disclosure of something that is hidden, and would remain hidden, except that God reveals it. Human effort, study, years of learning, will still not disclose that which can be known only by revelation. Jesus prayed:

> I thank thee, O Father, Lord of heaven and earth, because thou hast hid these things from the wise and prudent, and hast revealed them unto babes. (Matthew 11:25)

We may also think of divine revelation as information. We have all heard of criminal cases that have been retried because of new information that could substantially alter the outcome of the case. God's revelation is that information from the Holy One makes the difference. Facing death, the martyr receives convincing information with such clarity and power that all shadows of doubt flee. Not all revelation, however, is intended for the same purpose.

Normative Revelation—The Bible constitutes normative revelation. It establishes the norm (standard) for all Christians everywhere. Every Christian is to believe and receive normative revelation. Those who reject any aspect of the body of normative revelation are guilty of sin. The Bible is the Christian's ultimate and **final** authority. When it is properly interpreted, using hermeneutical principles rooted in Scripture, the words of Scripture come with the authority of God's actual words.

Private Leading—God gives His people personal insights into issues that affect us individually but that are certainly not, in any sense, normative for other people. The choice of spouse, occupation, clothing, and our decisions regarding specific issues that are morally neutral and are not specifically addressed in the Bible fall in this category. We are to pray to God that He would show us His will for us in this particular matter. Paul's Macedonian vision, cited earlier, is an example.

Signs, Wonders, Witness and Revival

When the early Christians met opposition to their witness, their prayer involved two requests: (1) That they would have boldness and not be afraid. (2) That God would show Himself in power by healing and by signs and wonders. Acts 4:29–31 records their prayer:

> And now, Lord, behold their threatenings: and grant unto thy servants, that with all **boldness** they may speak thy word, **by stretching forth thine hand to heal; and that signs and wonders may be done in the name of they holy child Jesus.** (emphasis added)

Does God still work miracles, and can we expect supernatural intervention? If He wants His work to continue and His gospel to be proclaimed, He will. The New World Order, the increasing use of surveillance technologies, and the militant madness to exterminate Christianity from the earth, along with the attempts at mind control through the use of magnets, drugs, and ultra-low frequencies, all present a terrifying arsenal of techniques to change our minds and to get us to deny Christ. The Bible speaks of "lying wonders" and of deception on a grand scale (2 Thessalonians 2:9; Matthew 24:4, 11). Has God left us to fend for ourselves in this terrifying world of deceit, tricks, and treachery, or should we cry out to Him for a manifestation of His presence and power? Just as God overcame seemingly insurmountable challenges in the early Church, those praying for revival believe that He can, and will, do that today.

There are new technologies that have the potential for being used in the most sinister of ways. Christians have never faced the arsenal of evil that can be used by the forces of evil. In both the United Kingdom and the United States, researchers are using magnets to change the values that people hold dearly and to weaken personal inhibitions.

Christians have Christian inhibitions about many things such as alcoholic beverages, lying and cheating, dating and marriage, and sexual behavior. Such inhibitions are good. Even little children have walls of modesty that God has placed in their hearts. There are some things that little children know are wrong, even without instructions. If these walls of modesty are violated, children are uncomfortable and will tell parents what has happened. However, the human mind can be "hacked," values changed, and inhibitions removed. This can be done surgically, chemically, electromagnetically, and in other sinister ways.

Having certain inhibitions are good and healthy (though not all inhibitions are good and healthy, as is true with false scruples, but that's another story). In the flesh we can't live a life pleasing to the Lord without inhibitions. They are like security lights outside a building that automatically turn on when an intruder steps beyond a certain point.

In experiments on both sides of the Atlantic, volunteers were asked to respond to the negative and positive emotional aspects of religion, in particular to rate their beliefs in the devil, demons, and hell, plus God, angels, and heaven. Experiments show that it is possible to alter and modify personal beliefs about these subjects without the individual being aware that his or her values are being manipulated—i.e., that someone is tampering with his or her mind.

In one experiment, participants were given two essays to read, both supposedly written by immigrants. One essay was extremely complimentary to the host country; the other was highly critical. Usually, individuals are defensive when a "foreigner" criticizes their country. However, scientists found that when a magnetic force was used to temporarily shut down the threat-response part of the brain, people were more likely to have positive feelings toward the immigrant who was critical. New experimentation is being developed in the area of TMS—Trans-cranial Magnetic Stimulation.[184]

The Pentecost Outpouring

In Acts chapter 2, we read that "there appeared unto them cloven tongues like as of fire, and it sat upon each of them. And they were all filled with the Holy Ghost, and began to speak with other tongues, as the Spirit gave them utterance" (vv. 3–4). Some who were present asked, "What meaneth this? Others said, These men are full of new wine" (vv. 12–13).

Peter denied that this was inebriation and said, "But this is that which was spoken by the prophet Joel" (v. 16). Yet, in Joel's prophecy, referred to by Peter, much more is included than what happened at Pentecost. Everything predicted by Joel did not occur on Pentecost:

> And it shall come to pass in the last days, saith God, I will pour out of my Spirit upon all flesh: and your sons and your daughters shall prophesy, and your young men shall see visions, and your old

men shall dream dreams: and on my servants and on my hand-maidens I will pour out in those days of my Spirit; and they shall prophesy: And I will show wonders in heaven above, and signs in the earth beneath; blood and fire, and vapor of smoke: The sun shall be turned into darkness, and the moon into blood, before that great and notable day of the Lord come. (Acts 2:17–20)

There is no indication that on Pentecost the Holy Spirit was poured out on "all flesh," or that "the young men had visions and that the old men had dreams; the sun did not turn into darkness, and the moon into blood." When Peter said "this is that which was spoken by the prophet Joel," he meant "this is like that," or "this is the beginning of that," or "this is a foretaste of that." We must believe that, sometime in the future, all of these manifestations will actually happen.

From the current work of God, it would be hard to deny that we are now seeing the outpouring that Acts 2 describes. But it would appear that there is much more to come. Though the work of God in Muslim lands is extraordinary, no one can convincingly say that this present work of God is the complete fulfillment of this prophecy in Acts 2.

The Next Great Awakening: When Will It Occur?

Since this chapter is titled *The Next Great Awakening*, a natural question that readily comes to mind is: "When will it begin?" It is this author's opinion that it has already started.

At present, the gospel is touching many more lives than ever before. Though biblical Christianity faces many challenges, God continues to raise up faithful servants who are ably equipped to deal with these challenges.

When many thought that science had dealt a death blow to the Christian faith, God raised up trained scientists and apologists like Henry M.

Morris and the Institute for Christian Research (ICR). ICR regularly addresses issues that may seem troubling to Bible-believing Christians and offers books and publications by PhDs in the scientific fields who also believe in the full inspiration and authority of the Bible. The same can be said for Ken Ham and Answers in Genesis, as well as Carl Baugh and the work of the Creation Evidences Museum in Glen Rose, Texas.

Many other examples could be cited. The decision of *Roe v. Wade* opened the door to abortion on demand, yet there was a tremendous pushback. Pro-life crisis pregnancy centers now number in the thousands. Even in emerging nations, pastors are teaching the sanctity of human life. Books, articles, and scientific studies show that human life begins at conception.

In his book *Dreams and Visions: Is Jesus Awakening the Muslim World?* author Tom Doyle includes Appendix 3: "The Global Shift—Christianity Soars Ahead of Islam," and cites the results of research:

- The majority of Islamic growth is through birth. An estimated 96 percent of Muslim growth is merely biological. Since Islamic tradition values large families, this inflates the numbers in their favor. Muslims who are born into the Muslim faith do not necessarily have the same commitment to Islam as do Christians who make a personal decision to become a Christian.
- The majority of evangelical growth is through conversion. Islam, on the other hand, often uses threats and persecution to build up the ranks. These "conversions" are not based on conviction but are merely "survival techniques."
- Eighty-five percent of the world has a Bible available in their native language.
- There have been 6.5 billion viewings of the Jesus film.
- It is estimated that when Father Zakaria Botros (a Coptic Christian apologist who debates Islamic clerics) is on televi-

sion in the Middle East, 60 million viewers watch. Al-Qaeda has honored him with the words "one of the most wanted infidels in the world," and has put a million dollar bounty on his head.

- In Iran, 7 to 9 million Persians watch satellite broadcasts of Hormoz Shariat, the "Billy Graham of Iran."
- The tight borders around Islamic nations can now be easily by-passed through the Internet. With Facebook and Twitter, young Muslims have now connected to the world, and they are having their say. The Syrian and Egyptian protests are movements that went viral.[185]

Satellite Television

SAT-7 identifies itself as "Christian Satellite Television by and for the people of the Middle East and North Africa," broadcasting in Turkic, Farsi, and Arabic. It has programs for women, Christian discipleship programs, and programs dealing with misconceptions often held about the Christian faith. Sat-7 Kids is the first and only Arabic Christian channel exclusively for children. It has been estimated that one out of every three children in Iraq views Sat-7 Kids and one out of every four children in Saudi Arabia views it.SAT-7 Kids seeks to make the gospel of Christ meaningful to kids in the Middle East, especially as they mature and take their place in a society where the future is so uncertain.

The FAQ section of the SAT-7 website addresses the question, "How can SAT-7 operate openly in Muslim majority nations?" The answer:

SAT-7 seeks to be a good member of the community, like the minority Christians who live in the Middle East and North Africa. By serving the local Christian community, by being a tool local churches can use, and by not broadcasting any programming that is political or that attacks any religion or denomination, SAT-7 has developed a good reputation within the region. The programs SAT-7 broadcasts help the majority community to understand the beliefs of Christians, dispelling misconceptions about the Christian faith that are common in the region. This sensitive and respectful approach helps the local Christian minority to be recognized as a valuable segment of local society. It has also enabled the ministry to maintain registered offices in Egypt and Lebanon, and will hopefully enable Sat-7 to open additional offices in other countries in the region in the future.[186]

The Call to Consistent Faith and Courage

It has always been God's desire to reach out to people all over the planet. He told Abraham, "And I will bless them that bless thee, and curse him that curseth thee: and in thee shall all families of the earth be blessed" (Genesis 12:3). Though Isaiah was a Hebrew prophet of old, the Lord spoke through him and said, "Look unto me, and be ye saved, all the ends of the earth: for I am God and there is none else" (45:22).

As the world becomes more deeply embroiled in conflict and confusion, the person and work of Jesus Christ are becoming increasingly more attractive to those whose hearts are being touched by the Holy Spirit and who desire peace and joy. It is this author's belief that God is preparing the world for a great end-time harvest. Despite the opposition, the gospel will be proclaimed over all the world, and then the end will come (Matthew 24:14).

[9]

The Rise of a Final End-Times Global Government

By Troy Anderson

t's arguably the biggest cover-up and political scandal in modern history.

Unbeknownst to much of the world, the elite are following what is known as "The Plan" to create a global geopolitical, economic, and religious system as predicted in Scripture.

Through a series of trade treaties, transnational laws, a "global citizen" indoctrination campaign, the UN plan titled *Transforming Our World: The 2030 Agenda for Sustainable Development*, and the Paris climate-change agreement, wealthy globalists are involved in an international political and economic takeover—what one former United States official calls a "global financial *coup d' etat.*"[187]

"It almost feels like pages being ripped out of a *Left Behind* novel," says Dr. Thomas R. Horn, the internationally acclaimed investigative author of *Petrus Romanus, Exo-Vaticana,* and *Zenith 2016,* and the chief executive officer of SkyWatchTV. "These are big-time, major prophecies unfolding right before our eyes."[188]

Kept largely secret for decades, these clandestine power brokers and their interlocking network of transnational corporations, international banks, government agencies, think tanks, foundations, and secret societies are creating what they call the "New International Order" and "Global Union."[189]

"One of the primary instruments for bringing this new global order is the United Nations and its climate change treaties like Agenda 21 and sustainable development," says Paul McGuire, an internationally recognized prophecy expert, Fox News, CNN, and History Channel commentator and the author of *The Babylon Code: Solving the Bible's Greatest End Times Mystery, The Day the Dollar Died,* and other books.

> None of these terms like eco-friendly, climate change, Agenda 21, sustainable development, social justice, and similar phrases actually mean what they pretend to mean or what the masses of people think they mean. In the manner of George Orwell's 1984, these are mind control words to conceal the true agenda and what is called "The Plan" of the United Nations, the secret societies, and the elite who control them.[190]

A Biblical "Whodunit"

In our bestselling investigative book *The Babylon Code* (www.faithwords.com/babyloncode)—the result of a five-year journalistic investigation involving more than one hundred interviews with faith leaders and prophecy experts such as Billy Graham, Dr. Tim LaHaye, Dr. Horn, and Joel Rosenberg—McGuire and I delve into the biblical riddle of Mystery Babylon and Babylon the Great in Revelation 17–18.

Combining a traditional journalistic investigative exposé with a mystery-solving journey into the Bible's greatest cryptogram, *The Babylon Code* follows the clues of a biblical "whodunit" that started in Genesis at the Tower of Babel and culminates in Revelation with the Battle of Armageddon.

The prediction involves Mystery, Babylon and foretells an international takeover by the world's elite—a global political and financial coup that will set the stage for the last days. This biblical mystery originates in ancient Babylon with the Tower of Babel and Nimrod, an archetype of the Antichrist and the tyrannical ruler of the first world government, economy, and occult-based religious system.

Babylon, the second most mentioned city in the Bible besides Jerusalem, plays a major role in the prophetic books of Isaiah, Jeremiah, Ezekiel, and Daniel, and remerges in Revelation as "Mystery, Babylon" and "Babylon the Great"—the final geopolitical, economic and religious system controlled by the Antichrist and False Prophet.

The 2030 Agenda and a World Socialist State

Since the book's release on October 6, 2015, prophecy experts and others have been astounded by the convergence and acceleration in end-time signs. In the subsequent months, the global elite took a number of steps to lay the groundwork for the creation of a world socialist state. As these events unfolded, geopolitical and prophecy experts sounded the alarm regarding secret trade pacts, laws undermining American sovereignty, the UN summit on sustainable development, and the Paris 2015 Climate Conference

In September, President Barack Obama, Pope Francis, and the UN General Assembly approved a sweeping document titled *Transforming Our World: The 2030 Agenda for Sustainable Development* at a UN summit in New York City that brought the world "one giant step closer to true global governance." The preamble calls for a "new universal agenda" for all humanity. The authors of the document wrote that the next fifteen years will be "some of the most transformative in human history."

"But one big question looms," wrote WND News Editor Leo

Hohmann in his article, "Obama Puts U.S. On 'Fast Track' To World Government":

> How does such an ambitious plan get implemented? The plan bypasses Congress and the legislatures of the worlds other 193 nations. Yet, the heads of state agreed to work toward implementation, largely through secret trade deals and backroom bureaucratic rule-making…. Very few members of Congress have likely even read the U.N. document that Obama agreed to implement.[191]

The only thing the elite are lacking now to fully create the "new global order" is a crisis big enough to garner public support in America and other nations for "full-on global governance." "Remember, the elite who are behind this are experts at manufactured crisis and their motto is *ordo ab chao*, which means 'order out of chaos,'" McGuire says. "This was a term coined by the Masonic leader Albert Pike. The new global order will be birthed by either a global financial crisis, the prospect of World War III involving Islam, Russia, Ukraine, NATO, Iran, Syria and Israel or a manufactured climate-change crisis."[192]

Presenting it as a way to address the world's mounting crises, global leaders approved the UN document in September 2015—a plan many believe will pave the way for the global super-state predicted in Scripture.

Patrick Wood, author of *Technocracy Rising: The Trojan Horse of Global Transformation*, argues that the anti-capitalistic sustainable development movement is a ruse to replace capitalism with a worldwide socialist system. "Any honest economist would instantly balk at such Pollyannaish promises of utopia, and the American public should do so as well," Wood told Cliff Kincaid, director of the Accuracy in Media Center for Investigative Journalism, in his article, "With Pope's Help, U.N. Bypasses Congress on Global Socialism." "These wild promises of prosperity for all are merely the candy coating to deceive the world into going along with its own economic destruction."[193]

We're All "Global Citizens" Now

The plan's goals, promoted by celebrities and rock stars during the Global Citizen Festival in New York in September 2015, seem laudable—promising to end poverty and hunger, protect the earth from "degradation," and create "inclusive societies" free from fear and violence. The authors of the UN report note that the world is facing "immense challenges." They wrote:

> Billions of our citizens continue to live in poverty and are denied a life of dignity. There are rising inequalities within and among countries. There are enormous disparities of opportunity, wealth and power.... Unemployment, particularly youth unemployment, is a major concern. Global health threats, more frequent and intense natural disasters, spiraling conflict, violent extremism, terrorism and related humanitarian crises and forced displacement of people threaten to reverse much of the development progress made in recent decades.... Climate change is one of the greatest challenges of our time and its adverse impacts undermine the ability of all countries to achieve sustainable development.... The survival of many societies, and of the biological support systems of the planet, are at risk.[194]

While the threat of climate change is controversial, many of the threats the UN authors list are credible and real. In fact, a recent report by Oxford University's Future of Humanity Institute titled "Global Challenges: 12 Risks That Threaten Human Civilization" detailed these and other threats. These include:

- Extreme climate change
- Nuclear war
- Global pandemic
- Ecological catastrophe

- Global system collapse
- Major asteroid impact
- Super-volcano
- Synthetic biology
- Nanotechnology
- Artificial Intelligence
- Unknown consequences
- Future bad global governance

In this report by one of the world's most prestigious universities, perhaps the most startling admission is that "poor global governance" could result in the creation of a "world dictatorship" or the "collapse of the world system." But even more stunning is the admission that many in the world's scientific community are fully aware of this. "The idea that we face a number of global challenges threatening the very basis of our civilization at the beginning of the 21st century is well accepted in the scientific community, and is studied at a number of leading universities," the authors wrote. "But there is still no coordinated approach to address this group of challenges.... This report has, to the best of our knowledge, created the first science based list of global risks with a potentially infinite impact where in extreme cases all human life could end."[195]

"Fast Track to a One-World Government"

Given the threat of what the authors of the report describe as a "world dictatorship" or a "global totalitarian state," McGuire, Wood, Hohmann, Kincaid, Horn, and others are concerned about the "2030 Agenda"—the replacement for "Agenda 21," the controversial UN "sustainable development" plan adopted at the Earth Summit in Rio de Janerio, Brazil, in 1992 that called for a "substantial flow of new and additional financial resources to developing countries...to deal with global environmental problems and to accelerate sustainable development," according to UN documents. However, critics say it involves an "age old socialist scheme of redistribution of wealth" to force Americans from the suburbs into cities. The Republican National Committee described it as "erosive of American sovereignty." It's been called "the most dangerous threat to American sovereignty" and an "anti-human document, which takes aim at Western culture." The goal of the new "2030 Agenda" is to persuade every nation to give up even more national sovereignty. "The U.N. vote is about to put America and the world on the fast track to a one-world government," McGuire says. "We are literally just one crisis away from that happening. It could happen overnight, and I don't think most people realize this."[196]

John Fonte—a Hudson Institute fellow and the author of *Sovereignty or Submission: Will Americans Rule Themselves or be Ruled by Others* —says "global governance" is simply a euphemism for a "world government." "What's emerged among the global elites (I call them transnational progressives) is what they call global governance—the setting up of laws and rules and institutions, global laws, that would be above the Constitution of the United States," Fonte says. "They would actually be superior to it or supranational—that is above national." This is what has happened in the European Union, the model for ten proposed regional unions worldwide, or the "Global Union." "The threat comes from the U.N.—from forces within the European Union and within the American elite at leading American law schools—trying to establish global governance," Fonte says. He stated further:

> They have said it openly. They are not going to do it by force. They are going to do it by judicial fiat—a judge says you've got to do X, Y and Z. We are a law-abiding people so we usually go along with judges. Laws change. We've seen the whole definition of marriage change within a few years. All of a sudden what was normal for thousands of years is now considered racist or bigoted or totally off the mark.

Following World War II, globalists openly talked about creating a world government, but they experienced tremendous backlash and changed their terminology. Fonte says:

> That's why they changed the term from world government to global governance. It's a sugar-coated pill so it will go down better. They say, "No, no no, we're not talking about world government. We have our governments. The United States government will still exist. It's just governance of the world. Global problems require global solutions." Certainly, you've heard the term. They repeat it over and over. There are global problems—climate change, worldwide pollution, world peace and atomic weapons. These are all global problems and require global solutions. In my book, I give them the benefit of the doubt. I said, "Okay, we'll call it global governance, but it's still bad. It's still the end of self-government. It's still the end of freedom. They've just changed the term."[197]

Lord Monckton, the former science adviser to British Prime Minister Margaret Thatcher, a British public speaker and journalist, warned in 2009 that the real agenda of UN climate change and Agenda 21 is to create "an all-powerful world government and to transfer wealth from Western nations to Third World nations through the force of new UN-sponsored international laws." The warning came as nations reeling from the global recession of 2007–2009 were amassing unparalleled levels of debt—prompting Harvard University economists to argue that the "endgame of the global financial crisis" is likely to require a "restructuring" of the world's economic system. In a recent Bloomberg interview, International Monetary Fund Director Christine Lagarde spoke of a coming "reset" of the global economy.[198]

"We see the world being deliberately brought to the brink of a financial crisis that is created through debt to the central banks in Europe and the Federal Reserve system in the United States," McGuire says. "The economies of the world have been strategically impacted by trillions of dollars in debt, the slowing of economic growth due to U.N. sustainable development policies and the impossible demands of attempting to pay off these debts through higher taxes."

In the not-so-distant future, financial experts anticipate that the sovereign debt crisis that began in Greece and Cypress will spread throughout Europe and ultimately to the US—igniting a global economic crash that will dwarf the Great Recession.

Two Hundred-Year-High Levels of Debt

Indeed, a recent International Monetary Fund report by two Harvard University professors found debt levels in the Western world have reached a two hundred-year high. "I believe that some very troubling times in terms of the US are coming and eventually that we're headed into the hardest economic times as a country that we've ever seen," says Michael Snyder, founder of the Economic Collapse Blog. "One thing I've been stressing with my readers lately is that we've been seeing so many of the patterns we witnessed just before the financial crash of 2008. They are happening right again in front of our eyes."[199]

Jay Peroni, the chief investment officer at Faith-Based Investor, says the global economy and markets are exhibiting the same signs that marked the beginning of previous economic downturns that took place over the course of many months. The current market could be "following the classic crash formula" of a stock market drop followed by a quick recovery and then the "real collapse." "Basically, what you tend to see whenever a crash has happened, if you go back to the last three major crashes in 1987, 2000 and 2007–08, is the market will have a pretty big drop—anywhere from 10–20 percent—and then you see a quick recovery...followed by the third leg which is a significant drop even worse than the first drop."[200]

Peter Schiff, an economist, frequent guest on national news programs, chief executive officer of Euro Pacific Capital, and author of *The Real Crash: America's Coming Bankruptcy*, believes the financial system is in a "big bubble" that is "going to burst." "I have a lot of concerns about the debt we have," Schiff says.

> I know it can't be paid back. The question is can the government default on it, find a more honest way to deal with it or are they just going to continue printing a lot of money, which is very dangerous. I think we're headed for a crisis in the U.S., and it is most likely going to take the form of a currency crisis. It will have a terrible impact. The U.S. basically lives on the fact that we have an overvalued currency. Americans are able to live beyond their means because of the overvalued dollar. When the dollar collapses, Americans will no longer have that luxury and our standard of living will be greatly reduced.[201]

Schiff believes the coming economic crisis is "inevitable":

We're already way beyond when it should have happened. We're living on borrowed time. The fact that this crisis has been delayed by so much by pushing the problem into the future means it's going to be that much worse. Literally, any day there could be an economic crisis. It's going to happen sometime probably over the next few years.

The Tree of Knowledge of Good and Evil and "Mystery, Babylon"

The coming global financial crisis—resulting in what many prophecy experts believe will be a concerted push for the end-time geopolitical and economic system predicted in Scripture—has its origins in Genesis.

Genesis tells the story of Adam and Eve, their fall after Satan tempted them to eat of the tree of knowledge of good and evil, and God's eventual destruction of mankind in Noah's Flood. Following the deluge, humanity sought to rebuild civilization and created a secret occult plan the apostle John described in Revelation as "Mystery, Babylon." It's a phrase that has puzzled Bible scholars ever since John penned those cryptic words nearly two thousand years ago: "And upon her forehead was a name written, MYSTERY, BABYLON THE GREAT, THE MOTHER OF HARLOTS AND ABOMINATIONS OF THE EARTH" (Revelation 17:5). Down through church history, theologians have sought to crack the end-times code of "Mystery, Babylon" and "Babylon the Great" (Revelation 18:2). Most Bible interpreters have thought that Babylon was some kind of code word for some other entity, such as the Roman Empire, Roman Catholicism, apostate Christianity, the European Union, the United States, or even a future reconstitution of the Babylonian Empire in the Middle East. However, the most logical conclusion based on Scripture, and the one detailed in *Halley's Bible Handbook*, is that "Mystery, Babylon" is a worldwide religious system, and "Babylon the Great" is a worldwide political and commercial system. As with many mysteries in Revelation and throughout the New Testament, the code is broken if one understands the references in the Old Testament.

Though seldom heard in sermons today, Genesis 10–11 and the Tower of Babel story are packed with prophetic significance, foreshadowing future events.

The first mention of Babylon in the Bible occurs in Genesis 10:9–10. These verses tell how Nimrod, the great-grandson of Noah and a "mighty one in the earth," was the ruler of ancient Babylon. Through Nimrod, Satan sought to develop an occult religious system to control the world. Nimrod created the world's first secret society—later described by the apostle John as "Mystery, Babylon." It's the source of all the occult and satanic religions throughout history. In ancient Babylon, Nimrod built the Tower of Babel, which some researchers believe was an astrological occult portal that permitted the entrance of demonic entities into the earthly realm. It was Satan's first attempt to create a one-world system at enmity with God. Nimrod believed humanity could achieve anything it imagined and become "as God" by building the occult-based tower, along with creating the first world government, economic and religious system.

But this was in disobedience to God's command following the Flood for mankind to multiply and fill the earth (Genesis 1:26–28; 9:1). Rather than spreading out over the face of the earth, humanity gathered in ancient Babylon to create a one-world, centralized government.

This new world state was religious in nature and believed government and Nimrod was its savior. God understood the dangers of this satanic unity: "Now nothing will be restrained from them, which they have imagined to do" (Genesis 11:6). So God judged mankind's attempt to centralize power by confusing their languages and dispersing humanity. Later, the city of Babel served as a model for the state-sponsored pagan mystery religions of the ancient world. Many ancient cities built ziggurats, perpetuating the idea of a centralized human government.

In the ensuing centuries, the occult teachings of "Mystery, Babylon" and the dream of a world government and religion were passed down from generation to generation through a series of secret societies in Babylon, Egypt, Rome, Europe, and—ultimately—to America. Throughout history, this esoteric knowledge has been utilized by "god-kings" who have ruled the world's most powerful empires through political, economic, and spiritual systems.

"Ever since ancient Babylon, a secret priesthood of Luciferian elites has conducted secret rituals and passed on secret Luciferian knowledge through what is known as 'Mystery, Babylon,'" McGuire says.

The Greek philosopher Plato spoke of this in the *Republic*, arguing that the ideal society is one ruled by "philosopher kings." The *Republic* was influential in the Roman Empire, the age of absolutist monarchs in Europe, and during modern political movements marked by an "infallible ruling elite." Sir Francis Bacon, the head of the Rosicrucian Order who played a leading role in creating the British colonies, wrote in his book, *The New Atlantis,* that a secret ruling elite would one day become the head of a utopian new world. "The names of these societies have been changed many times over the centuries," McGuire says. "For example, Sir Francis Bacon, a member of Britain's Parliament, was head of the Rosicrucian Order, which is believed to have later morphed into the Bavarian Illuminati, a fashionable 18th century secret society founded by University of Ingolstadt law professor Adam Weishaupt in 1776 that attracted some of Bavaria's leading intellectuals."[202]

Although the Bavarian government outlawed the Illuminati and other secret groups a decade later, many researchers believe members of these organizations later infiltrated the Freemasons, the political realm, European royalty, and the world's most powerful banking families. "The Illuminati philosophy was further spread—although unwittingly—by the Bavarian government which cracked down on the order in 1783," wrote Jim Marrs, a former *Fort Worth Star-Telegram* investigative reporter in his *New York Times* bestselling book *Rule by Secrecy.*

> Authorities saw the Illuminati as a direct threat to the established order and outlawed the organization. This action prompted many members to flee Germany, which only spread their philosophies farther. Secret Illuminati orders sprang up in France, Italy, England, and even the lands of America.... By 1790 the Illuminati appeared to have disbanded, but many members had simply fled to other countries while retaining their loyalty to the group's ideals. The Bavarian government tried to alert the leaders of other nations to what they saw as the danger of the Illuminati. Officials collected Illuminati documents into a publication entitled Original Writings of the Order of the Illuminati and distributed it to other European governments. But their warnings fell on deaf ears.[203]

Over the last two centuries, researchers believe the Illuminati helped inspire or morphed into a variety of powerful clandestine organizations in existence today, including Yale University's Skull and Bones (whose members have included both Bush presidents and Secretary of State John Kerry); the Bilderberg Group, Bohemian Grove, the Council on Foreign Relations, the Club of Rome, and The Trilateral Commission.

Surprisingly, a recent survey by the University of Chicago found that 51 percent of Americans believe that much of what happens in the world today is decided by a "small and secretive group of individuals—a "secret cabal." Today, many experts believe that this "secret cabal," or the Illuminati—often identified as the "original Marxist-Leninist group"—are far more powerful than it was in the late eighteenth century.[204]

"They are the scientific elite or the technocratic elite that the philosopher Plato referred to as the 10 god-kings," McGuire says.

Babylonian "Global Governance"

Today, the globalists behind the "New International Order" and the "Global Union" are still seeking a "Babel-like solution." They have the same belief systems as those in ancient Babylon. For most of human history, people have lived under pharaohs, Caesars, emperors, kings, feudal lords, dictators, and tyrants of various sorts. The conflict between tyranny and liberty dates to the beginning of human history. The powerful forces that sought to create an imperial empire in ancient Babylon are attempting to do the same thing again under the guise of "global governance" through trade treaties, international laws, and supranational government bodies and institutions. In recent times, the mainstream media has been filled with news about this emerging world system. For example, Pope Francis recently called for a "global political authority" to address climate change. *The Guardian* newspaper described it as "a kind of super-U.N. to deal with the world's economic problems and injustices." US Sen. Jeff Sessions, R-Ala., has criticized President Obama for pushing global trade pacts "encompassing up to 90 percent of world GDP" that would create a "secret Pacific Union"—compromising America's sovereignty and transferring power to "an elite set who dream of writing rules in foreign capitals." Sessions said the plan would transfer a "vast delegation of sovereign authority to an international union, with growing powers over the lives of ordinary Americans." "These 5,554 pages are like the Lilliputians binding down Gulliver," Sessions said.

> They will enmesh our great country, and economy, in a global commission where bureaucrats from Brunei have the same vote as the United States. Clearly, powerful forces will have their voices heard and find ways to profit immensely from this conglomeration.... At bottom, this is not a mere trade agreement. It bears the hallmarks of a nascent European Union.[205]

Greg Laurie, pastor of the fifteen thousand-member Harvest Christian Fellowship in Riverside, California, and president of Harvest Crusades, says America is losing its sovereignty in a piecemeal fashion to the globalists. He says:

> There was a statement by Chuck Hagel, our former secretary of defense, who said he sees a New World Order emerging, and he wasn't saying it critically. I thought, "Wow, he's really right." Things are shifting dramatically around the world. You can see these things that Scripture predicted: The idea that "no man could buy or sell" without mark of the Beast (Revelation 13:17) would have been completely impossible fifty or one hundred years ago, but with technology today we know that it's possible.[206]

Lt. Gen. William G. "Jerry" Boykin, executive vice president at the Family Research Council and former US deputy undersecretary of defense, says the world is moving toward "global Marxism." Boykin says:

> Remember, Karl Marx's goal was to dethrone God and destroy capitalism. Once you remove God, you are on the path to Marxism, and I believe very much that this is an end-time strategy

of the enemy. The Bible predicts that this would occur. If you go back to 1958, the Communist Party USA wrote a book called The Naked Communist. They laid out exactly what they were going to do to America. If you read what they said they were going to do and how much of it has already happened, it's shocking. They said they would promote pornography as a First Amendment issue. Haven't they done that? They said they would promote easy divorce and they would move the churches from revealed revelation to a social religion. In other words, it's just another place to go on Sunday. They said they would union-ize teachers and they would get behind the green movement, or climate change, and get people fired-up to shut down busi-ness. They wrote all these things and all of them have happened. Some people would blow this off as a conspiracy theory, but the reality is it is happening. You can't deny that. They wrote about it in 1958, telling us exactly what they would do. They wrote about how they would force Americans to celebrate and accept same-sex marriage. They have done exactly what they said they would in The Naked Communist.[207]

Chuck Missler, an author, former businessman, and the founder of the Koinonia House ministry, says the globalism movement is the "cause célèbre of today." "It's also very dangerous," Missler says.

It's all on the path to form a global tyranny. All this is anti-God. All these movements have an anti-biblical view of God. This is no surprise because the Bible talks about how this globalism idea will be the very instrument that is used to enslave people. That's what we see throughout the Old Testament and the New Testa-ment and in Revelation 13. Ultimately, it all culminates with the Battle of Armageddon and the world knowingly taking up arms against God. It's astonishing. I find it almost impossible to imagine mankind knowingly taking up arms against God. The climax is the Second Coming of Christ. He returns and sets up his kingdom forever.[208]

The UN and the elite are involved in a great seduction of humanity. It's the biggest cover-up in history, and plans are now underway to create the final satanic system that began in ancient Babylon, which has now returned just as the Bible predicted it would. "MYSTERY, BABYLON THE GREAT, THE MOTHER OF HARLOTS AND ABOMINATIONS OF THE EARTH," has come again. Ultimately, though, it's a counterfeit of the Kingdom of heaven, and as we read in the book of Revelation, Babylon will fall and be totally destroyed.

Just as He judged the first Babylon and its successors, God will destroy the final Babylon too, but this time for good. The satanic forces of Babylon will wage war with Jesus Christ and the armies of heaven at the Battle of Armageddon, but Satan will be defeated and Jesus will establish a new heaven, new earth, and the New Jerusalem, where there will be no more pain or sorrow and God will wipe away every tear. What humanity lost at the Garden of Eden—Paradise—will be restored.

The Age of Convergence

By Dr. Gordon McDonald, Koinonia Institute

We live in a cultural, technological, and spiritual time of instability. To have a reasonable "peek forward" into what could happen in the next ten months, let alone the next ten years, is daunting. Seemingly, there have never been so many "forces" in transition, changing so quickly and completely.

In 1967, Marshall McLuhan, in his much-read bestseller, *The Medium Is the Message*, warned that we had already reached a critical point in our ability to absorb and process change and still remain sane. I am sure he would have been surprised at our ability to survive the onslaught of technocultural development since. The real underlying question is, was he right? Did we survive or did our "new normal" become a form of institutionalized insanity? Could we even perceive our deteriorated mental and emotional condition if everyone (or most) had the same psychosis? When considering the possible changes in the next coming years, this is a very important question. When considering the path forward and its implications, we have to first determine how capable we are of "seeing" clearly.

Every day, we are "fed" many different analyses of what to expect in the near future. From consumer marketing to governmental controls to religious expectations, others make every effort to shape our behavior by their choice of information. Whether for the purpose of predicting group behavior or causing it, the constant din of forced perspective presses in on us. Every day, there is a race to find another, more effective method of this type of conditioned "education." Every day, we are challenged to protect our "true" view not only of how things really are, but also of how they will become.

We need to recognize these pressures. If we fall into believing that our perspective is not—and cannot—be influenced, or that it doesn't matter, we are certain to fall victim to miscalculations and misinterpretations at our detriment. It's been said in the past, "You can't know where you're going without first knowing where you've been." Although this is true, it is becoming more difficult to understand how far back you must be accurately cognizant.

Clearly, we are living in a time of accelerated development. Every day, a new and wondrous advancement is publically announced. That these "breakthroughs" are not new, but the general public is only now being informed, is either taken for granted or not realized. The truth is that most new technology is "weaponized" before public application. Many times what we see available to the public is three or four generations old. In reality, this technology would be considered extremely "old" and of little comparison to "current" levels of technological development. If all current development were to magically cease today, it would be years before those technological advances deep within the governmental science labs would come to the light of day. This delay inhibits an accurate assessment of where we will be in ten years. In times of such uncertainty, it is helpful to go back to the beginning for clarity.

In the Beginning

It is difficult to live in a fish bowl and realize it. It is almost impossible, from within a controlled environment, to notice your imprisonment—even the very medium in which you exist acts on and controls your perceptions. Like the view from inside a fish bowl, the view to the outside is distorted enough to be misunderstood. Only when you are elevated from the effects that surround you can you see what is truly taking place. You need an objective, informed perspective that is not bound by your own polluted misunderstanding.

Within this extreme environment of shifting shadows, there is a constant assault upon our senses and sensibilities. Clarity fades into the constant din of white noise we call "culture." The details and consequences of change, good or bad, become distorted or lost. In fact, this deception becomes so commonplace that we acquiesce to the fiction of its nonexistence. The seductions, trinkets, and other "shiny things" serve to distract from the reality of imprisonment.

But it wasn't always this way. In the beginning there were only two. No, not Adam and Eve. Adam and God. There was only one perspective from the One most qualified to provide it. God, the Creator Himself. Questions were unnecessary.

Life in the Garden was simple to predict. Since God Himself provided our every need, questions and their answers were of no consequence. Although each day may have been different, there was no "race" or competition for resources. Whatever the need, it was provided.

It is difficult to determine exactly how long this lasted. What we can say is that there was no technological change. There was no need for this type of change. We had perfect communion with our Creator and all our needs were provided. What else was there to chase after? If it hadn't been for the one "Rule," we could have peacefully and blissfully been satisfied with this forever. But one Rule is, obviously, one Rule too many.

Complications

There were suddenly many questions and few quick answers. Why is this animal lying in the way before us not breathing? And why am I covered in his skin? What are these feelings of needs? Food? Water? Air? Warmth? How do I ensure their continuity? At first this must have been frighteningly confusing.

Adam and Eve had to come to grips with providing for themselves what God had done so completely and casually. Life became much more complicated. Gone were the days of gentle, leisurely strolls through a food-laden Garden. Just as the enormity of this came into focus, they had children. Oh, my! Seriously, life became MUCH more complicated. The paradox of joy and pain.

We started with no questions, not even simple "yes or no" ones, but from then on, the questions became many, both complicated and life-threatening. The world changed in that moment of realization that we would have to compete and struggle to provide support for our own existence and that of our families. Seemingly, the environment itself transformed from a servant into a wild beast.

Made in the Image of God

We weren't abandoned without abilities. We had been made in the image of God Himself. We could imagine. We could hope. We could devise. We could analyze. We could cooperate. Certainly we could do these things at a miniscule capacity compared to God, but we had enough of these abilities to supply our basic needs.

At first we used our abilities to supply our rudimentary needs. But soon we realized we could supply not only for summer needs but winter also. In the midst of this, we realized that we controlled the definition between our needs and our wants—I'm certain that was a happy day indeed. We found that different people had different needs and abilities. Life quickly became a group activity. Like-minded families and individuals banded together to solve their common problems and support their self-interests. It also seemed some were "gifted" at taking what others had earned. They, also, gathered with like-minded individuals.

There was yet another pressing need: cooperative defense. People found that as they cooperated they could jointly fulfill their needs, wants, and aspirations. In fact, they were so good at it and were making such incredible strides that God Himself had to step in and make life even more complicated. Through their cooperation, they were growing in knowledge too quickly, with only a rudimentary understanding of the consequences. There was a simple godly solution to this: Confuse their communication. Life was replete with an overwhelming number of highly important questions.

As local populations grew, the necessity for communication and cooperation within those populations also grew. Not only did you have to agree with your wife, and not only did you have to get your children to agree with you (and each other), but now you had to agree with other people. Life continued to progress to complexity.

First tribes, and then countries, with their administrations and armies, were formed—some more aggressive than others. Cultures developed within these groups, and soon everyone was so concerned with themselves and their own "culture," they no longer saw or felt anything outside their own "fish bowl."

In their business and political intrigues, they had forgotten their Creator. This course would have ended in utter destruction, except for the truth from the beginning. The One who had created them also loved them, in spite of their rebellion. He offered them a desperately needed perspective. Some, not most, became aware of the fish bowl in which they were confined.

Those who ignored Him turned their God-given gifts toward building a world of their own making. All the different facets of life that

God had always wanted to provide, they made efforts at duplicating. They created solid ground where there was none. They stored up vast amounts of food for long-range security. They made lights to push back the darkness. They made roads to take them wherever they wanted to go. Their "needs" became confused with their "wants," and these started to multiply and have not ceased to this very day.

As you can imagine, the people became overwhelmed with the enormity of their tasks and were frustrated by their paltry successes and unexpected outcomes. Undeterred, though, they redoubled their efforts. Categories of discovery and investigation began to proliferate. Specialization took place within the work forces. As they pressed on, they discovered that the more closely they looked at the world around them, the more questions they had. Then they found out why God had to step in so many years ago. They rediscovered synergy between groups.

The Two Shall Become One

Just as many small creeks can come together to create a tributary, and those can come together to form a mighty and powerful river, human development has this same feature. Discoveries are built upon previous discoveries. Advances are a result of previous advances. Made in the image of God, man's innate ingenuity has accomplished wondrous things. But don't confuse recreation with creation. Man has taken what God created and cleverly used what has existed before to put it to work for himself. God created something that didn't previously exist and put it to work for us.

In the early years of population expansion, man developed crafts to float on the water. He used these to gather food resources and travel reasonable distances without having to walk and carry his own supplies. This was an effective method for hundreds of years. Most of this seafaring technology depended upon the coastlines for a frame of reference.

There were explorers, but generally the majority was afraid of what lay beyond the horizon.

Separately, there were also those who were fascinated with the night sky. The movements of the celestial, yet-to-be-defined bright spots were intriguing. As early students of the skies studied these "lights" and their movements, they discovered that the lights were consistent in their placement and trajectories. They also discovered that one's location could be determined by the change in position of the celestial lights. This was an enormous change in perspective. At this point, mankind thought they had at least determined the size and shape of the fish bowl. Little did they know.

It didn't take long for these two technologies—one linked to the sea, the other to the skies— to converge into the ability to break free from coastal navigation. With the invention of the astrolabe [ancient astronomical computer] and the mariner's quadrant, within about four hundred years, almost the entire earth had been mapped and "discovered."

Ocean transportation had a relatively low impact for hundreds of years. Celestial navigation was developing slowly and separately during that same period. When the two technological "trends" became mature and convergent, they changed forever the course of human history in a short period of time. This is an example of the vast transformative power of convergence.

Once you realize this perspective, the concept of convergence becomes apparent everywhere. From strides in pest control and selective seed development to material development and propulsion and aircraft design, the convergence of technologies has become so commonplace, and so powerful, that we neglect to either recognize its scope or wonder at the continual parade of miracles it has produced over the centuries.

With the advent of artificial human body parts, convergence has yielded amazing new technology. Through the cooperation of biology and materials science we now have artificial organs such as skin (but one thousand times more sensitive), muscles (again, one thousand times stronger), bones, hearts, livers, eyes, and a multitude of other, so-called lesser body parts. All of these discoveries are in their infancies (but are they really?). Publically, within the next ten years they will proliferate.

Ten years ago, Japanese researchers successfully grew a brain cell onto a silicon computer chip. This convergence of organic biology and inorganic silicon technology culminated in successfully growing the ganglia of a brain cell to specific "leads" on the computer chip without rejection. The brain cell survived. That was ten years ago. Assuming a normal development speed, that technological path is well matured and advanced.

We are in the period of major convergence. In our time, areas of development that have been converging for thousands of years are themselves converging with like lines. This has brought amazing changes to the world around us and raised the standard of living for the entire industrialized world in a dramatic fashion. As the pace of this development accelerates, we are only now realizing its massive impact "Are we able to absorb, process and survive?"

Assumptive Truth

Assumptions are always dangerous. They are only as good as the completeness of the information upon which they are built. Since they are generally a shortcut, they rarely reflect complete and accurate perspectives. However, the speed at which the world is operating and moving requires prolific use of such a cost and timesaver. More often than not, this device is passed off as truth rather than presented as the theory it actually is. You must assume that most of what you are told is only theory. That doesn't mean it is false, only that it carries a certain risk of error.

A good case in point is convergence. While it is easy, once alerted, to see and understand, it is also easy to misunderstand its implications and consequences. Generally, our expectations are that tomorrow will be the same as today and the next day will be the same as well. Even if we are in a situation that is less than desirable, we find it hard to believe that tomorrow will be better than today.

Technological development is a victim of this human trait. While in the stream of development, we don't realize the speed of the flow that is occurring around us. New developments are taken for granted to occur at a "normal" pace. This produces a cognitive simulation of linear development. The true speed at which change is happening is not realized.

The very nature of intellectual development is *exponential*, not linear. Each discovery is built upon the previous work. These discoveries become broader in their effects as successive "generations" are accumulated. Each generation increases the impact. The impact growth inflates at an exponential rate.

If it is true that technology and its impact is increasing faster that we can adapt to, then it is also true that our perception of its impact is lagging at an exponential rate. This can be a dangerous situation in which "the creature" can be outgrowing "the creator."

Ray Kurzweil, an acclaimed futurist, has stated that we presently aren't developing at a commonly believed 10:1 ratio, but, thanks to the exponential nature of development, it is closer to 20,000:1 and increasing. If this is even half true, the impact on the near future and our capability of adequately dealing with it, is staggering.

010010010111011101101010010110110001101100

From the time God confused the language of the masses, who "were on the verge of being able to accomplish whatever their minds could conceive" (Genesis 11:6), communication has been the most sought-after commodity in history. Whether by conquest, treaty, technology, transportation, or religion, the desire for ever-faster and voluminous communication has been the insatiable quest behind all human development.

The more we discover, the more questions we have. The more power we acquire through information, the more we want.

Just stop and think. After thousands of years of development, the fastest common communication at the birth of the United States (1776 or so) was a lantern at night. Even this carried a bare minimum of information. In the last 240 years, through global synergy within the science community, we are now transmitting, at the speed of light, trillions of bits of information at a time, every second of every day. So for the first few thousands of years, we achieved a single signal light at night, and in the last 240 years, communication has increased to trillions of bits per second without distance restrictions.

Through the technological development of communication, we have returned to the Tower of Babel. Every area of discovery is becoming an information-oriented endeavor. We are no longer isolated from each other. Once again we have one voice and one language. There are no impediments to the free trade of ideas and insights. There are no restrictions on "intuitive jumps" or breakthrough "mistakes." What we must ask ourselves is: "Are we any more emotionally or intellectually ready?" We have once again told God to His face "I will." Now nothing will prevent us from doing whatever our minds can conceive.

Not All Things Are Equal

With this as a basis, we can see the medium within which we are confined. A sinful world, rejecting the simplicity of the Creator, is driving itself at an ever-increasing rate into the desert of confusion and questions. Now as development, technological and otherwise, converges back on us, it raises the specter that conditions have proceeded far beyond our control.

Since all of these avenues of discovery are combining, we find ourselves under conditions in which progress itself is growing at exponentially. It would be simple, of course, if this development were progressing in a linear fashion as commonly thought: 1, 2, 3, 4, 5, 6, 7, 8, 9, 10. Unfortunately, all the data and analysis of the process implies an exponential rate, 1, 2, 4, 8, 16, 32, 64, 128, 256, 512, and so on, and increasing. In the space of ten permutations, the exponential ratio has outgrown the linear ratio by 502 times. At thirty permutations (only thirty, mind you), it outpaces at a rate of a billion, and at forty, a trillion.

An example of this is the Human Genome Project. Halfway through the project, it had taken seven years to sequence 1 percent. Critics touted that this meant the project would take seven hundred years, and thus was useless. In fact, 1 percent is only seven permutations from 100 percent—and, as it turns out, it was seven years later that the project was completed.

Statistical analysis has shown that the cost of computation from 1890 until now has decreased a trillion times. Your smart phone that you carry is estimated to be several billion times less expensive computationally than in 1960. Interestingly enough, these exponential advances have been impervious to effects of economic downturns, cultural dislocation, or war (global or regional).

It is said that technological growth in the nineteenth century exceeded that of the previous nine centuries. And growth in the first twenty years of the twentieth century exceeded all advancement of the nineteenth century. Since then, there is no evidence of convergent development slowing down.

Every area of development and discovery is progressing at exponentially and converging with each other for application. All areas (artificial intelligence, solar energy efficiency, the resolution of 3D printing, age extension, disease prevention, DNA sequencing, and all others) are past their 1 percent. As we have seen, from 1 percent to 100 percent is only seven permutations. The expected technological changes by 2020 are overwhelming: machines that have passed the computational goal of duplicating (or passing) the capabilities of the human brain; nano machines capable of being inserted into the human bloodstream that can connect to the cloud network. Technologically, we are advancing so rapidly that it has become a challenge to even measure the rate of progress.

Remember our primary question: At what point are our immature minds overwhelmed by our attempt to process this volume of information delivered at such a rapid pace? It is folly to believe this level of information flow and capability will have no psychological effect on the human condition going forward. There is only one hope for mankind. There is only one place of safety. Alone we can't turn away from the temptation of "knowing," and yet we are incapable of containing, assimilating, and wisely implementing at this ever-increasing rate.

The Truth or Lack of It

Much like going down the road in an automobile at a high rate of speed, if one looks out the side window, it's a blur—detail is lost. In today's technology convergence, we no longer (if we ever could) have the controls to slow down the "car." In fact, it is continuing to accelerate exponentially. Fueled by our insatiable hunger to "do it ourselves," we are left victim to our own faulty perceptions. Led by the scant amount of misleading information we can attain, we will, by definition, make a seriously wrong turn. If we try to convince ourselves we can see clearly, even though our entire life we have been looking out the same window, we deceive ourselves and will make a disastrous decision.

The conditions we are under are of our own making. We are afforded the opportunity to give up the "wheel" and God hears our defiant refrain, "I can do it myself." Truth is what many profess to be searching for, but this search without God's total control only promises an endless stream of more "important" questions.

Fortunately, we have acceptance from a patient and graceful God who only requires us to recognize our need.

Things to Come

We have talked about the dangers of losing sight of the truth of things by adopting a "polluted" perspective. Whether caused by the pace of change or by simply a faulty foundation, the result is the same: a distorted and inaccurate understanding of our surroundings. The only real defense of this is to gain an objective and accurate worldview. Since the "fishbowl" we are contained in includes the entire earthly environment, such a viewpoint would be extremely rare and, in fact, impossible.

In the coming years, those who acquire such an advantage and have an objective source to clear the distortion will not be tolerated. In our fishbowl, the majority rules, and the majority does not like to be proven inadequate. It does not like to view its nakedness. To it, we Christians are an irritation.

If Marshall McLuhan was in any way correct in his assessment of our lack of resiliency under these modern conditions, we can make some expectations. If the population is experiencing a degradation of cognitive stability, those who aren't will not only become more apparent, but will be ostracized.

Persecution of the Right

Persecution of those who maintain and demonstrate a more accurate and effective worldview will increase with more and more negative, ruthless actions. As the exponential ratio takes its toll on the population, these singled-out groups will be required to endure real social and personal threat.

This should not be a surprise. During the insanity of the Roman Empire, this exact sociological process took place in the martyrdom of the Christians of the time. Christian groups were tortured, killed, and publically displayed with impunity. This was a localized event. When the entire environment is fully involved in the same process, there will be nowhere to hide. Persecutions will become commonplace and seen as justified. Men will call good evil and evil good. As the Church continues to point out the failed logic of risking everything for the unconfirmed promise of a technological advance, it will be ostracized as an impediment to the advancement of mankind.

Even now there are symptoms of such aberrant belief behavior. Several legal actions are being filed to legalize human-robot marriages, anticipating the arrival of anatomically correct, interactive mechanical devices. They are using the Supreme Court's decision on homosexual marriage as their precedent in their proceedings. Cross-species DNA splicing has become a popular topic of research, regardless of possible unintended consequences. Splicing certain extremely virulent virus strains in an attempt to capture beneficial traits continues. There is ongoing research into creating more destructive bombs by splitting the smallest building blocks of matter, quanta. All of these and more can be a point of contention between an insane worldview and one dedicated to the good of all.

If it were just a single developmental path, the prognosis would not be so dire. We find this faulty thinking repeated within many avenues of not only scientific, but social, areas of development.

Mohammed's Moment

Islam has some two billion followers worldwide. Although not all are fundamentalist to the Koran's instructions, even a reasonable percentage will have a world-altering effect going forward. With fundamentalist educational programs for adults as well as children, and success being measured by their own deaths, this religious movement will grow tremendously in the coming years. Fueled by oil and drug sales, they will claim success first in the Mideast and next in most of Africa.

Because of the lack of common moral restrictions, the rest of the industrialized world will also find no cover. The West, unwilling to accept that an open society affords little interior protection from those wanting to do harm, will ultimately find itself a soft target. A major terrorist event involving weapons of mass destruction, either within the US or Europe, is inevitable.

With a belief system that promises riches for behavior that plays to basic negative, human instincts, a vast economic separation will occur between the Haves and the Have-Nots. With a vast population to recruit from, the probability of a solution—peaceful or otherwise—is an adverse expectation. Tensions will expand, first between other Mideast tribal states and then to the rest of the global society. Technological advances in the near term will have little effect in reducing hostilities. Other convergences in present religious "differences" can transpire to support the growth of the conflicts. There will be islands of cessation, both geographically and temporally, but only on a temporary basis.

There will be attempts to solve these differences with a peaceful resolution. The Catholic Church will attempt to broker a deal. The global community will attempt the same. The military industrial complex will create new weapons advances, and/or use current ones, in a desperate attempt at its own solution. All these will fundamentally fail in their objectives. What will occur is a compromise of cultural moralities as a result of attempted conciliatory political and economic solutions. Religions worldwide will find themselves more ecumenically aligned. Governments will find themselves much more willing to cross previously stated philosophic "lines in the sand." Fundamental Islam will continue to grow.

Another Kind

As referenced before, our world culture has already begun to accept the inevitability of artificial intelligence. Although the marriage between these types of "species" is a bit extreme, the recognition of the need and desire for its eventuality is, or should be, staggering. Whether from a desire to show God that "we can create also" or from the pride that we can control whatever we develop, there is a race for both social and industrial robotics implementations.

We are somewhat at the mercy of fantasy media representations when we visualize what this entails. Of course, there will be robots built that simulate the human form. First, the bipedal, symmetrical, equal-in-height forms, and then the attempt to duplicate the anatomically-correct variety.

These will represent the "limited" service devices that will, first, do the tasks that save us time and money. Later-generation models will take an increasing role in every aspect of practical living. As robotics and computational technologies converge into more sophisticated devices, no task will be too great to "offload" to this willing worker. There will be a "natural" progression toward complete dependence on this technology.

The question of societal security will be rationalized into a blind faith in our intellectual ability to impede the machine's capability to "correct" its own deficiencies. Whether we have the time to arrive at this nightmarish scenario will hinge on just how correct the principle of "exponential growth" turns out to be.

All of the aforementioned is what will go on publically. Far more is going on is the dark. Industrialization of robotics has been developing and growing for decades now. Huge cost savings have been achieved by this technology. The hardware-engineering development and its precision have fueled this behind-the-scenes activity.

The only hindrance to greater integration has been the convergence and inclusion of more sophisticated computer hardware and software. We now live in a time when this convergence is showing its exponential nature. Once the back office and production systems are fully realized in this manner, our lives, good or bad, will be dependent upon machines that very soon will be able to calculate faster and more accurately than our own brains.

In each of these technology "trends," it is important to understand where it is on the development path. The farther down the path, the less time until crisis. As fully mature trends find convergence with others, the impact is greater.

Recently, a report by the World Economic Forum (WEF) gave its assessment of the state of robotic development in the world and projected its practical consequences. It reported that the analysis showed that by 2020, "Disruptive labor market changes, including the rise of robots and artificial intelligence, will result in a net loss of 5.1 million jobs over the next five years in 15 leading countries." The International Labor Organization, part of the United Nations, is predicting an increase in global unemployment, as a result of robotics, of eleven million by 2020.

Since both organizations used different, but massive, samples, the total unemployment figure is staggering. Two-thirds of all job losses are expected in the white-collar office and administrative sectors. The WEF has labeled this issue as "the fourth industrial revolution." This will lead to the complete change of everything. Every sector will suffer loss—some more than others, of course. There will be a demand for certain skilled workers, including data analysts and specialist sales representatives. Of the jobs lost, women will lose more than five jobs for every one gained. Men will see approximately one job gained for every three lost.

The critics point out that more than five million jobs is a small portion of the entire work force of the fifteen major economies WEF evaluated. And all things being equal, that is true. But all things aren't equal, as we have discussed. Remember, after 1 percent is reached, there are only seven turns to 100 percent in an exponential environment. The projections are for just under four years from now. On the first turn, the impact doubles, and on the second it quadruples. Our target of ten years out portrays another tech stream in crisis with large social and political changes occurring at an ever-increasing rate.

Biohobbyism

Recently, a bioengineer in England asked to be able to take the lives of thirty babies through gene editing at the embryonic stage to advance the knowledge of human development. This was not an unusual request. Just before that in Washington, DC, at the International Summit on Human Gene Editing (HGE), the experimental use of children at the embryonic level to possibly cure specific genetic disorders was advocated. The safeguards and restrictions on human experimentation are changing.

HGE is the creation of a genetically modified (GMO) human. Any HGE changes made to a child at the embryonic stage will become "permanent" and passed down to successive generations. This emerging technology is a profound threat to the human race. The hope is to produce a cure for many inherited diseases and prevent certain contagions. While this sounds altruistic at first hearing, the risk of mistake or unintended consequence in an area little understood is extremely high.

Because of the risk of permanent, unintended consequences, there has been a backlash within the scientific community of late. But as an example of how little control in reality one has after the "box" is opened, it is becoming far too profitable, easy, and inexpensive to set up your own "lab," no matter your education and training. HGE is against the law in more than twenty-nine countries. Sadly, China, North Korea, and the United States are not among them.

After World War II and the horrific human experimentation performed by the Nazis, most of the countries of the world came together at the Nuremberg Medical Trials and ruled that this type of experimentation without consent was a war crime. This culminated in the public hanging of seven Nazi doctors. As a direct warning to the medical community worldwide, the Nuremberg Code was adopted by most of the Western nations, except the United States. This decision became the founding tenet of modern bioethics. If the embryo after HGE is determined to be a human, then those who tampered with it would be in violation of informed consent protections.

In April 2015, China announced its use of a new technology known as CRISPR (Clustered Regularly Interspersed Palindromic Repeats), used for the purpose of simplified gene editing. This new genetic modification technology is fast, simple to use, and inexpensive. A recent Chinese biotech start-up named Amino has brought this technology to everyone in a kit that retails for just under seven hundred dollars. Yes, for less than a good smart phone, you, too, can edit genes in the comfort of your own garage.

The seminal material is not included, but the kit contains instructions, hardware, and chemicals necessary for gene editing. And it turns out that human material is not that hard to acquire. More than five hundred thousand human embryos have been made available through the in vitro fertilization (IVF) process. Prospective cryogenically frozen IVF embryos are routinely released by their parents.

Whether the excess is from a successful IVF procedure and parents not wanting to pay for their upkeep or those actively donating their "leftovers" to science, these children become part of a group that the National Institutes of Health have declared "non-persons." It is just a matter of time until a rogue individual seeking fame and money, using CRISPR technology, produces a GMO child with unknown, permanent consequences to the human condition. The field of bioengineering technology is outpacing bioethics by magnitudes. The technology trend is clearly on the increase with little to inhibit its growth.

This is yet another technology trend that is well past the experimental phase. With easy access to the tools of the trade and the promise of explosive income, this area will grow to a level of unimagined heights within the next few years. The dangers are clear, but the genie is out of the bottle. The threat of change to who we are, whether through integration with machines or fundamental changes to our flesh and bone, is real, inevitable, and imminent.

Pick a technology trend. Pick any. Look into its recent developmental trajectory and apply the exponential expectation. Look for the convergences and the powerful leaps they produce. They're not hard to see.

They're everywhere. In the next few years, all that we know will change. As we awaken to the chaos of the real world, we have to remember that there is a way out. If this world is racing toward a technology collapse, there is the promise of a better one coming, if you listen. The promise is clear. It is offered to just one, you. He says, "Fear not, for I have overcome the world."

A Reduction to the One

God is a just God. Just as He saved us from ourselves in the beginning by choosing a people by which to introduce Himself, He will at the end once again show us extreme mercy. While we are lost in this sea of confusion, deception, and complexity, He as the patient and loving Father will gradually reduce our personal choices to one. As over our history as a species we have disregarded God and sought our own answers, resulting in an exponential growth in questions, His use of convergence will increase and resolve, forcibly, all of our questions back to just one.

From the beginning, everything that really matters has been a "yes" or "no" question. As we introduced increasing amounts of complexity to hide from His calling, the complexity of our choices will once again reduce to a single "yes" or "no." So that His justice will never be questioned, all the confusion and deception produced by the enemies of God, and the blurry complexity of our own doing, will be made clear and transparent. One clear question: "yes" or "no." One binary choice. A reduction to the simplest of terms possible.

Do you trust Him?

And I saw another angel fly in the midst of heaven, having the
everlasting gospel to preach unto them that dwell on the earth,
and to every nation, and kindred, and tongue, and people,

> Saying with a loud voice, Fear God, and give glory to him; for the hour of his judgment is come: and worship him that made heaven, and earth, and the sea, and the fountains of waters. (Revelation 14:6-7)

A Final Communication

After studying and watching the end times for some twenty-five years or more, a perspective has gradually grown. Commonly, the question of Jesus Christ's Rapture or His Second Coming has been a continual hunt for any nuance of God's Word that could bring further clarity.

Maybe we have been looking in the wrong direction. With Jesus' insistence that "no man knows the day or hour" (Matthew 24:36, Mark 13:32) and the elaborate convolutions of questionable logic meant to explain how He really didn't mean what He said, maybe only the last generation could clearly "see."

There is no argument that this has been a valuable life-long effort. Any motivation to dig deep into God's nature and intentions can transform even the coldest of hearts and free one's perspective to see clearly in a distorted world. If it were not for a single verse, this approach would be the only one necessary.

There is a hint of evidence embedded within the New Testament that is seldom given the weight or importance for determining the signs of the times.

> And except those days should be shortened, there should no flesh be saved: but for the elect's sake those days shall be shortened. (Matthew 24:22)

This was written in a time when the very statement would be deemed preposterous. In the last generation or so, contemplating the consequences of this scenario has been the full-time endeavor of multitudes of political and military individuals and groups around the world.

As we try to assimilate the consequences that, within the next ten to fifteen years, man's understanding of his total environment is on pace to increase by a trillion times, we are met with Marshall McLuhan's dire prediction and our question: Is the probability of a catastrophic planet-killing event also increasing exponentially? If so, the time to Jesus' return could be much nearer than we suppose.

I want to leave you with this thought, but not to cause fear. Only being outside the comfort and protection of God should cause fear. But as the world around us changes so dramatically, we need to self-evaluate how we are changing and submit everything we have held back from God.

He shortens the time for our sake. Don't waste this precious opportunity.

[11]

The Hybrid Age Begins

By Sharon Gilbert

And whereas thou sawest iron mixed with miry clay,
they shall mingle themselves with the seed of men: but they shall
not cleave one to another, even as iron is not mixed with clay.
—DANIEL 2:43

So as we evolve, we become closer to God. Evolution is a spiritual
process. There is beauty and love and creativity and intelligence
in the world—it all comes from the neocortex. So we're going to
expand the brain's neocortex and become more godlike.
—DR. RAYMOND KURZWEIL

ay Kurzweil wants to become a god—or at least "godlike." In an
informal talk[209] given to a small group of graduate students at Singularity University in September 2015, the man who leads Google's
artificial intelligence lab expressed his belief that humans will have the
option to access all world knowledge—and hence become "omni-
scient"—by the year 2030. According to the write-up at the *Huffington
Post* on October 1, 2015, the futurist inventor predicted that:

...in the 2030s, human brains will be able to connect to the cloud, allowing us to send emails and photos directly to the brain and to back up our thoughts and memories. This will be possible, he says, via nanobots—tiny robots from DNA strands—swimming around in the capillaries of our brain. He sees the extension of our brain into predominantly nonbiological thinking as the next step in the evolution of humans—just as learning to use tools was for our ancestors.[210]

If only Dr. Kurzweil knew his Bible better, he'd realize that the idea of mingling metal (or machine) with carbon-based life-forms is nothing new. In fact, the prophet Daniel explained this concept to King Nebuchadnezzar following a disturbing dream given to the king by the Lord God YHWH (pronounced Yahweh or sometimes Jehovah). In this dream, the head is made of gold, the chest and arms of silver, the belly and thighs of bronze, and the legs of iron; while the toes are made of "iron mixed with miry clay," The angel explains this vision to Daniel, commenting that these "feet" represent a "mingling" of human "clay" with something else:

> And whereas thou sawest iron mixed with miry clay, **they shall mingle themselves with the seed of men**: but they shall not cleave one to another, even as iron is not mixed with clay. (Daniel 2:43, emphasis added)

Of course, if Dr. Kurzweil were to read this passage (and particularly the next verse), he'd also see that such hybrid creations will not be permitted to continue for long:

> And in the days of these kings shall the God of heaven set up a kingdom, which shall never be destroyed: and the kingdom shall not be left to other people, but it shall **break in pieces and**

consume all these kingdoms, and it shall stand for ever. (Daniel 2:44, emphasis added)

God has no intention of allowing "self-evolved" hybrid humans to exist for long. He didn't permit it before the Flood, and He will quickly stamp it out again just before Christ returns to set up His millennial kingdom. If you are a student of Bible prophecy and have been paying attention to recent developments, then none of this is a surprise. But just in case you doubt the sincerity of men like Kurzweil, let's examine the current science and technological trends and discover where the world's leading scientists are steering and altering mankind.

Global Future 2045

In June of 2013, thirty-four of the world's brightest thinkers presented papers to a gathering of approximately eight hundred attendees (who had each paid $800) regarding the future of mankind. The speaker list reads like a "Who's Who" of transhumanism (a philosophy and/or movement that advocates self-directed evolution of the human species, using genetic editing, hybridization, and eventually mind uploading to a computer). Speaking on the movement's core topics of artificial intelligence, genetics, and robotics were: Dr. Raymond Kurzweil, Natasha Vita-More, Dr. George Church, Dr. Hiroshi Ishiguro, Dr. Ed Boyden, Dr. David Dubrovsky, Dr. Ben Geortzel, Dr. Amit Goswami, and Dr. Alexander Kaplan.

It isn't a surprise to find neuroscientists, geneticists, roboticists, quantum physicists, artificial intelligence researchers, and futurists at an event like this; however, the roster also included several experts in spirituality: Tibetan Buddhist Lama Phakyob Rinpoche, Canadian Archbishop (retired) of Ottawa Lazar Puhalo, Russian yoga master Swami Visnudevananda and fellow yoga master Mahayogi "Pilot" Baba.

Strange bedfellows, you might think, but those who push the transhumanist agenda and the drive toward artificially extending human life spans and capabilities through technology often travel hand-in-hand with new-age, "spiritual" thinkers. In fact, the mysterious founder of the Global Future 2045, Dmitry Itskov, recently met with the Dalai Lama and received his "blessing" for the 2045 Avatar Project.[211]

In a March, 2013 interview with the online news source *Digital Trends*, Itskov discussed his philosophy:

> We believe that to move to a new stage of human evolution, mankind vitally needs a **scientific revolution coupled with significant spiritual changes**, inseparably linked, supplementing and supporting of each other. The vector of future development provided by **technological advancement should assist the evolution of the consciousness of humanity**, the individual and society, and be the transition to neo-humanity.[212] (emphasis added)

Itskov's utopian dream centers on something called the Avatar Project. If you've seen James Cameron's blockbuster CGI film *Avatar*, then you get the idea. Humanity will, according to Itskov and his colleagues, soon live inside eternally renewable extensions called avatars. It's a new play on an old theme (eugenics, which we'll visit in a bit)—but first, let's examine Itskov's idea more closely.

The Avatar Project, as envisioned by Itskov, is not directly connected to DARPA's Avatar Program[213] (more on DARPA in the next section), but the basic idea is the same. While DARPA plans to create robotic 'avatars' for human soldiers to operate either directly or remotely, Itskov's vision is for a three-step road toward human immortality.

Phase 1: Avatar A would be a robotic construct that humans could interface with via implanted hardware (or perhaps as Kurzweil explains by using nanobots).

Phase 2: Avatar B adds a "human brain life-support system" to Avatar A, allowing the human/robot construct to better integrate.

Phase 3: Avatar C will emerge when the human's "mind" (Kurzweil and George Church might call it "our connectome" translated into computer language) is uploaded to the computerized brain of Avatar B.

This three-phase system provides a false immortality without the requirement for salvation or remission of sins. It is little more than the alchemist's homunculus or golem filled with "something" spiritual to give it life. It is iron (machine) mixed with clay—or worse, a mingling of human seed with something inhuman. It also brings another passage in Scripture to mind:

> And he had power to give life unto the image of the beast, that the image of the beast should both speak, and cause that as many as would not worship the image of the beast should be killed. (Revelation 13:15)

DARPA's Dream of a Supersoldier

The Defense Advanced Research Project Agency (DARPA), originally called ARPA, was founded in 1958 to provide a secret place for men and women of science to imagine and eventually create technologies that would keep the United States at the forefront of military capabilities. Following on the heels of the Manhattan Project, our country's original "black op," ARPA has financed pioneering research into ways to build a better soldier and a more efficient and informative theater of war. Beginning in the Korean and Vietnam eras of the late '50s and early '60s, this research and development branch of the Pentagon field-tested new ideas in intelligence-gathering via acoustic devices, cameras, and computer-driven analytics that culminated in the digital warfare we know today. Unmanned aerial vehicles (UAVs), commonly called "drones," along with field robots such as ATLAS and the Cheetah, have brought science fiction-based dreams into the sobering reality of twenty-first-century combat.

News reports about DARPA's "brain and body" research have emphasized the restoration of function and memory to soldiers injured in battle as being the primary goal. Who among us doesn't know a man or woman who has experienced trauma in a theater of war? Many reading this can relate personally, concerned about loved ones who have come home with physical or mental ailments, and nearly all of us can name a friend or an acquaintance with post-traumatic stress disorder (PTSD). The need for physical and emotional healing is real, but this lofty goal may be serving as a lovely smokescreen for a larger, sinister agenda.

In fact, in her remarkable new book, *The Pentagon's Brain*, Annie Jacobsen reveals much of the darker truths behind DARPA's motives:

> **It is likely that DARPA's primary goal in advancing prosthetics is to give robots, not men, better arms and hands.** Robotics expert Noel Sharkey, who serves as a United Nations adviser and chairman of the International Committee for Robot Arms Control, explains: "You hear DARPA talk about a robot they are designing, being able to turn a valve inside a Fukushima-type power plant. Yes, that is an example of robotics keeping humans safe. But that robotic hand will also soon be able to turn a valve onboard, say a ship." A ship **that a robot has been sent to take over in a military operation.**[214] (emphasis added)

DARPA not only researches and finances research into robotics, but also serves as a major partner in the BRAIN Initiative. An "About Us" page on the Initiative's website explains the general purpose and description of this massive scientific endeavor:

> The Brain Research through Advancing Innovative Neurotechnologies (BRAIN) Initiative is part of a Presidential focus aimed at revolutionizing our understanding of the human brain. By

accelerating the development and application of innovative technologies, researchers will be able to produce a revolutionary new dynamic picture of the brain that, for the first time, shows how individual cells and complex neural circuits interact in both time and space. Long desired by researchers seeking new ways to treat, cure, and even prevent brain disorders, this picture will fill major gaps in our current knowledge and provide unprecedented opportunities for **exploring exactly how the brain enables the human body to record, process, utilize, store, and retrieve vast quantities of information, all at the speed of thought.**[215] (emphasis added)

Whenever most media outlets publish an article or news item about the BRAIN Initiative, the emphasis is placed on medical applications such as curing Alzheimer's, treating PTSD, or helping students to learn better or faster. However, with DARPA involved, you can bet that medical applications are only the beginning. With a supersoldier and/or avatar as the ultimate goal, neurological studies that map the human connectome will open the door to an entirely new world of military possibilities. Autonomous drones powered by AI will eliminate the need for antiquated "biological units" in the field of operations. Supersoldiers who are more like the Cybermen of Doctor Who than *Homo sapien* soldiers, will have no need for sleep, will run without tiring, and interface with AI drones for lightning-fast decision-making and fearless combat responses. Metal with carbon. Iron mixed with clay. It is a nightmare in white-hot metal, and it's coming soon to a theater of war near you.

One of the primary, founding goals of DARPA was to prevent the United States military from being "surprised" by geopolitical events, particularly in the realm of technology. When Russia launched Sputnik in October of 1957, it appeared to the American public that the Eisenhower administration was caught with its collective "pants down." However, the CIA and Eisenhower knew better. A new, super-secret "black ops" program based out of Area 51 had constructed a supersonic spy plane called the U-2. Though the world and the Kremlin knew nothing about it, our nation's secret U-2 pilots had overflown the Soviet Union multiple times, gathering photographic evidence of top-secret rocket bases where German scientists nabbed by the Soviets after World War II (in the Soviet version of Operation Paperclip) were outpacing their American equivalents.

This Cold War rivalry never truly disappeared, and developments in the Middle East and particularly now in Syria indicate that the rivalry between Russia and the United States is heating up again. In an odd, twenty-first century echo of the 1950s and 60s, a recent report from the government-sanctioned station Russia Today (RT)—which presents news and opinion to global audiences in native languages—trumpets Russian advances in artificial intelligence:

> In a step towards creating independent artificial intelligence comparable to Skynet from the "Terminator" franchise, a Russian company has successfully tested software capable of undertaking decisions and carrying them out without any human intervention.
>
> The United Instrument Manufacturing Corporation (OPK), an integral part of the Rostec arms corporation, says it has developed the Unicum (Latin for "the only one") software package that **gives military or civilian robots enough artificial intelligence to perform complicated tasks completely on their own.**
>
> Powering a group of up to 10 robotic complexes, the Unicum artificial intelligence (AI) communicates and distributes "roles" among the robots, chooses the "commander" of the robotic task force and assigns combat mission to each individual machine.[216] (emphasis added)

While Sputnik was a major step in Soviet/US military brinkmanship, today's rush to build a true artificial intelligence is likely to affect the entire world. RT's use of the term "Skynet," the artificial intelligence that rules the twenty-first century world of the *Terminator* films, is chilling, but the term is apt, because it implies Russian world domination, which is probably the intent of the article. Vladimir Putin certainly gives the impression that he would love to run the world, but then so would most US presidents. True to its original goal of making sure our tech is better than anyone else's, DARPA wants to make sure our AI emerges before "their" AI. This race toward AI, and eventually a super-AI (SAI, an artificial intelligence that surpasses human ability) rides upon a wave of bureaucratic fear that the country that produces the first SAI (sometimes referred to as an ASI or even ISA, which has prophetic implications, discussed in a bit) will achieve and maintain global dominance.

Picture a battle scenario in the not-too-distant future, when autonomous robots running a "sentient" artificial intelligence, operate not only as individual units but like a collective consciousness. This very scenario is depicted in Joel 2:

> Blow a trumpet in Zion; sound an alarm on my holy mountain! Let all the inhabitants of the land tremble, for the day of the Lord is coming; it is near, a day of darkness and gloom, a day of clouds and thick darkness! **Like blackness there is spread upon the mountains a great and powerful people; their like has never been before, nor will be again after them through the years of all generations.**
>
> Fire devours before them, and behind them a flame burns. The land is like the garden of Eden before them, but behind them a desolate wilderness, and nothing escapes them.
>
> Their appearance is like the appearance of horses, and like war horses they run.
>
> As with the rumbling of chariots, they leap on the tops of the mountains, like the crackling of a flame of fire devouring the stubble, like a powerful army drawn up for battle.

Before them peoples are in anguish; all faces grow pale.

Like warriors they charge; like soldiers they scale the wall. They march each on his way; they do not swerve from their paths.

They do not jostle one another; each marches in his path; they burst through the weapons and are not halted.

They leap upon the city, they run upon the walls, they climb up into the houses, they enter through the windows like a thief.

The earth quakes before them; the heavens tremble. The sun and the moon are darkened, and the stars withdraw their shining.

The Lord utters his voice before his army, for his camp is exceedingly great; he who executes his word is powerful. For the day of the Lord is great and very awesome; who can endure it. (Joel 2:1–11, ESV, emphasis added)

While there is debate about what exactly comprises this end-times "army," the description is powerful and terrifying. Joel 1 makes it clear that this invasion devastates the people living in Israel at the time. There is also a hint that this invasion occurs midway through the final seven years of Daniel's prophetic timeline (that is the "mid-Tribulation" period) for we read in Joel 1:

Gird yourselves, and lament, ye priests: howl, ye ministers of the altar: come, lie all night in sackcloth, ye ministers of my God: **for the meat offering and the drink offering is withheld from the house of your God.** (Joel 1:13, emphasis added)

The withdrawal of the daily sacrifice is a major part of Daniel's vision, related to us in chapter 11:

For the ships of Chittim shall come against him: therefore he shall be grieved, and return, and have indignation against the holy covenant: so shall he [Antichrist] do; he shall even return, and have intelligence with them that forsake the holy covenant [that is, break the treaty]

And arms shall stand on his part, and they shall pollute the sanctuary of strength, and **shall take away the daily sacrifice**, and they shall place the abomination that maketh desolate. (Daniel 11:30–31, emphasis added)

The army of Joel 2 shows superhuman capabilities, so it is either a troop of super-soldiers, cyborgs, or robots (or a combination of all three), directed by a super-artificial intelligence that allows this army to behave like one massive, demonic organism. It is also possible that this horde is actually a supernatural troop of spiritual beings, loosed from the abyss and led by their king, Abaddon (also called Apollyon). Yet, there may be a third interpretation, combining a cyborg/robotic force possessed and controlled by spiritual entities. Whichever proves to be true when this invasion comes to pass, the current race toward super-artificial intelligence by the United States, Russia, and many other countries (and terrorist organizations) will play a major role.

I mentioned above that the acronym for a super-artificial intelligence can vary depending on who is using it, but one such acronym is ISA (Intelligence Super Agent, with the idea of this entity being a master controller within an artificial system). "Isa" is what Islam calls "Jesus," and Islamic eschatology claims that Isa will return along with the Mahdi in the final days of planet earth. Given that programmers and robotics experts are racing to build a silicon version called "ISA" is disturbing at best, but it tracks with Christian eschatology of an "image of the beast."

Google's Robotics and Human Engineering Game

As mentioned in the opening to this chapter, Google's chief of engineering and resident transhumanism specialist is Dr. Raymond Kurzweil.

Google, by the way, is a founding supporter of Kurzweil's dream project, Singularity University. And ever since Dr. Kurzweil's arrival at the massive Google complex in 2012, the parent company (now known as Alphabet) has purchased a wide variety of tech and research companies that form an interesting mosaic. Prior to 2012, the majority of Google's purchases and/or mergers involved companies that helped expand their search engine market share or improve the company's ability to curate and display pinpoint advertising to you and me. However, the list since 2012 includes:

- Boston Dynamics (robotics)
- Viedle (facial recognition software)
- DNN Research (Deep Neural Networks)
- Behavio (social prediction)
- Flutter (gesture recognition software)
- Schaft, Inc. (robotics, particularly humanoid robots)
- Industrial Perception (robotics)
- Redwood Robotics (you can guess what they research)
- Meka Robotics (ditto)
- Nest Labs (home automation)
- Titan Aerospace (high-altitude UAVs, aka drones)
- Quest Visual (augmented realty)
- Skybox Imaging (satellite company)
- Dropcam (home monitoring)
- Jetpac (artificial intelligence)
- Polar (social polling)
- Dark Blue Labs (artificial intelligence)

It doesn't take a genius like Kurzweil to note the trend in these acquisitions and how such a portfolio of technology companies will allow Alphabet (Google's massive parent corporation) to shape the future of our interconnected world. One might even say that Alphabet's suite of capabilities forms the nucleus of a future Skynet (with apologies to Russia), eventually controlling and curating the flow of information throughout the world. Add robots, UAVs, satellites, and home/business integration, and such a company could truly control everything and everyone connected to its "cloud."

In 2014, *Fortune* magazine ran a special report about Google's own version of DARPA, a division called Advanced Technology and Projects Group (ATAP), led by former DARPA director Regina Dugan:

> ATAP's projects are more narrowly focused on mobile, but they, too, could easily land a leading role in a sci-fi movie script. There's a digital tattoo that you can paste onto your forearm and use to unlock your smartphone. There's Ara, a project to reinvent the smartphone so that it can be assembled on the fly to a customer's specs. It would give users the ability to choose hardware components to fit their needs—a camera, sensor, battery, or, say, an oximeter that measures pulse rates and blood oxygen levels—just as they choose apps. There's Tango, a prototype tablet that can see the world around itself in 3-D to map the inside of your home, for instance, or help a blind person navigate.[217]

And like DARPA, Dugan's ATAP will partner with outside groups:

> The core ATAP group involved just a dozen scientists and engineers, who joined with some 40 outside partners, including universities in the U.S. and Europe and NASA's Jet Propulsion Laboratory. In all, ATAP has worked with 326 partners—universities, startups, large system integrators, government and nonprofit organizations—in 22 countries.

So, if you think Google is just a search engine, think again.

CCTV and the Selfie Culture

In many ways, the citizens of the world have voluntarily signed up to be catalogued and collated. One of my favorite television programs from the 1960s was a visionary summer replacement series called *The Prisoner*. Enigmatic actor Patrick McGoohan starred and helped produce and even sometimes direct this claustrophobic examination of fascism taken to its logical extreme. The main character is never given a name, only a number. He's a man known simply as "Number Six," a number that in many ways represents mankind as a whole, for Adam was created on day 6, and carbon (the atomic element most prevalent in our bodies) has six electrons, six neutrons, and six protons.

The basic premise to the series is that Mr. McGoohan's character has suddenly and unexpectedly resigned from a sensitive position with a government agency (probably MI6 or something like it) and plans to leave London. However, while packing in his apartment, our hero is rendered unconscious by a mystery man using a gaseous agent, only to awaken in a duplicate of his flat in a place called "The Village" with no idea how he arrived or where he is geographically.

The Village is an insular place, where everyone is spied upon through CCTVs and listening devices, and where obedience is demanded with a practiced smile. It is a very creepy little place to say the least, and it is never quite explained just who built it—but there are hints. In fact, the finale is the subject of much debate even today regarding just what really happened to Number Six at all. It is possible that all the action occurred within his own mind, or that by discovering that he is—in reality— Number One, the enigmatic shadow man who runs The Village—our hero reveals that fascism only exists by the implied permission of those governed. In other words, he is responsible all that is happening—he is at fault because he didn't try to stop it.

I bring this up because you and I volunteer a vast amount of personal information to the keepers of the Internet (think of it as a worldwide "Village") with our daily Tweets, Facebook posts, and Instagram photos. Our cell phones have become a cyber-extension of ourselves, constantly pinging who knows which websites and reporting our locations, our conversations, and our surroundings to shadowy third-party companies and secretive organizations. GPS tracking software built into each mobile device follows our footsteps, and computer algorithms tag us and digitize us into little more than numbers to crunch and collect—tracing not only our present positions, but also predicting where we will go and what we will do, and with whom.

Walk into any fast food restaurant, and you are likely to find tables filled with families, business people, and teenagers engaged not in conversation with each other but rather in texting their friends or followers and posting pictures of their food. It sounds crazy, and honestly it really is. Why do we do this? Why have we allowed technology to recreate us from the ground up? What happened to engaging with humans through actual conversation, touching, and face-to-face sharing? Isn't it a bit ridiculous when someone you've never actually shaken hands with knows more about your life than your spouse, your children, or your parents?

Number Six in *The Prisoner* famously shouted again and again that he was "a man and not a number," yet we seem to revel in the faceless nature, the anonymity, of Internet engagement. Humanity is volunteering for the matrix, lining up for the latest gadgets to keep us ever more connected to an addiction that grows worse and worse with each passing year. Technology can be wonderful; it can inform, educate, and connect. But it can also be used for evil—to spy on us, to stupefy us, and to so distract us that we are no longer sensitive to one another's needs. Compassion and empathy are dying on the vine as privacy erodes and false anonymity empowers stalkers, mockers, and digital devils.

Our lives are on display almost around the clock. Nearly everywhere you look today, you'll find a camera—on a street corner, in a business, in a parking lot, on our neighbor's porches, in our children's toys, on a hundred cell phones within shouting distance, and now even on commercially sold drones. Nearly every morning, I find a new story about someone who discovers a remote-controlled quadcopter (a drone with four helicopter-type rotors) hovering outside his or her window, the onboard camera photographing intimate moments inside a bedroom or a teenage daughter taking a dip in the family pool. Many communities are discovering there are no municipal regulations to cover these intrusions, and some unlucky victims have themselves been arrested for daring to damage the invasive drone! If the drone's owner had actually *broken into* the victim's home to take photographs, he'd likely have been prosecuted for breaking and entering and perhaps even accused of sexual misconduct, but if he uses a drone, then he is not technically breaking the law in many districts of the country.

As mentioned above, even our children's toys are connected to servers. The Elf on the Shelf and a new Interactive Barbie are just two of the toys intended to provide security and friendship for our children. Our Alphabet creature Google has even patented the following:

> An anthropomorphic device, perhaps in the form factor of a doll or toy, may be configured to control one or more media devices. **Upon reception or a detection of a social cue, such as movement and/or spoken word or phrase,** the anthropomorphic device may aim its gaze at the source of the social cue. In response to receiving a voice command, the anthropomorphic device may interpret the voice command and map it to a media device command. Then, the anthropomorphic device may transmit the media device command to a media device, instructing the media device to change state.[218] (emphasis added)

For the "anthropomorphic device" to respond to spoken cues, it will be "listening" all the time. ALL THE TIME. This means that the toy that sits near our child's bed or on a shelf in the living room has the potential to hear and record *and report* all spoken words inside the home.

And who "hears" these words other than the "doll"? A third-party provider? A foreign power? A hacker? A stalker? A neighborhood pedophile?

Actually, we have no way of knowing or controlling who is listening or watching. Electronic eyes and ears are everywhere, and because we have become so accustomed to seeing them and to "'being seen," we no longer consider a panopticon state to be abnormal. We're happy in The Village so long as we have a reality show to watch or a ballgame to enjoy. As long as we keep our addictions fed, then we will continue to volunteer all that The Village requires of us.

The Glass Bubble of Perceived Reality

And while we're on the topic of social media and its effect on our private lives (or what's left of them), perhaps we should discuss how you and I are being altered by the ubiquitous curation taking place. Curation? "What is that?" you might ask. Well, simply put, curation is having others choose what we will experience—with others acting as a "curator." Museum curators choose which items to display to the public and which to "store," and they determine how the public items will be displayed, thereby influencing our perceptions.

In the very early days of Facebook and Twitter, members were able to see most if not all posts and tweets published by their friends. Likewise, their friends could "see" most if not all of that member's posts and tweets, and this immersive environment allowed for a rich and diverse experience on social media, which was the initial draw for most of us. However, because nothing is truly free on "free" sites, social media providers like Facebook and search engines like Google quickly realized that all those clicks could be monetized, which means that you and I become both a producer and a consumer. *We are the product these sites sell.* Our lives and our pictures provide opportunities for advertisers' algorithms to learn more about us, and as these integrated algorithms "learn," they decide which ads to serve us, which news to report, and even which posts to publish. Our "likes" and comments provide context and clarification for further analysis, which then leads to additional and more precise curation. Therefore, with each passing day, you and I are drawn farther and farther into a contextual bubble created for us by computers.

We view the world that the algorithm chooses for us to see, skewed and shaped to provide us a pleasurable experience—and this feedback loop feeds the addiction. Hybridization can be more than just mixing metal with carbon in a literal sense; it can also mean being refashioned and *reshaped by a machine*. Honestly, if you consider our present reality, in which we who spend our lives buried in a landslide of social media likes and shares are being drawn into a virtual web created by a software monster, then it is incumbent upon us to wake up and withdraw. The more content we share, the more personal information and precious time that we sacrifice to the swelling beast system within the World Wide Web, the more we will be deluded by its perceived beauty, for it will only reflect back that which we feed it. Curation. We see ourselves in a magic mirror, and the more we like it, the more we look.

Now, having said this, let me emphasize the importance of ministry within the pages of the World Wide Web, for there is still much that can be achieved for the Kingdom of God. But remember that while you tread there, you do so on an alien landscape owned and operated by programs and people who have little room for God and may themselves be victims of lying shapes and shadows that inspire and suggest and lie—and who have been given dominion of our planet—for now. But Christ is returning, and the current world order will give way to the millennial reign. Hallelujah!

Memes in Media: Video Games, Television, and Film

Similar to the way the World Wide Web shapes our reality (and as a consequence shapes us and our thoughts), entertainment and even the daily news we watch and consume contribute to who we are and what we believe. Earlier, I mentioned the television program *The Prisoner* and how its plot echoed not only fascism but also the virtual mire in which we all now live. However, while some entertainment uses fiction to reveal a true "man behind the curtain," as Toto did in *The Wizard of Oz*, entertainment and media can also *conceal* that man or even obscure his devices behind curtains of "memes."

What is a meme? Simply put, it's an idea that spreads like an infection, moving from person to person, infecting and affecting the opinions of each person it touches. The word is based on the Greek word *mimeme*, which is the noun form of the verb *mimeisthai*, meaning "to imitate." A "mime" imitates something, as does a "mimic." Though the idea is an old one, the field of study is relatively new. In fact, the field known as "mimetics" emerged only within the last thirty years—arising at about the same as the World Wide Web.

Internet memes have become so commonplace that meme posters provide content on many of today's Facebook and other social media posts. It's like having someone sneeze an idea in your direction, which then takes hold like a cold virus and changes you from the inside out. Mimetics as a "science" has been confirmed by Richard Dawkins, who refers to memes as "units of cultural transmission." This quote comes from a 2012 article penned by Rupert Sheldrake, a scientist I've often referred to in my talks at various conferences, because Sheldrake is a driving force behind the idea of morphic fields. The article appeared at New Dawn Magazine online on May 11, 2012, and includes this section about memes:

> Morphic resonance has many implications for the understanding of human learning, including the acquisition of languages. Through the collective memory on which individuals draw, and to which they contribute, it should in general be easier to learn what others have learned before.

Morphic fields could revolutionise our understanding of cultural inheritance, and the influence of the ancestors. Richard Dawkins has given the name "meme" to "units of cultural transmission," and memes can be seen as cultural morphic fields. Morphic resonance also sheds new light on many religious practices, including rituals.[219]

Before I unpack a bit more about memes and how media outlets exploit them, let me give you a little background on Rupert Sheldrake and morphic field theory. Sheldrake's ideas may sound "out there," but he is not just a fringe kook; in fact, Dr. Sheldrake received his doctorate in biochemistry from Cambridge University in England. Though not all his colleagues agree with Sheldrake's ideas of morphic resonance and how such "fields" influence human behavior and ideas, as a Christian, I have to admit that it makes some sense. You and I live in a world that is held together by an unseen deity that we know as Jesus Christ (Colossians 1:17, "He is before all things; and in Him all things hold together."). Yet, our world, due to its fallen nature, has been relegated to the control and influence of fallen angels and demons. When YWHW chose Jacob to father the nation of Israel, He also carved out a land for His people that would stand as a beacon of hope among a world run by these supernatural entities. (If this concept is new to you, I would refer you to the work of Dr. Michael S. Heiser, an expert in ancient languages, who serves as consultant to Logos Bible Software. Heiser's writings explain the concept of a Divine Council and how God apportioned the nations to the dominion of fallen angels following the fall of Babel.[220])

The world of spiritual entities is by its very nature unseen, therefore it is entirely within the realm of possibilities that Sheldrake's "morphic field" represents a nonbelieving scientist's attempt to explain how our world responds to changes within the spiritual dimensions. With this in mind, then, let us continue to explore memes and propagated viral ideas and beliefs within media and how humanity is shaped by them.

Video games: I began playing video games back in the stone age of the genre when playing Pong or Space Invaders felt like stepping into the future. Since then, game play has become so accessible and affordable that nearly every household in America has at least one if not dozens of gaming systems. In the thirty years since Nintendo first emerged in our country, bringing with it Mario and Zelda, other platforms and thousands of games have come to dominate our children's bedrooms and their minds.

While many video games provide storylines and activities that may concern parents and grandparents, two types of interactive formats allow for profound meme transmission—role-playing games (RPGs) and first-person shooters (FPS). RPGs include games such as Zelda, where the player takes on the role of the main character (note that in some RPGs, character redesign and gender/name are included options). It is the story that drives the game. Some players enjoy the strategy required to get past enemies, while others derive more satisfaction from engaging the "bosses" on each level through fighting techniques. Oftentimes, as with Zelda, the story is rooted in folklore or mythology. Ancient pagan gods often serve as plot devices, and the player must follow the quest that these gods assign to them. Other times, the storyline may take on overtly dark themes involving zombies, vampires, alien invaders, or wizards. Video games don't necessarily program our children (or the adults who play them), but the virtual world certainly can influence thoughts and beliefs. And gaming can become addictive—not just to the game, but also to the social interaction provided by online gaming. World of Warcraft (WOW) is a case in point. WOW has proven so addictive for many of its players that online addiction forums like WOWaholics.org have emerged to help former players kick the habit.

Those who follow the podcast and blogs produced by my husband Derek P. Gilbert and myself will most likely smile when I say that an episode of Doctor Who illustrates nicely just how addictive and destructive media can be. In season 2, episode 7, "The Idiot's Lantern," an alien entity falls like lightning to the earth and inhabits television signals in a small district of London. This alien, called "The Wire," subsists on electrical energy and must "feed" in order to maintain its life force. Anyone who is watching a program during such a "feeding session" loses his or her face and mind. They become blank and without thought: essentially zombies. The Wire gobbles them up and laughs the whole time about the foolishness of the foolish earthlings. A secondary theme permeates this well-done episode: Nazis and totalitarianism. Each television aerial sitting atop each row-house roof is intentionally shaped to resemble a swastika, and even the father of the primary family looks a bit like Hitler, and he most certainly behaves like the German dictator by acting the part of dictator within his own home and spying on his neighbors. Media, it seems, can indeed render us little more than mindless minions of an unseen hand.

Television and Film: Since we have referenced a television program and TV in general as spreading memes, let's examine many of the current trends in entertainment. Take a look at the Fall 2015 lineup of programs available on cable or satellite setups, and you'll find several primary themes. So-called reality programs abound, and I'm at a loss to explain why, except perhaps for a human failing toward voyeurism. Humans have always been nosy and curious and prone to gossip, but I'm completely baffled by the success of these programs. They remind me a bit of the wrestling matches that aired every Saturday evening when I was growing up, where flamboyantly fierce men faced each other in a ring, and audiences cheered for their favorite (usually the "nice guy") while booing the "villain." It was and continues to be theater. Then, as now, wrestlers rehearse their throws and holds to make them appear realistic but mostly harmless. In essence, these men (and now women) are stunt experts, putting on a show for the masses. Reality programming parallels this idea, but instead gives us self-obsessed celebrities and celebrity wannabes who line up to become the next big thing. A few of the programs are structured as contests, but it's probable that the outcome has been determined in advance, just as in the old wrestling shows. It is all theater masquerading as real life, yet, it shapes and influences our real lives, particularly the fashion and lifestyle trends. Politically correct behavior is reinforced through programming and social media, and though you and I might be able to see past the façade, more often than not our children and grandchildren cannot, and so they are shaped and molded according to the world before they even begin school, all from "the idiot's lantern."

Film, like television, plays an important role in shaping society and personal belief systems. The memes propagated via movies creep into our thoughts, though we may not realize it. Governments know the power of a well-constructed (and well hidden) meme. Nazis employed commercials, rallies, architecture, and film to motivate and control the masses, and the Allied nations followed suit. Hollywood writers and directors partnered with our federal government during World War II to put a positive spin on the war and encourage families to live sacrificially as patriotic citizens, including being willing to serve in the military. Media had the opposite effect during the Vietnam era, as nightly news interrupted evening meals and bedtime routines with disturbing images of a war that America could not win, and this imagery helped ignite a social revolution that turned families and sexual mores on their collective heads.

I've heard it said that among all various plotlines available to writers, you can reduce all to just seven basic storylines:

1. Overcoming the Monster
2. Rags to Riches
3. The Quest
4. Voyage and Return
5. Comedy
6. Tragedy
7. Rebirth

While some lists may differ (I've seen lists as long as a dozen or so), it's obvious that all entertainment stems from a small list of conflicts or quests. Over the millennia of storytelling, and in particular the age since the emergence of the novel, writers all across the globe have managed to work these few plot constructs into a dazzling variety of genres and adventures. How is it then, that over the past decade or so, filmmakers appear to have settled on formulaic films that beat a constant drum of transhumanism and apotheosis? Consider for a moment how often a hit movie revolves around superhuman characters, alien seed/panspermia (that then gives rise to superhumans), genetic improvement of humans, supernaturally changed and improved humans, and so on and so on. There is now an entire subgenre of films based on Marvel, DC, and Dark Horse comics feature incredible CGI (computer-generated imagery) and stunts with movies about X-Men, Avengers, Blade, Spiderman, Ghost Rider, Thor, Guardians of the Galaxy, Superman, Constantine, V for Vendetta, Watchmen, Batman, Wonder Woman, Green Lantern, Timecop, The Mask, Tank Girl, Alien v. Predator, Hellboy, The 300, Sin City, and the list goes on. Sequels to successful films have almost replaced original thought, and remakes of previous hits serve well when you need an "original" movie idea.

I'll admit to enjoying movies and television, but when Derek and I watch either, we do so with our eyes open and try to discern what memes are being spread. Transhumanism is a major theme in most current movies, and it's echoed in the small screen as well as in programs like *Heroes*, in which genetically enhanced individuals (as with Marvel's X-Men) are all that stand between the earth and doom. But superheroes need not always be genetically enhanced men and women; they might also be a supernatural hybrid. What teenager doesn't believe himself or herself to be "'different'"? It is part and parcel of emerging from childhood to adulthood to undergo an uncomfortable season of change, is it not? Movies like the immensely popular *Twilight* series, based on the also popular books, features a young girl torn by her love for both a vampire and a werewolf. In fact, blood alteration and blood-letting seem to go hand in hand in film these days.

And speaking of blood, for *God's Ghostbusters*, I wrote a chapter about virtual sin and the idea that those who actually are drawn to blood and gore films, those who nurture a secret thrill upon watching such, may actually be participating (though they may not realize it) in virtual bloodletting, which may also precipitate a spiritual response. Bloodletting in fiction is nothing new. In Bram Stoker's seminal novel *Dracula*, the insane man Renfield quotes Scripture in chapter 18 as he tries to explain his odd behavior to Dr. Seward and his guest Mina Harker:

> Why, I myself am an instance of a man who had a strange belief. Indeed, it was no wonder that my friends were alarmed, and insisted on my being put under control. I used to fancy that life was a positive and perpetual entity, and that by consuming a multitude of live things, no matter how low in the scale of creation, one might indefinitely prolong life. At times I held the belief so strongly that I actually tried to take human life. The doctor here will bear me out that on one occasion I tried to kill him for the purpose of strengthening my vital powers by the assimilation with my own body of his life through the medium of his blood, relying of course, upon the Scriptural phrase, "**For the blood is the life**" [Deuteronomy 12:23]. Though, indeed, the vendor of a certain nostrum has vulgarized the truism to the very point of contempt. Isn't that true, doctor? (emphasis and Bible reference added)

Victorian readers in the 1880s were shocked by Stoker's depiction of a narcissistic and bloodthirsty count named Dracula, but even though Stoker presented the character as repulsive and thoroughly depraved, this despicable character morphed into an anti-hero with magnetism and charm within twenty years, and even caused the female audience to swoon when portrayed by Bela Lugosi onstage and later in the 1931 film. By the early twenty-first century, vampires had undergone drastic changes, transforming into a victim in *Interview with a Vampire* and more recently into a twenty-something heartthrob who is simply misunderstood and only wants to love Bella (the heroine of the *Twilight* series). In fact, most if not all of our current superheroes are "misunderstood" and claim their sole purpose is to help humanity. However, unlike our Savior who gave His blood so that you and I might have eternal life, the vampire would take our blood to give himself eternal life. As with the women in the early twentieth century who fainted at the overt sensuality of Lugosi's Dracula, teens and twenty-somethings are fawning and fainting over the supernatural romances so popular today. We have been slowly moved from a rigorous and righteous path toward the pagan stand of superhero trees that populate the treacherous and false forests of the "Holy-woods" (Hollywood).

Don't let film and television draw you and your loved ones into dangerous places, dear reader. Instead, if your child insists that she must read it because all her friends are doing so, then read the book or graphic novel with her, and discuss it from a biblical point of view. Use these fads and fancies as golden opportunities to overcome the world's twisted, viral memes with sound teaching.

As I mentioned earlier, many of today's films and television programs, even many video games, began their lives in the printed word. And so we must turn to books and their memes.

Bell, books, and candles in the wind: An old expression goes something like this: Give a man a fish, and you feed him for a day; teach a man to read, and you feed him for life. The originator of this proverb is much disputed. Some say it is Lao Tzu, others that it is Maimonides, but regardless of the source, the premise is sound, particularly if that man reads the Bible. However, being able to read does not always mean the reader has discernment or even good taste in literature, so books and today's graphic novels beloved by the younger set can serve as excellent sources for mind-shaping memes. The Stoker book, *Dracula*, is a case in point—as is another nineteenth-century novel, *Frankenstein*. Both of these books broke new ground when released in 1897 and 1818, respectively. It's interesting that the two books so often mentioned together were published a generation apart. Like with our twentieth century, the nineteenth began and ended with vastly different societies. Industrialization began in the early nineteenth and found its apex in the early twentieth, while one might say that our Information Age began in the late nineteenth and is ongoing.

Literature is a powerful medium, for it can be savored in utter privacy. Who among us doesn't remember sitting up until the wee hours of the morning with a great book in one hand and a flashlight in the other, doing our best to devour every page, every word, beneath the shelter and secrecy of a quilt or blanket? I grew up in a household of six daughters, and privacy was at a high premium in our house, for although we moved several times during my youth, we seldom had more than three bedrooms to share amongst a family of eight. Hiding beneath the covers at night gave me a private world, and running off to the woods in the daytime did the same. But there was always something special about staying up late to read that eclipsed daytime adventures. My fare generally ran to science fiction or mysteries, and this has definitely informed my writing style today. A writer must first be a reader, and the printed word holds a significant power from generation to generation. Words can change us. They shape opinion and ignite revolutions, but they also soothe the soul and can lead to eternal life. Our Savior is the very embodiment of this latter aspect, for He is called the Word (Greek: *logos*) in John. When God spoke, He was there. He lives in every word inspired by the Spirit, and He leads us to everlasting salvation when we hear His call.

But words can harm as well as heal. Memes in media in recent years, as seen in news articles, blogs, short stories, novels, nonfiction, and graphic novels, depict Christians and our Christ as mean and meaningless.

Young readers are influenced by textbooks, young adult fiction, and the social media posts their parents never see. Teens are "radicalized" online through the written word. Wives and husbands are lured from their families by online trysts and pornographic websites—via the written word often accompanied by graphic depictions and pictures. Books written by experts can convince us that black is white and orange is black just by using persuasive arguments and twisted truths. Horoscopes, alien archeology, panspermia, paganism, feel-good psychology, diluted gospel, and veiled propaganda are published daily to make publishers rich and readers spiritually poor, to sow dissension and unrest while harvesting souls.

And then there are the magazines and pornographic websites. Serial killer Ted Bundy once told Dr. James Dobson that pornography hooked him as a youth and contributed to his thirst for murder. And while Bundy's manipulative personality as a sociopath may have directed his conversation, there is a dark nugget of truth within his comments:

> I wasn't some guy hanging out in bars, or a bum. I wasn't a pervert in the sense that people look at somebody and say, "I know there's something wrong with him." I was a normal person. I had good friends. I led a normal life, except for this one, small but very potent and destructive segment that I kept very secret and close to myself. Those of us who have been so influenced by violence in the media, particularly pornographic violence, are not some kind of inherent monsters. We are your sons and husbands. We grew up in regular families. **Pornography can reach in and snatch a kid out of any house today. It snatched me out of my home 20 or 30 years ago.** As diligent as my parents were, and they were diligent in protecting their children, and as good a Christian home as we had, there is no protection against the kinds of influences that are loose in a society that tolerates....[221] (emphasis added)

It's chilling to read these words, knowing that Bundy was once a small, impressionable boy and that his life could have taken so many different paths. Words matter, and they have power, but when coupled with illicit ideas and pictures, they can rage like a firestorm intended to destroy our God-given rights and possibilities. Children deserve protection from words that hurt, and they must be exposed to the Word who heals. Humans are being slowly and irrevocably enticed to leave God aside, to toss Him into the rubbish heap like so much trash, and rush into a pagan future awash in gore, idolatry, and sex magic masquerading as popular fiction. We are being programmed to believe a lie, when the truth stands before us, waiting to light our pathway and our steps. You can stand in the gap between your children and words that harm by knowing what they are reading—and if you cannot dissuade them, join them in the discussion by reading the book with them. What you don't know can hurt *them*. Memes change minds, and they spread efficiently and swiftly; before you know it—all are infected. As Paul said to the church at Galatia, "a little leaven leavens the whole lump" (Galatians 5:9). Tiny changes in what we read, what we hear, and what we see can lead to massive changes in our culture and our world. It can alter our futures, and even lead to shameful policies like our next topic.

The New Eugenics: Just the Old Eugenics Rebranded

As I mentioned earlier, much of what drives the transhumanism movement is revealed in an oft-repeated phrase, "self-directed evolution." The road to a "better human," and, by implication, a "better world" (according to adherents), is paved with bricks made of self-improved gold. Just enter the phrase "self-directed evolution" into your Google search engine, and you'll find loads of videos, articles, and books that repeat the theme. What today's mobile minions may not realize is that this is a phrase and a dream that reaches back to the late nineteenth century and the eugenics movement.

. While the space constraints of this chapter make it impossible to cover eugenics in depth, let me give you a brief introduction. If this topic is new to you, then you might be inclined to connect Adolf Hitler and his search for the Ubermuench (Superman) to the start of eugenics, but Hitler actually based his idea on programs created in the United States. As Darwin's theory of evolution took hold across the Western world, researchers began to unravel small pieces of the genetics puzzle. By 1900, chromosomes had been observed and debated for about fifty years, but the function and design of these "colored bodies" (the actual meaning of the term "chromosomes") mystified early cell biologists. At about this same time, the mid-nineteenth century work of Gregor Mendel came to light, allowing scientists to recognize and record patterns in inheritance. Concomitant geopolitical issues were, in many ways, similar to today, and these concerned many academics; therefore, some of these men and women began to theorize about ways to improve the human condition, and by doing so produce enlightened humans not prone to war or disease because of their superior bodies and brains. Hence, philosophy, changes in religious belief, scientific advancement, pandemics, war, and geopolitics bubbled together inside a sinister cauldron and produced the eugenics movement.

Perhaps the first official eugenics organization arose within the American Breeders Association, an academic membership founded in 1903. An excerpt from the 1910 premier issue of the organization's magazine featured an editorial on the subject of eugenics. Written by Charles B. Davenport, the article calls for serious academic study into human breeding:

The association of research in Eugenics with the American Breeders Association is a source of dignity and safety. It recognizes that in respect to heredity man's nature follows the laws of the rest of the organic world. It recognizes that human heredity is a subject of study for practical ends; **the ends namely of race improvement.**[222] (emphasis added)

According to the eugenics archive at the University of Missouri's website, Charles Davenport was a leading architect of the American eugenics movement.

As the wave of new adherents to the eugenic cause increased, the movement took on an **almost religious or spiritual character.** Charles Davenport, Director of the Eugenics Record Office, came to realize the need for a canon or dogma for the movement and developed the Eugenics Creed. The creed underwent some minor modifications over time, but it remained the central doctrine of the eugenics crusade.

Eugenics Creed
- I believe in striving to **raise the human race to the highest plane of social organization**, of cooperative work and of effective endeavor.
- I believe that **I am the trustee of the germ plasm** that I carry; that this has been passed on to me through thousands of generations before me; and that **I betray the trust if (that germ plasm being good) I so act as to jeopardize it**, with its excellent possibilities, or, from motives of personal convenience, to unduly limit offspring.
- I believe that, having made our choice in marriage carefully, we, the married pair, should seek to have 4 to 6 children in order that our carefully selected germ plasm shall be reproduced in adequate degree and that this preferred stock shall not be swamped by that less carefully selected.
- I believe in such a selection of immigrants as shall not tend to adulterate our national germ plasm with socially unfit traits.

- I believe in repressing my instincts when to follow them would injure the next generation. (emphasis added)

The first congress for eugenicists met in England, led by Charles Darwin's son, Maj. Leonard Darwin, but after that, the focus and primary driver of the movement shifted to America, with Davenport as its leading proponent. My own alma mater, Indiana University (IU), as well as many academic institutions throughout the country, taught courses in and emphasized selective breeding to improve the human species. IU's biology department's primary building is even named for David Starr Jordan, one of these early academicians who served as chair of the school's Natural Sciences department and eventually as university president (1885–1891). Jordan later left Indiana to become the first president of the newly founded Stanford University. According to a website dedicated to preserving the works and history of Jordan's life, the biologist had some beliefs that reflected many within the rarified air of academia at the time:

> Like many prominent intellectuals and leaders during the turn of the 20th century, **David Starr Jordan believed in the ideas of race supremacy and characterized himself as a Nordicist.** While he didn't believe that the Nordic race was perfect in all forms, he did prefer the kind of citizens that upheld the virtues maintained by his puritan ancestors. As a promoter of freedom, **Jordan believed that all men were born free and equal in a political sense, but that biological inequality not only prevailed between races but within races as well.** As a distinguishing factor from other Nordicists, Jordan recognized the cultural and intellectual contributions of other races as superior to the Germanic peoples in many different realms.[223] (emphasis added)

Well-known supporters of eugenics included Theodore Roosevelt, Winston Churchill, Herbert Hoover, Margaret Sanger, H. G. Wells,

Linus Pauling, John Maynard Keynes, John Harvey Kellogg, George Bernard Shaw, John D. Rockefeller, Alexander Graham Bell, and, of course, David Starr Jordan and Charles B. Davenport. Ways and means to enforce this "self-directed evolution" ran the gamut from state fairs that awarded "fitter family" prizes to enforced sterilization within prisons and mental hospitals (criminality, "feeble-mindedness," and even "poverty" being considered indicators of being "unfit").

With this very brief introduction to eugenics as practiced in the early days of genetic studies, it quickly becomes clear why the very phrase used by these twentieth-century "breeders," that of "self-directed evolution," brings it all back around. Transhumanism and the post-modern drive toward Human 2.0 is neo-eugenics wearing a very thin veneer. And it is also the oldest lie in history: that humanity is somehow defective in our God-created state. The Nachash (the serpent) convinced Adam and Eve that they lacked a very important dimension to their design and that by following him they would find that missing spark that could render them "gods."

Which brings us back around to Dr. Raymond Kurzweil's dream of "godhood." Metal and clay combine to form a better human, or so Raymond Kurzweil believes. Computers and carbon-based organic matter. If you're under forty, then you probably don't remember a television series called *The Six-Million-Dollar Man*, but it entertained millions in the 1970s. Lee Majors starred as a former astronaut whose body was nearly destroyed when his experimental aircraft crashed. So, rather than lose a great astronaut, a scientific organization (similar to DARPA) rebuilt the body of Steve Austin (played by Majors), giving him super abilities. He could run faster, jump higher, and see with a 20-X zoom capability. Rather than repairing Austin, the Office of Scientific Intelligence made him "better." This is exactly what DARPA and commercials enterprises like Google are trying to do today: improve the human condition through technology. The super soldiers of Joel 2 may already exist. Metal mixed with clay may already breathe and walk upon this earth.

Collective Intelligence: The Needs of the Many Outweighs the Need of the One

While researching current trends in human evolution and technology, particularly artificial intelligence and sociological theory, I came across a curious term that relates to our topic of human change and hybridization: collective intelligence. This is a sociological idea that claims groupthink is wiser than individual-think. Another way to couch this idea in current terminology is to say that collective intelligence (CI) is crowdsourced wisdom. In other words, the whole is greater than the sum of the parts. There is a spiritual equivalent to this in the Body of Christ, where the potential of the collective is much greater than the additive capabilities of all members. However, we do not truly make full use of this potential, because we have never achieved a full and complete union of the members—we fight, we disagree on doctrine, we pull away, and even wound one another. We have an autoimmune disorder of sorts.

The secular world of government and corporate entities also form a corporate entity that will serve as the body of the coming world leader whom we call the Antichrist. Collective intelligence, or "hive mind," will enable this group to cooperate and obey the "head" because they will be incorporated into perfect union where free will no longer exists. This is why, when a person accepts the "mark" and worships the beast, he or she loses all chance at redemption: Free will and choice are gone. That door is now closed to him or her. Each member of the Antichrist body will serve only his head. This is fascism "writ large." Fascism is nothing more than dictatorial control of a population by binding it under one ruler or form of rule. The Village mentioned earlier is a prime example. The Village citizenry have a form of happiness, but it is derived from fear, not joy. The citizens obey because they know nothing else; to do otherwise would be to die. They have lost their individuality, and therefore have become nothing more than cells within a massive "Village Body."

This is the idea behind collective intelligence, and though sociologists may not foresee it, this concept is a way to describe the rising global entity that we currently call the Internet. Like it not, we who populate the Internet—we "netizens"—are being shaped by this technology. Hashtags and viral ideas serve, and memes are more than just reflections of the netizen landscape; they are orders from the core. These memes affect us and shape opinion, and by doing so, they transform us. It is an ongoing process that will culminate in the physical integration of all who worship the beast into the Antibody—with the Antichrist as its head.

Yesterday, I came across a sobering article that claims smart phones will become redundant within five years. Five years! Already, we see "smart watches" serving as adjunct appliances to our smart phones and tablets, and eventually those will be obsolete. What will replace this ubiquitous technological appendage? Wearables, virtual reality, and implantables. Computer chips, neural dust, and genetic editing will very soon negate the need for external devices. Recent success in getting past our God-designed neural firewall (the blood-brain barrier) will allow our brain cells to be hacked and "upgraded." In fact, Raymond Kurzweil's vision of a brain chip (probably a nano-device or neural dust) that gives the host constant wi-fi access to a virtual world is already being bench-tested, so it is very likely that human trials will begin, assuming they have not already commenced within DARPA or its associated labs—or elsewhere in the world, such as in China or Russia.

Humans who volunteer for this pervasive matrix risk losing their free will as the price of receiving the kick of being constantly connected. Internet addiction is real, and I can imagine many scenarios in which an implantable device would be considered desirable: medical applications in which wireless therapeutics replace worn-out or defective cells and tissues; patients with memory problems, soldiers with PTSD, students who need to score higher grades, or those who want to learn a new language instantly, upgrade their intelligence, or perhaps unlearn a habit like smoking or overeating. Other applications might be the treatment of depression or just serving as an internal "friend" to the lonely or vulnerable. It's easy to see how neural implants (already being used in several medical applications with a physical device that provides deep-brain stimulation) will be sold as useful, if not indispensable, to all humans, not just patients.

Science fiction is quickly becoming science fact, and it is not unlikely at all that neural connections will be hailed as the means of achieving world peace! Speaking of neural connections and brain hacking, let's now discuss the elephant in the room: Gene editing and CRISPR Cas9.

Better Living through Biochemistry

Evolutionists and transhumanists have much in common. Both believe that humanity arose from a long procession of transitional forms that began with a singular catalytic event in which life spontaneously emerged from basic chemicals. Honestly, this belief system requires much more faith than believing in creation, but since that is the position of many scientists and philosophers, it is logical that evolutionists would applaud a technology that permits scientists to guide humanity toward the next phase of development.

When Charles Darwin outlined his theory in the nineteenth century, biology was a relatively new discipline, and cell biologists knew practically nothing about the magnificent intricacies of the human cell, let alone the specific functions and biochemical makeup of DNA. Scientific thought in the late nineteenth and early twentieth centuries knew only that certain traits could be inherited, and that careful "breeding" practices, judiciously employed, would yield desirable traits. This is how eugenics was born. Fast forward one hundred years to the present, and we see the rise of neo-eugenics (transhumanism) that uses biochemical means *to force change* within an organism. Breeding is so last century! Now, a visit to the lab can fix problems *in situ* (Latin for "local" or "on site"—in other words, fix them in living cells in real time). This was possible even when I studied genetics back in the 1990s, but today's molecular tools are much more precise, efficient, and economic. CRISPR Cas9 has kicked it up a whole lot of notches (to paraphrase TV chef Emeril). This new gene-editing system paves the way for germline engineering.

So, what is CRISPR? As mentioned earlier in the book, the acronym stands for Clustered Regularly Interspersed Palindromic Repeats. A palindrome is a word that is spelled the same backwards as forwards, and palindromes within DNA code work in similar fashion: The lettered code reads the same backwards and forwards. DNA is composed of biochemical subunits called nitrogenous bases, which can be thought of as letters of the genetic alphabet. These are guanine, cytosine, thymine, and adenine. G, C, T, and A. The structure of these bases allows them to connect to each other in specific ways using hydrogen bonds. By connecting, these bases form molecular rungs of the DNA ladder. The side pieces of this ladder are two ribose sugar backbones where the ribose molecules are linked by phosphodiester bonds. You needn't worry about memorizing or even really understanding this, but if you're familiar with biochemistry, then it makes sense. What I want you to understand is the beauty and complexity of God's design. This is not a random structure that arose from a series of catalytic events. This is a gorgeous and efficient system that reveals God the Creator! Not only is DNA elegantly designed, but it is compacted in ways that early twentieth century eugenicists could never have imagined.

Each cell in the human body contains approximately six feet of DNA that's stored inside a miniscule "main office" called the nucleus. Six feet! Though as long as some men are tall, this molecule is only two nanometers in width (a human hair is about one hundred thousand nanometers wide). So, how does DNA keep from getting all knotted up, and how does it even fit? God's design is amazing. Proteins called histones, shaped like nanoscale "balls" help to organize this strand, sort of like spooling a long thread. There are five types of histones, and within these there are even more subtypes, but each type has its own function. This remarkable system organizes the superfine thread of DNA and also helps to regulate gene expression (unwinding when the cell needs to make a protein from the 'recipe' contained in the gene).

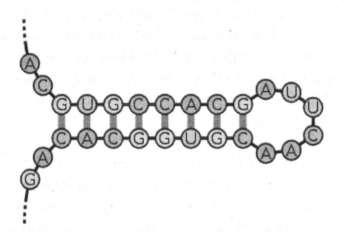

CRISPR was discovered in bacterial cells as a means to fight off viruses (bacteriophages). The palindromic repeats mentioned in the CRISPR name are actually areas that form palindromic pairings rather than strict palindromes. In DNA, A pairs with T, and C pairs with G. Therefore, the sequences GTGCCACG and CGCTGGCAC, when placed near each other on the same side of the ladder will want to pair and form a hairpin, which opens up the DNA (shown in this illustration). The diagram here is of RNA, which uses uracil (U) in place of thymine (T) when transcribing a gene into the RNA "protein template." (RNA plays a crucial role in the assembly line of gene to finished protein, but that's a tale for another book.)

The hairpin areas like the one above are called the CRISPR "locus," and the areas between these "hairpins" are called spacers, where the Cas genes (Cas stands for "CRISPR associated") are located. When researchers discovered these repeats and made the connection between their presence throughout the bacterial genome and "editing," it was a short trip from discovery to implementation. Today, CRISPR kits that contain the Cas9 gene (or another type of Cas gene; there are lots of them with different numbers) along with an RNA guide (essentially a short piece of RNA that leads the kit to the gene to be altered or to the insertion site for a new gene) and other required catalytic proteins can be purchased by any lab or educational institution online for prices beginning at just a few hundred dollars. In fact, the prices are so reasonable that labs across the world are using these kits in experiments that they hope will not only reveal more truths about human DNA, but will lead to patentable discoveries and even patentable creatures. Humans and animals can now be rewritten *in situ*, but also via germline engineering. In fact, an article recently posted online heralded ours as an age when dragons and unicorns might become real![224]

What do I mean by germline engineering? Human cells are either somatic (part of the current body) or reproductive (ova and spermatozoa). Altering a somatic cell only affects the current person, but altering/editing a reproductive cell potentially affects *all descendants*. Eugenicists dreamt of removing what they considered to be undesirable traits, such as feeble-mindedness, alcoholism, and so-called sexual immorality (believed by eugenicists to be inheritable traits that weakened a population and led to increased crime). (Note: What eugenicists were really doing was trying to breed sin out of humans, but that is never going to happen. Each of us is born as an inheritor of sin. Though we might try to use our free will to be sinless, it is an impossibility for us. Only Christ managed to live a perfect, sinless life, and it is His substitutionary atonement that frees us and grants us access to heaven with the promise of a brand new, eternal body. Eugenics is not a means to eradicate sin, nor is it the road to godhood. Technology has no power to negate God's judgment.)

Neo-eugenics, also called transhumanism, or the Humanity + movement (H+), is hailed by proponents as the way to achieve the eugenicists' dream and transform humanity into the perfect creature, i.e., gods. Germline editing is their means of achieving this end, but editing is not the only way to alter somatic and even reproductive DNA. A new discipline called epigenetics can effect changes in parent and offspring alike.

Epigenetics was discovered only a few decades ago, so it is relatively new. Essentially, it involves the regulation of gene transcription (remember those histone proteins?) and switching (turning genes on and off). Generally speaking, most switching is achieved through a chemical change called "methylation." Simply put, this is adding a methyl group (a carbon with three hydrogens, CH_3) to a molecule. When a gene is methylated, it is turned off. In fact, research now indicates that cancer cells have a higher percentage of methylation than healthy cells. It is however dangerous to assume that artificially enforced switching (through medical intervention) will result in healthy cells. The field of epigenetics is in its infancy, and every day researchers are discovering how God's design uses selective and even transient switching in some cell types. Still, researchers are a curious lot, and laboratory methylation experimentation is happening across the globe as I type this, in hopes of discovering more secrets of how our cells function—and quite frankly in hopes of finding patentable and marketable drugs and therapeutics.

There is a fascinating spiritual aspect to genetic expression via epigenetic switching. We find it in Exodus, where God is giving the law to the Hebrews through His servant Moses:

> Thou shalt not bow down thyself to them, nor serve them: for I the LORD thy God am a jealous God, **visiting the iniquity of the fathers upon the children unto the third and fourth generation of them that hate me.** (Exodus 20:5, emphasis added)

> Keeping mercy for thousands, forgiving iniquity and transgression and sin, and that will by no means clear the guilty; **visiting the iniquity of the fathers upon the children, and upon the children's children unto the third and the fourth generation.** (Exodus 34:7, emphasis added)

Epigeneticists view their insights and research as ground-breaking, yet this idea of an action taken by a living human that can affect subsequent generations is an epigenetic fact, and we find it in the Old Testament that we've studied for thousands of years! Epigenetics is here to stay, and it will only grow as a means to improve human beings by conquering disease and making us stronger, fitter, and better (or so goes the belief). It is another way of expressing the eugenics goal of self-directed evolution. CRISPR Cas9 and epigenetic switching are just two biochemical ways to achieve this goal.

As discussed throughout this chapter, our entire technological ecosystem, built upon the backbone of servers and nodes, television screens and tablets, implantables, and wearables, is herding humanity toward an ancient goal: "Ye shall be as gods." It is the same twisted promise made in a garden so many millennia ago, and it continues today, gilded with the shimmer of a golden age of technological advancement.

You and I are in a transitional phase, and we have very little time left. Humanity is being changed, cell by cell, thought by thought, decision by decision. The enemy is using the good intentions and curiosity of scientists and philosophers to steer us toward an end game, and the stakes couldn't be higher. *Our immortal souls are on the line.*

Both Matthew and Mark recorded Christ's words of warning and promise. When asked by His disciples for signs and prophecies concerning the last days and the coming of the next age, Christ tells them to expect wars and rumors of wars, and He refers to the prophet Daniel's visions. He tells them (and, through Scripture, tells us) about a coming time when sorrows will be multiplied and famines, pestilences, earthquakes, and affliction will define and terrorize our world. He also warns that these signs will occur incrementally, like birth pangs, growing more and more intense as the time of His return nears.

You and I are living in that time, and with each passing year the signs intensify, growing fiercer and more frequent. In fact, the Lord warned it would become so bad that mankind's very existence would be threatened:

And except those days should be shortened, there should no flesh be saved: but for the elect's sake those days shall be shortened. (Matthew 24:22)

And except that the Lord had shortened those days, no flesh should be saved: but for the elect's sake, whom he hath chosen, he hath shortened the days. (Mark 13:20)

In each occurrence, the word translated as "flesh" is *sarcos*, which can refer to the carnal nature or to the actual body of a person. The word translated as "saved" is *sozo*, a Greek word meaning "safe" or "preserved." Salvation may not be the only issue here, and perhaps not even physical survival. One wonders if Christ may also be warning us that the human species might one day change, potentially becoming incapable of salvation. That if left unchecked (if the days were not shortened), our bodies will become so altered, so hybridized, so genetically mutated and morphed by the enemy of God that these hybrids would no longer qualify us as human in His eyes. At the very least, such hybridized beings might no longer be capable of free thought or free choice, for their constant connectivity to a hive mind will have erased all independence.

Praise His name that Christ promises to put an end to such foolishness before it is too late! But, even though we can trust in Christ to keep a lid on the enemy, we also know that the Lord is allowing us to continue to wallow in our sin and foolishness as a species—for now. If as experts predict, genetic editing and technological hybridization is already a possibility and that we will be post-human soon, then we who call Christ our Savior and King must shout the truth about these planned alterations from the roof tops! We must sound the warning bell and proclaim Christ's redemptive story with our every breath.

Mankind *is being changed by the enemy*, but Christ offers eternal change of the heart, where it matters most. Thank you, Jesus!

America and Coming Revival

By Paul McGuire

The Pilgrims and Puritans, who entered into a covenant with God based on the covenant the children of Israel made with God outlined in Deuteronomy 28, originally founded America. America became the most unique nation in human history, providing more economic prosperity and opportunity for more people than any other nation in the history of mankind. In addition, America has provided more freedom and more rights to people than any other nation on earth. The reason for the uniqueness of America among all the nations on earth is based on the powerful truth that America is the only nation besides ancient Israel organized under the belief that it is the biblical God and not man who is the source of all our blessings, prosperity, and freedom.

Conversely, every single nation on earth that was organized around the belief that man can be the source of prosperity and freedom has failed dismally. In addition, those nations that were organized around the belief in a non-biblical God or "false gods," sooner or later began to self-destruct. The truth that individual and national freedom and prosperity are directly tied to the worship of the biblical God is met with the fiercest opposition in today's politically correct culture. But, whether or not it is politically correct thinking does not dismiss the historical reality that it is true.

Just as it is impossible for any man or woman to be saved apart from faith in Jesus Christ, history shows us that no nation can save itself apart from the biblical God. The reason for this is that Christianity is truth and not a religion. It is no accident that America's totally unique form of government, along with its Constitution and Bill of Rights, flowed from a powerful biblical revival called the First Great Awakening, which happened prior to the American Revolution. The First Great Awakening began under the preaching of Jonathan Edwards, and it released the power of God upon the thirteen original colonies, along with divinely energizing a biblical worldview, directly impacting government, law, science, education, theology, media, and culture.

It is not that our Founding Fathers were not influenced by Illuminism, Deism, and Freemasonry, but that the power of the Third Great Awakening overarched all other beliefs in the establishment of our nation. The strong, biblical Christians who founded America believed that they could not save themselves, and that "life, liberty and the pursuit of happiness" were granted by the Creator and not by any manmade government. The French Revolution, which later produced the Communist Revolutions, was based on the idea that man could save himself and that man's reason and logic could produce Paradise on earth. These man-centered governments all produced mass deaths, bloodshed, tyranny, oppression, dictatorships, and horrific oppression. The humanistic Communist revolutions, which were a direct outgrowth of the philosophies of the French Revolution, produced in excess of 250 million deaths, caused mass starvation, and resulted in people being sent to brutal concentration camps. Ideas have consequences, and it is no accident that that ideas contained in the Humanist Manifesto I and the Humanist Manifesto II—which, like the philosophies of the French Revolution, are based on Utopian ideas of a manmade Paradise on earth—have ended up producing the most threatening forms of intellectual, societal, and political fascism of our time. The ideas of the Humanist Manifesto that exploded into life during the 1960s counterculture, above all, proclaimed "free speech." In fact, the 1960s counterculture was birthed in part by the "Free Speech Movement" that originated on the campus of the University of California at Berkley.

However, as is the case with all humanistic movements, what began as "free speech" has transformed into a social dictatorship in which social engineering and political correctness control with totalitarian force all those who would actually seek to exercise "free speech" by saying anything that is not deemed by the Orwellian "thought police" of the media, university professors, and self-appointed cultural leaders as "politically correct." The content of speech is so controlled and restricted in America that anyone who dares to say anything out of the "politically correct" humanistic dogma can be fined and arrested, and have their careers or livelihood destroyed. The specific targets of this "New Reign of Terror" are those who attempt to espouse beliefs that reflect a biblical worldview or those who would seek to speak out against the mythologies of Darwinian evolution, Marxist economics, climate-change theories proposed by people like Al Gore, or the utopian promise of a world socialist government promoted by the United Nations.

When this author was visiting and speaking in Paris, France, while finishing the book entitled *Mass Awakening* that outlined how America and other nations will inevitably experience either spiritually dark mass awakenings or biblical great awakenings, depending upon what belief system these mass awakenings are built upon, I could not help but notice the historical monuments in Paris that testified of the reality of the "Reign of Terror" (1793–1794) produced by the ideas of the French Revolution. One of the leaders of the Reign of Terror was Maximilien Robespierre, a French lawyer who believed the maxim popular in all Communist revolutions that "the end justifies the means." He stated that "terror is nothing else than justice, prompt, severe, inflexible."

Over the last one hundred years, Christians in America, unlike the

Christians of the First and Second Great Awakenings, abandoned their responsibility before God to be stewards of this nation and to obey the words of Jesus Christ to "occupy until I come." As such, the institutions of American society have been infiltrated and largely taken over by humanistic radicals who have sought to destroy America as we know it and turn it into a manmade humanistic and socialist state that is intended to be part of a world government.

Due to the apathy of American Christians and their leaders, America has been high-jacked by radicals who have caused the American people and its institutions to turn away from the God of the Bible and toward viewing man and manmade government as being our Savior. There is a direct and measurable correlation between America's decline in every single area and its rejection of biblical principles in favor of humanistic principles.

Today, America is in the greatest crisis it has been in since the founding of our nation. The questions before us are: "Will America or at least a 'remnant' of Bible-believing Christians repent of our sin of turning from God and cry out to Him for a Third Great Awakening? Or will we continue to be seduced in the church and the nation by the lie of the 'serpent of old,' who told Adam and Eve, 'You shall be as gods'?"

This is the ultimate question for each of us as individuals and collectively as a nation. It is this question that plays out with great subtlety in the pulpits of America, where the truth of God's Word has been replaced with subtle lie that we can save ourselves through humanistic, motivational sermons. These messages at their root proclaim the lie that we can save ourselves through our own human intelligence and willpower. This question also plays out in the science of transhumanism, which promises that in the next couple of decades we can save ourselves from death and achieve artificial immortality through technologies like gene therapy, computer-brain implants, and the merger of man and machine into some kind of cyborg, android, or robot. On a national level, Americans believed, until only recently, that the American dollar, economy, military, science, technology, and government, only with American know-how, could save us from the plight of lesser-developed nations. Now that belief is fundamentally challenged as America is plagued with economic problems, social problems, a war on terrorism, and the real prospect that the dollar will no longer be the world's de facto global currency.

The question of man's ability to save himself began in the Garden of Eden, where Adam and Eve were tempted by 'the serpent of old' who promised them, "you shall be as gods," and seduced them to reject God's Word and eat from the tree in the middle of the Garden that activated the law of sin and death. At that moment, Adam and Eve began to die, and they could do nothing to save themselves. It was there where modern humanism began, as Adam and Eve attempted to save themselves by hiding their nakedness before God with fig leaves. But, the reality was that Adam and Eve were naked and ashamed before God and could do nothing to stop the death force that had entered their bodies.

Following the lies of the "serpent of old," the humanist movement, along with New Age and occult spirituality, believes that man can self-evolve and achieve eternal life through science and create an artificial paradise or Utopia. The seduction to be "like gods" lies inside the heart of every fallen man and woman. Mankind has been trying to be God for thousands of years, and man has attempted to create heaven on earth apart from God beginning in ancient Babylon.

America is now at the final turning point, having now largely rejected the truth that its success as a nation came from the biblical God and adhering to the principles of God's Word. The nation has embraced the great humanist lie that we are gods—and, like all the nations that embraced that lie, America will collapse into the brutal darkness of man's totalitarianism. There is only one way out of this crisis, and that is not in any human program or another manmade idea. The way out of our crisis can only be found in turning away from or repenting of the lie that we are gods, for that is the root of our problem.

This repentance must begin in the Church, because the Bible teaches that "judgment begins in the house of God" (1 Peter 4:17). In practical terms, this means repenting of and turning away from any form of doctrine or teaching that says we can save ourselves through humanistic, psychological motivation, human willpower, and manmade ideas based on corporate marketing principles vs. the power of God. The root of all these teachings is that "we are gods." It is the desire of God to send a Third Great Awakening upon America, but He cannot send it upon His people when they continue to insist that they can save themselves. The root of this is pride—the root of all sins. When as individual Christians, the church and the seminaries of America begin to repent of this root sin, and when we begin to humble ourselves before God and cry out to Him for a Third Great Awakening, it is that at that moment God will send a Third Great Awakening.

Yet, despite all the rhetoric about man being God, men and women still cannot save themselves from death and they cannot save themselves from all kinds of things such as diseases, famines, war, and myriad unsolvable problems. The technocratic societies of America and Europe, along with other nations that flowed from the philosophies of the French Enlightenment, believe that scientific and social progress is evolving as mankind moves towards the utopian belief in a world socialist state ruled by a scientific elite. But, not only has this elite failed to save mankind, but the human race skirts the precipice of an economic, geopolitical, and social apocalypse. The scientific elite, who do not believe in the reality of the biblical God, believe that mankind is here due to the random chance of evolution, where "only the fittest survive." As such, the elite believe that they are gods and have assumed for themselves the power to eliminate billions of people on planet earth and control all of mankind with the Draconian technology of a science fiction-like surveillance state. Finally, they believe that, as gods, they have the right to create a global feudal state where, through the science of eugenics, they will bring in a new world order with the kind of genetically engineered caste system depicted in Aldous Huxley's *Brave New World*. Once again, the humanistic principle emerges: "The end justifies the means."

The sinful nature of fallen men and women expressed in the elite who claim to be gods produces a counterfeit salvation and a Frankenstein-like messiah, who will eventually emerge on the world scene as the Antichrist that Bible prophecy predicts.

Prior to the Flood of Noah, some men and women thought they could be become gods by mating with the fallen angels. According to the Book of Enoch, two hundred fallen angels descended upon Mount Hermon and mated with human women, creating a hybrid race of Nephilim, which possessed both human and fallen-angel DNA. On Mount Hermon, the fallen angels gave mankind advanced science and technology, and mankind believed that they could be immortal like gods through science and technology.

Ten philosopher-kings or god-kings ruled ancient pre-Flood civilizations like Atlantis. The Greek philosopher Plato wrote in *The Republic* that Utopia, or heaven on earth, could be achieved through rule by an elite using science and technology. In the mid-1600s, Sir Francis Bacon, the head of an occult movement called the Rosicrucians, which later became the Illuminati, planned for America to be the head of the new world order and the New Atlantis.

In 1776—the same year the Illuminati were formed—America was born. The nation, the most unique and advanced in the history of mankind, was birthed out of an odd mixture of Illuminati, occult, and Freemason philosophy. In addition, America—and its unique form of a constitutional government with a Bill of Rights—was created from the fires of the First Great Awakening and a strong biblical worldview that man's rights are inalienable and given by the Creator and, as such, cannot be taken away from any man or manmade government. The biblical idea that this Creator God granted us "life, liberty and the pursuit of happiness" along with a Bill of Rights that included the freedoms of speech and religion, the freedom to assemble," the freedom of the press, and the Second Amendment right to bear arms in order defend those freedoms from a tyrannical government, made America's form of government unique in all of human history.

Like the interspecies breeding of fallen angels and human DNA, America's guiding philosophy was a hybrid mixture of biblical truths and a strange mixture of Illuminism and Freemasonry. The idea of god-like "illumined ones" hinted of a new breed of man, who were gods of messiahs. America, unlike all the humanistic governments in which rights and freedoms were granted by human governments and could be taken away by the whims of human government (which was the case in the French Revolution, the Communist Revolutions, the National Socialist Revolution of Nazi, Germany, and the humanistic and emerging global government of the United Nations), produced more freedom and more economic prosperity for more people than any other nation on earth.

However, today, America's unique Constitution and Bill of Rights, along with its guiding philosophy that flows directly out of the First Great Awakening, has been eroded and undermined by a subversion of its Constitution and Bill of Rights. As a result, it is in the greatest crisis it has ever been since its founding in 1776.

We must understand that, as biblical Christians, we should never embrace a non-biblical fatalism. God did not call us before the foundation of the world to be here for such a time as this, to surrender to fatalism, and to do nothing to save our nation. America is of vital importance in the last days, and although none of us can undo God's sovereign prophetic Word in relationship to the prophetic Scriptures, God does expect us to obey His commandment to the church to "occupy until I come" (Luke 19:13). This is not Christian reconstructionism, nor does it undo Bible prophecy. In the long term, God's prophecies about the end times will all be fulfilled, but as long as this Church Age lasts, we are responsible to seek the face of God in repentance and prayer for our nation, and petition God for a biblical revival and a Third Great Awakening. If the Lord should grant us this Third Great Awakening, we must understand, as Jonathan Edwards and Charles Finney did, that a true, biblical, Third Great Awakening is not something mystical. The power of the First and Second Great Awakenings rested on the fact that these were biblical spiritual awakenings. Also, a strong intellectual, moral, political, scientific, cultural, and theological content flowed out of these Awakenings, which transformed many aspects of American society. The fathers of the First and Second Great Awakenings did not succumb to the non-biblical anti-intellectualism of the current evangelical Church. The power of a true biblical revival must awaken the intellectual force of minds that are redeemed by the Word of God and are able to effectively promote a biblical worldview into our nation.

Notes

1. http://www.nytimes.com/2013/02/13/world/europe/pope-benedict-xvi-resignation.html?_r=0.
2. Eric Schmitt, "In Battle to Defang ISIS, U.S. Targets its Psychology," *New York Times,* December 28, 2014, last accessed February 18, 2016, http://www.nytimes.com/2014/12/29/us/politics/in-battle-to-defang-ISIS-us-targets-its-psychology-.html?_r=0.
3. Ibid.
4. David Commins, *The Wahhabi Mission and Saudi Arabia* (London, New York: IB Tauris, 2006), vi.
5. Front page of the As-Sunnah Foundation of America website, *ASFA*, last accessed February 17, 2016, http://sunnah.org/wp/.
6. Zubair Qamar, "Wahhabism: Understanding the Roots and Role Models of Islamic Extremism," under the "Introduction" header, last accessed February 17, 2016, http://www.sunnah.org/articles/Wahhabiarticleedit.htm.
7. Ibid.
8. "ISIS Spokesman Declares Caliphate, Rebrands Group as 'Islamic State,'" Jihadist News, last updated June 29, 2014, last accessed February 17, 2016, https://news.siteintelgroup.com/Jihadist-News/ISIS-spokesman-declares-caliphate-rebrands-group-as-islamic-state.html.
9. Eric Schmitt, "In Battle to Defang ISIS," http://www.nytimes.com/2014/12/29/us/politics/in-battle-to-defang-ISIS-us-targets-its-psychology-.html?_r=0.

10. George Weigel, "ISIS, Genocide," https://www.firstthings.com/web-exclusives/2016/02/ISIS-genocide-and-us; emphasis added.

11. Anugrah Kumar, "Over 100 NGOs, Leaders to Obama: ISIS Atrocities against Christians, Other Minorities, Are Genocide," *Christian Post*, February 18, 2016, http://www.christianpost.com/news/obama-ISIS-atrocities-christians-minorities-genocide-international-religious-freedom-roundtable-158043/.

12. Ibid.

13. "Leading Sunni Sheikh Yousef Al-Qaradhawi and Other Sheikhs Herald the Coming Conquest in Rome," *MEMRI: The Middle East Media Research Institute*, posted December 6, 2002, last accessed February 18, 2016, http://www.memri.org/report/en/0/0/0/0/0/0/774.htm.

14. "Leading Sunni Sheikh," http://www.memri.org/report/en/0/0/0/0/0/0/774.htm.

15. "In New Message Following Being Declared a 'Caliph,'" *MEMRI: The Middle East Media Research Institute*, posted July 1, 2014, last accessed February 18, 2016, http://www.memrijttm.org/content/view_print/blog/7607; emphasis added.

16. "Pertaining to the Conquest of Constantinople and the Appearance of Dajjal and Descent of Jesus Son of Mary (Jesus Christ)," *The Only Quran*, last accessed February 18, 2016, http://www.theonlyquran.com/hadith/Sahih-Muslim/?volume=41&chapter=9.

17. Sophie Jane Evans, "ISIS's Chilling Death March to the End of the World: Jihadists Release Video Depicting Their Apocalyptic Vision of a Future Battle Culminating in Rome," *DailyMail*, December 11, 2015, last accessed February 18, 2016, http://www.dailymail.co.uk/news/article-3356503/ISIS-s-chilling-death-march-end-world-Jihadists-release-video-depicting-vision-future-battle-culminating-Colosseum.html.

18. Sam Prince, "WATCH: New ISIS Video Shows Armageddon Battle with the West," *Heavy News*, December 11, 2015, last accessed February 18, 2016, http://heavy.com/news/2015/12/new-ISIS-islamic-state-news-video-see-you-in-dabiq-rome-muslim-extremists-rome-crusaders-colosseum-malahim-meeting-at-dabiq-italy-west-war-uncensored-full-youtube/.

19. Video can be seen at the following article: Anthony Bond, Kara O'Neill, Kelly-Ann Mills, "ISIS Release Chilling New 'End of the World' Video Showing Final Battle with Crusaders," *Mirror News*, December 11, 2015, last accessed February 18, 2016, http://www.mirror.co.uk/news/world-news/ISIS-release-sickening-new-video-6995563.

20. Tyler Durden, "ISIS Releases New Apocalyptic Video Depicting 'Final' Battle with 'Crusaders' in Syria," December 12, 2015, *Zero Hedge*, last accessed February 18, 2016, http://www.zerohedge.com/news/2015-12-12/ISIS-releases-new-apocalyptic-video-depicting-final-battle-crusaders-syria.

21. http://time.com/3745462/vatican-ISIS-syria-iraq-middle-east/.

22. http://www1.cbn.com/cbnnews/world/2014/August/Pope-Francis-US-Action-against-ISIS-a-Just-War.

23. https://en.wikipedia.org/wiki/Just_war_theory.

24. http://www.cruxnow.com/church/2015/03/13/vatican-backs-military-force-to-stop-ISIS-genocide/.

25. http://www.breitbart.com/big-government/2015/11/15/paris-pope-francis-tells-christians-ready-end-world/.

26. http://www.dailymail.co.uk/news/article-3356503/ISIS-s-chilling-death-march-end-world-Jihadists-release-video-depicting-vision-future-battle-culminating-Colosseum.html.

27. http://www.nbcnews.com/storyline/pope-francis-visits-america/ISIS-magazine-dabiq-singles-out-pope-francis-ahead-u-s-n431681.

28. http://nypost.com/2015/03/10/pope-francis-if-im-assassinated-at-least-make-it-painless/.

29. http://www.ncregister.com/daily-news/pope-francis-consecrating-the-world-to-mary-culminates-fatima-celebration/.

30. Thomas Horn, Cris Putnam, *Petrus Romanus* (Crane, MO: Defender, 2012), p. 454.

31. Thomas Horn, *Zenith 2016* (Crane, MO: Defender, 2013), p. 371.

32. http://catholictruthblog.com/2013/12/30/was-pope-francis-canonically-elected/.

33. Rev. Herman Bernard Kramer, *The Book of Destiny* (Belleville, IL: Buechler, 1955), p.277.

34. http://nation.foxnews.com/2016/01/10/report-obama-wants-become-un-secretary-general-netanyahu-doing-everything-he-can-stop-him.

35. http://www.discoveringislam.org/end_of_time.htm.

36. James E. Smith, *What the Bible Teaches about the Promised Messiah* (Nashville: Thomas Nelson, 1993), p. 38; Walter C. Kaiser Jr., *The Messiah in the Old Testament* (Grand Rapids: Zondervan, 1995), p. 38.

37. Robert Jamieson, Andrew Robert Fausset, and David Brown, commentary on Numbers 24, in *A Commentary, Critical and Explanatory, on the Old and New Testaments*, vol. 1 (Hartford: S. S. Scranton & Co., 1871), p. 113.

38. John Walvoord, *Daniel: The Key to Prophetic Revelation* (Chicago: Moody, 1989), p. 68–69.

39. Tacitus, *The History*, New Ed ed., bk. 5.1, ed. Moses Hadas; transs. Alfred Church and William Brodribb (New York: Modern Library, 2003).

40. Flavius Josephus, *The Complete Works of Josephus, The Wars of the Jews or The History of the Destruction of Jerusalem*, bk. 3, chap. 1, par. 3.

41. Ibid., chap. 4, par. 2.

42. Alexander Arthur, *A Critical Commentary on the Book of Daniel.* (Edinburgh: Norman Macleod, 1893), p. 103.

43. Carl Friedrich Keil, and Franz Delitzsch, *Commentary on the Old Testament.* Vol. 9. (Peabody, MA: Hendrickson, 1996), p. 685.

44. Ammianus Marcellinus, *Rerum Gestarum*, 19.1; cf., Wood, Leon. *A Commentary on Daniel*, (1973, Zondervan, Grand Rapids), p. 208.

45. Harvard University Library. Visual Information Access, http://via.lib.harvard.edu/via/deliver/deepcontentItem?recordId=olvwork279755%2CFHCL%3A4627754.

46. H. C. Leupold, *Exposition of Daniel* (Columbus, OH: Wartburg Press, 1949), p. 346.

47. G. H. Lang, *The Histories and Prophecies of Daniel* (London: Paternoster Press, 1940), p. 113.

48. John F. Walvoord, *Daniel: The Key to Prophetic Revelation.* (Chicago: Moody, 1989), p. 184.

49. Hippolytus of Rome: *Commentary on Daniel* (T.C. Schmidt, 2010), p. 144.

50. Ephrem the Syrian, as quoted in *Ancient Christian Commentary on Scripture,*

volume XIII, gen. editor Thomas C. Oden (Downer's Grove, Il, InterVarsity Press, 2008), p. 250.

51. Jerome, *Jerome's Commentary on Daniel*, translated by Gleason L. Archer Jr. (Grand Rapids, MI: Baker, 1977) 85.

52. Ibid.

53. Theodoret of Cyrus, *Commentary on Daniel*, translated by Robert C. Hill (Atlanta, GA: Society of Biblical Literature, 2006), p. 209–211.

54. H. A. Ironside, *Lectures on Daniel the Prophet* (New York: Loizeaux, 1920), p. 150.

55. Albert Einstein, in an interview with Alfred Werner, *Liberal Judaism* 16 (April–May 1949), p. 12. Einstein Archive 30–1104, as sourced in *The New Quotable Einstein* by Alice Calaprice (2005), p. 173.

56. The family depicted in this narrative is entirely fictional and was derived solely from the imagination of this chapter's author. The details of living through an atomic blast, however, are as close to reality as the innumerable historical accounts of the bombing of Hiroshima relate.

57. Compare the description of the second trumpet of Revelation's visions and prophecies. Many students of Bible prophecy believe they see, in that passage, a foreshadowing of the Hiroshima and Nagasaki bombing that eventually ended World War II—another potentially prophetic event that was ultimately responsible for the rebirth of Israel, a twenty-five-hundred-year-old prophecy. Even if the timing of WWII and the specific revelation of the second trumpet are rejected on eschatological grounds, there are still many who see the potential of this vision perhaps being a description of an even greater nuclear detonation occurring during the trumpet days sometime after the Rapture of the Church. Of course, there is also a school of eschatological thought that supposes this vision may speak of Tribulation-days meteor impact.

"And the second angel sounded, and as it were a great mountain burning with fire was cast into the sea: and the third part of the sea became blood; And the third part of the creatures which were in the sea, and had life, died; and the third part of the ships were destroyed" (Revelation 8:8–9).

58. Mark Selden, "Living with the Bomb: The Atomic Bomb in Japanese Consciousness," http://japanfocus.org/-Mark-Selden/2043/article.html.

59. "U.S. Planned to Drop 12 Atomic Bombs On Japan," August 2015, http://www.thedailybeast.com/articles/2015/08/14/u-s-planned-to-drop-12-atomic-bombs-on-japan.html.

60. Amanda Macias, "Nine Nations Have Nukes—Here's How Many Each Country Has," http://www.businessinsider.com/nine-nations-have-nukes-heres-how-many-each-country-has-2014-6.

61. Mark Newton, "5 Ways The World Will End, As Told by the Experts Who Know," http://moviepilot.com/posts/2015/03/11/5-ways-the-world-will-end-as-told-by-the-experts-who-know-2767642.

62. Greek: *throeó*, Strong's #2360, http://biblehub.com/greek/2360.htm.

63. Phobia—the definitions listed were derived directly from the dictionary "definition box" that that is the first feature of a Google online search for the definition of the English word "phobia."

64. Greek: *odin*, Strong's #5604, http://biblehub.com/greek/5604.htm.

65. Coming Soon to a City Near You—Before Armageddon!" http://www.biblebelievers.org.au/nl085.htm.

Note: The term "Armageddon" comes from the Hebrew word *Har-Magedone*. The meaning of this word is "Mount Megiddo." The Battle of Armageddon is usually defined as the future battle in which God will intervene and destroy the armies of the Antichrist as predicted in biblical prophecy (Revelation 16:16; 20:1–3, 7–10). According to the Scriptures, there will be a multitude of people engaged in the battle of Armageddon, as all the nations gather together to fight against Christ. The word "Armageddon" only occurs in Revelation 16:16. The reference concerning this battle in Revelation 20:8 mentions the terms "Gog" and "Magog." The names "Gog" and "Magog" also appear in Ezekiel 38–39, two chapters that appear to describe a World War III scenario that first unfolds in the Middle East and the surrounding area. The Ezekiel 38–39 war is aimed specifically at the prophetically returned nation of Israel. Scholars are divided concerning the precise timing of the Battle of Armageddon.

66. "World War III (Battle of Armageddon)," http://www.bibleplus.org/prophecy/rev/26_armageddon.htm.

67. Pope Francis Calls for a New System of Global Government to Tackle Climate Change," http://www.independent.co.uk/environment/pope-francis-calls-for-new-system-of-global-government-to-tackle-climate-change-10330124.html.

68. Greg Laurie, "Foreshocks of Armageddon," August 2015, http://www.wnd.com/2015/08/foreshocks-of-armageddon/?cat_orig=faith. This article is used as one example of an internationally recognized pastor, crusade evangelist, author, and popular end-times' commentator who teaches that Jesus' words in Matthew 24 speak of an end-time global war scenario.

69. WND.com, "Is World War III Coming Soon?" April 2015, http://www.wnd.com/2015/04/is-world-war-iii-coming-soon.

70. Vikas Shukla, "China Warns of World War 3 Unless the US Backs Down on South China Sea," May 28, 2015, http://www.valuewalk.com/2015/05/china-warns-of-world-war-3.

71. WND.com, "World War III Is Shaping Up in Syria," Sept. 29, 2015, http://www.wnd.com/2015/09/wwiii-is-shaping-up-in-syria/#lSBfVqBpx0Vi565m.99.

72. Joel Richardson, "Ezekiel's Magog: Russia or Turkey?" June 2012, http://www.wnd.com/2012/06/ezekiels-magog-russia-or-turkey.

73. WND.com, "Islam Is the Cause of Turkey's Violent History," http://www.wnd.com/2015/10/islam-is-the-cause-of-turkeys-violent-history/?cat_orig=faith.

74. Drew Desilver, "World's Muslim Population More Widespread Than You Might Think," June 7, 2013, http://www.pewresearch.org/fact-tank/2013/06/07/worlds-muslim-population-more-widespread-than-you-might-think.

75. The Joker, Batman, "The Killing Joke," written by Alan Moore, ttp://genius.com/Alan-moore-the-killing-joke-annotated.

76. Henig (2002), *The Origins of the First World War* (London: Routledge) ISBN 0-415-26205-4.

77. Edward R. Kantowicz (1999), *The Rage of Nations* (Grand Rapids, MI: Eerdmans) ISBN 978-0-8028-4455-2, p. 149.

78. The following two respected references (one secular and one Christian) illustrate the truth of the footnoted proposition: "Gulf War Started Arab Spring," http://www.nytimes.com/2013/04/07/opinion/sunday/the-arab-spring-started-in-iraq.html?_r=0. "Arab Spring Led to ISIS," http://www.cbn.com/cbnnews/insideisrael/2015/August/Arab-Spring-to-ISIS-The-Mideast-Misconception.

79. Sheikh Muhammad Ahmad Hussein claimed Al-Aqsa was built by Adam or by angels "during his time." It was, in fact, opened in the year AD 705. Ilan Ben Zion, "Jerusalem Mufti: Temple Mount Never Housed Jewish Temple," *The Times of Israel*, October 25, 2015, (http://www.timesofisrael.com/jerusalem-mufti-denies-temple-mount-ever-housed-jewish-shrine/.

80. Exodus 25:22; Numbers 7:89; 1 Samuel 4:4.

81. Jeremiah 3:16.

82. Ted Belman, "The Temple Mount Controversy," *American Thinker*, November 30, 2014, http://www.americanthinker.com/articles/2014/11/the_temple_mount_controversy.html.

83. Dr. Timothy R. Furnish, "Intervening (in Syria) Like It's the End of the World?," *MahdiWatch*, September 6, 2013, http://www.mahdiwatch.org/2013.09.01_arch.html#1378502364220.

84. Matthew Lee, "Now Is Time for Palestinian State," *Washington Post*, October 15, 2007, http://www.washingtonpost.com/wp-dyn/content/article/2007/10/15/AR2007101500703_pf.html.

85. Dahlia Scheindlin, "Israelis, Palestinians Support 2-State—But Why Bother?", *+972 Magazine*, January 7, 2012, http://972mag.com/surveys-israelis-and-palestinians-support-two-state-peace-but-why-bother/32311/.

86. Jerusalem Old City Initiative, http://www.cips-cepi.ca/event/jerusalem-old-city-initiative/, retrieved 12/12/15.

87. Aaron Klein, "International Mandate to Control Sections of Israel's Capital," *WND*, December 15, 2013, http://www.wnd.com/2013/12/u-s-plan-gives-jerusalem-holy-sites-to-vatican/.

88. Mary Chastain, "Turkish President Erdogan: Muslims Lost

Their Way to Jerusalem," *Breitbart.com*, May 18, 2015, http://www.breitbart.com/national-security/2015/05/18/turkish-president-erdogan-muslims-lost-their-way-to-jerusalem/.

89. "Turkey to Israel: No Renewal of Ties Without Unlimited Access to Gaza," *Jerusalem Post*, December 26, 2015, http://www.jpost.com/Israel-News/Politics-And-Diplomacy/Turkey-to-Israel-No-renewal-of-ties-without-unlimited-access-to-Gaza-438463.

90. Uri Blau, "Netanyahu Allied Donated to Groups Pushing for Third Temple," *Haaretz*, December 9, 2015, http://www.haaretz.com/settlementdollars/1.690821.

91. Adam Eliyahu Berkowitz, "Leading Israeli Rabbi Says the Arrival of the Messiah is Imminent," *Breaking Israel News*, July 3, 2015, http://www.breakingisraelnews.com/44534/leading-israeli-rabbi-messiah-imminent-jewish-world/.

92. Adam Eliyahu Berkowitz, "Prominent Rabbis Sternbuch, Amar Hint That the Messiah is 'Just Around the Corner'," *Breaking Israel News*, December 9, 2015, http://www.breakingisraelnews.com/55777/turkeysyria-conflict-unfolding-prominent-rabbis-hint-messiah-around-corner-jewish-world/.

93. Rivkah Lambert Adler, "18th Century Jewish Mystics Predicted Future Conflict Between Russia, Turkey Ripe with Messianic Implications," *Breaking Israel News*, November 29, 2015, http://www.breakingisraelnews.com/54943/200-years-ago-war-between-turkey-russia-prophesied-sign-redemption-jewish-world/.

94. Andrey Ostroukh, "Russia Suggests Turkey Planned Downing of Warplane," *Wall Street Journal*, December 23, 2015, http://www.wsj.com/articles/russia-suggests-turkey-planned-downing-of-warplane-1450899609.

95. Berkowitz, December 9, 2015.

96. Adam Eliayahu Berkowitz, "Torah Scroll Being Written to Present to Messiah Upon His Arrival," *Breaking Israel News*, December 15, 2015, http://www.breakingisraelnews.com/56244/rabbi-sets-out-mission-write-torah-scroll-present-messiah-upon-arrival-jewish-world/.

97. "Rabbi Kaduri's Most Recent Words," *ArutzSheva*, January 24, 2006, http://www.israelnationalnews.com/News/Flash.aspx/97225#.VoWcU8YrLMg.

98. Rivkah Lambert Adler, "Rabbi Kaduri 'Jesus as Messiah' Claim Proven as False," *Breaking Israel News*, June 17, 2015, http://web. archive.org/save/http://www.breakingisraelnews.com/43554/ rabbi-kaduri-jesus-as-messiah-claim-discredited-as-false-jewish-world/.

99. Pew Research Center, "Many Americans Uneasy with Mix of Religion and Politics: Section IV—Religious Beliefs," August 24, 2006, http://www. people-press.org/2006/08/24/section-iv-religious-beliefs/.

100. Dr. Timothy R. Furnish, "Mahdism (and Sectarianism and Superstition) Rises in the Islamic World," *History News Network*, August 13, 2012, http://historynewsnetwork.org/article/147714.

101. A recent survey by the Pew Research Center found that between 73 percent and 99 percent of Muslims in Turkey, the Palestinian territories, Israel, Jordan, and Lebanon had an "unfavorable" view of ISIS. Jacob Poushter, "In Nations with Significant Muslim Populations, Much Disdain for ISIS," *FactTank*, November 17, 2015, http://www.pewresearch.org/fact-tank/2015/11/17/ in-nations-with-significant-muslim-populations-much-disdain-for-isis/.

102. Furnish, 2012.

103. Daniel L. Byman and Jennifer R. Williams, "ISIS vs. Al Qaeda: Jihadism's Global Civil War," February 24, 2015, http://www.brookings.edu/research/ articles/2015/02/24-byman-williams-isis-war-with-al-qaeda.

104. Paul Alster, "Israel, Hamas Strange Bedfellows When It Comes to Reining in ISIS in Gaza," *FoxNews.com*, July 23, 2015, http://www.foxnews.com/ world/2015/07/23/israel-hamas-strange-bedfellows-when-it-comes-to- reining-in-isis-in-gaza.html.

105. "ISIL Warns Hamas in Video Message," *Al Jazeera*, July 1, 2015, http://www.aljazeera.com/news/2015/07/isil-warns-hamas-video- message-150701042302630.html.

106. William Young (Senior Policy Analyst for RAND Corp.), "ISIS Aims to Occupy Mecca," *Newsweek*, January 17, 2015, http://www.newsweek.com/ islamic-state-aims-occupy-mecca-300205.

107. Ishaan Tharoor, "Why Turkey's President Wants to Revive the Language

of the Ottoman Empire," *Washington Post*, December 12, 2014, https://
www.washingtonpost.com/news/worldviews/wp/2014/12/12/why-turkeys-
president-wants-to-revive-the-language-of-the-ottoman-empire/.

108. Catherine Shakdam, "Is Turkey Attempting to Resurrect the Ottoman
Empire on the Back of the 'Black Army'?," *Al-Akhbar*, October 29, 2014,
http://english.al-akhbar.com/node/22243.

109. Dr. Timothy R. Furnish, "Apocalypse Row: Netanyahu, Nukes, and
Iranian Eschatology," *zPolitics*, March 2, 2015, http://zpolitics.com/
apocalypse-row-netanyahu-nukes-and-iranian-eschatology/.

110. Furnish, March 2, 2015.

111. "Hamas-ISIS Cooperation Adds New Layer to Middle
East Threats," *Breaking Israel News*, December 25,
2015, http://www.breakingisraelnews.com/56935/
hamas-isis-cooperation-adds-new-layer-mideast-threats-terror-watch/.

112. Adam Eliyahu Berkowitz, "ISIS Leader Threatens 'Palestine
Will Be Graveyard for Jews'," *Breaking Israel News*, December
27, 2015, http://www.breakingisraelnews.com/57118/
isis-leader-threatens-palestine-will-be-graveyard-for-jews-terror-watch/.

113. And there have been. We recommend *The Unseen Realm* by Dr. Michael S.
Heiser for an accessible yet scholarly treatment of this concept.

114. Psalm 74:12–17. Isaiah 27:1 prophesies that Yahweh will kill Leviathan "in
that day," the Day of the Lord—the future time when the Lord pours out
His wrath on an unbelieving world.

115. Actually, it began even before Joshua led the tribes across the Jordan. On
the advice of the prophet-for-profit Balaam, the king of Moab, Balak,
sent women to seduce the men of Israel into the worship of Baal-Peor (see
Numbers 25:1–15). In this context, the heresy of Baal-Peor can be seen as a
supernatural response to the crossing of the Red Sea.

116. William Booth and Ruth Eglash, "Jewish Activists Want to Pray on
Jerusalem's Temple Mount, Raising Alarm in Muslim World," *Washington
Post*, December 2, 2013, https://www.washingtonpost.com/world/
middle_east/jewish-activists-set-sights-on-jerusalems-temple-mount-

raising-alarm-in-muslim-world/2013/12/02/d0561dc4-4e00-11e3-97f6-ed8e3053083b_story.html.

117. Zafrir Rinat, "Israel is Due, and Ill Prepared, for a Major Earthquake," *Haaretz*, January 15, 2010, http://www.haaretz.com/israel-is-due-and-ill-prepared-for-a-major-earthquake-1.261497.

118. See www.GodsHolyMountain.org.

119. "New Initiative Would Build Temple Next to Dome of the Rock," *Koinonia House eNews*, June 23, 2009, https://www.khouse.org/enews_article/2009/1477/.

120. Jake Wallis Simons, "The Rabbi, the Lost Ark, and the Future of the Temple Mount," The Telegraph, September 12, 2013, http://www.telegraph.co.uk/news/worldnews/10287615/The-rabbi-the-lost-ark-and-the-future-of-Temple-Mount.html.

121. "The Red Heifer: Introduction," The Temple Institute, https://www.templeinstitute.org/red_heifer/introduction.htm.

122. Raphael Poch, "New Jersey Red Heifer Disqualified for Temple Service," *Breaking Israel News*, July 12, 2015, http://www.breakingisraelnews.com/45005/new-jersey-red-heifer-disqualified-jewish-world/.

123. "Architectural Plans for Third Temple Have Begun," *ArutzSheva*, July 26, 2015, http://www.israelnationalnews.com/News/News.aspx/198621#.VoBeH8YrLMg.

124. 1 Samuel chapters 4 through 6.

125. Moira Schneider, "African 'Jewish' Tribe Displays Its Lost Ark," *Jewish Chronicle Online*, April 22, 2010, http://www.thejc.com/news/world-news/30865/african-jewish-tribe-displays-its-lost-ark.

126. Simons, 2013.

127. Dr. Timothy R. Furnish, "Mahdism (and Sectarianism and Superstition) Rises in the Islamic World," *History News Network*, August 13, 2012, http://historynewsnetwork.org/article/147714.

128. Nicola Nasser, "Syria, Egypt Reveal Erdogan's Hidden 'Neo-Ottoman Agenda'," *Global Research*, November 20, 2013, http://www.globalresearch.ca/syria-egypt-reveal-erdogans-hidden-neo-ottoman-agenda/5358781.

129. 1 Corinthians 10:11: "Now all these things happened unto them for examples: and they are written for our admonition, upon whom the ends of the world are come."

130. For an excellent study into this idea, check out the DVD, *Which Rapture Are We Waiting For?* by Doc Marquis.

131. This particular scenario applies if you, like me, subscribe to a pre-Tribulation Rapture belief.

132. Genesis 19:1 (KJV): "And there came two angels to Sodom at even; and Lot sat in the gate of Sodom: and Lot seeing them rose up to meet them; and he bowed himself with his face toward the ground."

133. Genesis 19:15 (KJV): "And when the morning arose, then the angels hastened Lot, saying, Arise, take thy wife, and thy two daughters, which are here; lest thou be consumed in the iniquity of the city."

134. "Hebrew Lexicon: H2474 (KJV)." Blue Letter Bible. Accessed 19 August 2015.

135. "Hebrew Lexicon: H5869 (KJV)." Blue Letter Bible. Accessed 19 August, 2015. http://www.blueletterbible.org/lang/Lexicon/Lexicon. cfm?Strongs=H5869&t=KJV.

136. "Hebrew Lexicon: H212 (KJV)." Blue Letter Bible. Accessed 19 August, 2015. http://www.blueletterbible.org/lang/Lexicon/Lexicon. cfm?Strongs=H212&t=KJV.

137. See Exodus 14:25 and 1 Kings 7:30–33.

138. For example, Enoch 61:10 reads: "And He will summon all the host of the heavens, and all the holy ones above, and the host of God, the Cherubic, Seraphin and Ophannin, and all the angels of power, and all the angels of principalities, and the Elect One, and the other powers on the earth (and) over the water On that day shall raise one voice, and bless and glorify and exalt in the spirit of faith, and in the spirit of wisdom, and in the spirit of patience, and in the spirit of mercy, and in the spirit of judgement and of peace, and in the spirit of goodness, and shall all say with one voice: 'Blessed is He, and may the name of the Lord of Spirits be blessed for ever and ever.'"

139. Maimonides, *Yad ha-Chazakah: Yesodei ha-Torah.*

140. Pseudo-Dionysius, *De CoelestiHierarchia* ("*On the Celestial Hierarchy*")

141. For example, Daniel 7:9 reads: "I beheld till the thrones were cast down, and the Ancient of days did sit, whose garment was white as snow, and the hair of his head like the pure wool: his throne was like the fiery flame, and his wheels as burning fire."

142. I do not believe the *ophanim* mentioned in Scripture as surrounding the throne of God would be in this group. The Bible does not directly mention fallen *ophanim*, so this is merely a possibility from silence.

143. For more information on this, refer to my book *Cherubim Chariots: Exploring the Extradimensional Hypothesis.*

144. This refers only to spatial dimensions, not temporal.

145. E. A. Abbot, *Flatland: A Romance of Many Dimensions,* 1884.

146. In two-dimensional reality, this actually would be translated as a circle, but since Flatlanders lack the ability to see the entire shape, it would look to them as a line. Similarly, in our three spatial dimensions of reality, we cannot see around to the back side of solid and opaque objects that are right in front of us.

147. See my books *Quantum Creation* and *Cherubim Chariots.*

148. For more information on this, refer to the National UFO Reporting Center at http://www.nuforc.org/.

149. *Encounters with Angels: Interview with Emma Heathcote* ,http://www.shareintl.org/archives/angels/ang_gfencounters.htm.

150. "Mystery 'Angel' Priest Appears at Missouri Car Crash, Performs 'Miracle,' Then Disappears (UPDATE)," http://www.huffingtonpost.com/2013/08/08/mystery-angel-priest-car-crash-_n_3725992.html.

151. Ibid.

152. "The Butterfly People of Joplin," http://www.stltoday.com/news/local/metro/the-butterfly-people-of-joplin/article_cca48b1a-282b-587d-902b-cd5f09ca8516.html.

153. Abby Holman, "The Butterfly People of Joplin," http://www.missourilife.com/blogs/mo/the-butterfly-people-of-joplin/.

154. *Monsters and Mysteries in America*, S03E08 - *Mantis Man, Spottsville Monster, Tornado Phantoms.*

155. 2 Corinthians 11:14: "And no marvel; for Satan himself is transformed into an angel of light."

156. R. Leo Sprinkle, quoted in *Encyclopedia of Extraterrestrial Encounters*, pg. 136–140, Ronald D. Story, Editor.

157. http://www.ascension-research.org/jesus.html.

158. Another example of this can be found at http://www.askrealjesus.com/, which is a heretical website dedicated to mysticism while posing as "true Christianity." Again, if you are researching topics like this, make sure you have a solid foundation in the Bible. It is also a good idea to go into it prayerfully, asking God to not allow any deceptions to overtake you, and pray against anything heretical in the name of Jesus Christ.

159. For an in-depth analysis of these two passages, refer to my book *Cherubim Chariots: Exploring the Extradimensional Hypothesis.* .

160. Wikipedia.org/wiki/Pine_Tree_Flag (accessed 9/21/15). See also Jennifer LeClaire, *The Next Great Move Of God: An Appeal To Heaven for Spiritual Awakening* (Lake Mary, Florida: Charisma House, 2015), p. 42–45.

161. Taken from Michael L. Brown, *Outlasting The Gay Revolution: Where Homosexual Activism Is Really Going and How to Turn the Tide* (Washington, D.C.: WND Books, 2015), p.85.

162. Ibid., 94.

163. The Sentinel Group (www.sentinelgroup.org) offers videos, messages, and testimonies of revivals taking place in different parts of the world.

164. There are some 5-Point Calvinists (TULIP proponents: Total Depravity, Unconditional Election, Limited Atonement, Irresistible Grace, Perseverance of the Saints) who would argue that if you don't adhere to TULIP you cannot possibly understand grace. There are also those in the Arminian camp who would hold that if you believe in TULIP you can't possibly win the lost. Yet evangelists from both groups have been used by God to win the lost by preaching a gracious gospel.

165. See LeClaire, 86–87.

166. Tom Doyle, *Breakthrough: The Return of Hope to the Middle East* (Colorado Springs: Authentic Publishing, 2008) 1. Two other volumes are helpful for those wishing to understand God's plan and purpose for the sons of Ishmael: *Making Our Peace with the Warriors of the Sand: What the Bible Says Positively about Our Estranged Arab Cousins,* by Jeffrey L. Seif and Ihab Griess (Crane, Missouri: Defender, 2010), and also *The Holy Land Key: Unlocking End-Times Prophecy Through the Lives of God's People in Israel,* by Ray Bentley (Colorado Springs: WaterBrook Press, 2014).

167. cbn.com/biblestudy/breakthrough-in-the-middle-east, accessed 10/9/15.

168. *Captive In Iran* (Carol Stream, Illinois: Tyndale House, 2013).

169. http://www.nytimes.com/2015/08/14/world/middleeast/isis-enshrines-a-theology-of-rape.html, (Accessed 9/10/15).

170. Tom Doyle, *Dreams and Visions: Is Jesus Awakening the Muslim World?* (Nashville: Nelson, 2012) 260–261.

171. *Captive in Iran*, 6.

172. Ibid., 92.

173. Eddie L. Hyatt, *America's Revival Heritage: How Christian Reformation and Spiritual Awakening Led to the Formation of the United States of America* (Grapevine, TX: Hyatt International Ministries, 2012), p. 25.

174. Ibid., 26–28.

175. Ibid., 34–35.

176. Ibid., 40–41.

177. Ibid., 43–46.

178. Hyatt, 47.

179. Ibid., 47–50.

180. www.jonathan-edwards.org/Narrative.html, accessed 10/9/51.

181. Elmer Towns and Douglas Porter, *The Ten Greatest Revivals Ever: From Pentecost to the Present* (Ann Arbor: Servant Publications, 2000), p. 7–8.

182. R. T. Kendall, *Holy Fire: A Balanced, Biblical Look at the Holy Spirit's Work in Our Lives* (Lake Mary, Florida: Charisma House, 2014), p. 43–44.

183. Taken from Tom Doyle, *Killing Christians: Living the Faith Where It's Not Safe to Believe* (Nashville: W Publishing Group, 2015), p. 99–100.

184. www.thedailybeast.com/articles/2015/10/14/this-magnet-could-change-everything-you-think-you-believe. See also: Cris Putnam and Thomas Horn, *Exo-Vaticana: Petrus Romanus, Project L.U.C.I.F.E.R, and the Vatican's Astonishing Plan for the Arrival of an Alien Savior* (Crane, MO, 2013); Nick Begich, *Controlling the Human Mind: The Technologies of Political Control or Tools for Peak Performance* (Anchorage, Alaska, 2006).

185. Doyle, *Dreams and Visions,* 263–266.

186. www.sat7.org.

187. 101 Catherine Austin Fitts, "Financial Coup d'Etat," *Solari Report,* August 8, 2011, https://solari.com/blog/financial-coup-detat.

188. Dr. Thomas R. Horn, telephone interview with Troy Anderson, May 19, 2015.

189. Mark Corner, "Towards a Global Sharing of Sovereignty," Federal Trust for Education & Research, August 2008, http://www.fedtrust.co.uk/wp-content/uploads/2014/12/Essay44_Corner.pdf ; Drew Zahn, "Kissinger: Obama Primed to Create 'New World Order': Policy Guru Says Global Upheaval Presents 'Great Opportunity,'" WND.com, January 6, 2009; www.worldnetdaily.com/index.php?pageID=85442.

190. Paul McGuire, "Bilderberg, Babylon and Agenda 21," NewsWithViews.com, October 12 ,2015, http://www.newswithviews.com/McGuire/paul271.htm.

191. Leo Hohmann, "Obama Puts U.S. on 'FastTrack' to World Government," WND.com, September 30, 2015, http://www.wnd.com/2015/09/obama-puts-u-s-on-fast-track-to-world-government; George Russell, "UN Brewing Up New- and Expensive- Global 'Sustainable Development Goals,'" FoxNews.com, October 3, 2013, http://www.foxnews.com/world/2013/10/03/un-brewing-up-new-and-expensive-global-sustainability-development-goals.html.

192. Leo Hohmann," Obama Puts U.S .On 'Fast Track' to World Government," WND.com, September 30, 2015, http://www.wnd.com/2015/09/obama-puts-u-s-on-fast-track-to-world-government.

193. Cliff Kincaid, "With Pope's Help, U.N. Bypasses Congress on

Global Socialism," Accuracy in Media Center for Investigative Journalism, September 24, 2015, http://www.aim.org/aim-column/with-popes-help-u-n-bypasses-congress-on-global-socialism.

194. United Nations, "Transforming Our World: The 2030 Agenda for Sustainable Development," September 2015, http://www.un.org/ga/search/view_doc.asp?symbol=A/RES/70/1&Lang=E .

195. University of Oxford Future of Humanity Institute and the Global Challenges Foundation, "Global Challenges 12 Risks That Threaten Human Civilisation," February 2015, http://globalchallenges.org/wp-content/uploads/12-Risks-with-infinite-impact-full-report-1.pdf.

196. Leo Hohmann, "Obama Puts U.S .on 'Fast Track' to World Government," WND.com, September 30, 2015, http://www.wnd.com/2015/09/obama-puts-u-s-on-fast-track-to-world-government; United Nations Sustainable Development, " United Nations Conference on Environment & Development, Rio de Janerio, Brazil, 3 to 14 June .1992, https://sustainabledevelopment.un.org/content/documents/Agenda21.pdf ; Caitlin Dickson,"Agenda21:The U.N. Conspiracy That Just Won't Die," The Daily Beast, April 13, 2014, http://www.thedailybeast.com/articles/2014/04/13/agenda-21-the-un-conspiracy-that-just-won-t-die.html.

197. John Fonte, telephone interview with Troy Anderson, June 9, 2015.

198. Leo Hohmann, "Obama Puts U.S .on 'Fast Track' To World Government," WND.com, September 30, 2015,http://www.wnd.com/2015/09/obama-puts-u-s-on-fast-track-to-world-government ; JohnMorgan, "Harvard Economists to IMF: Global Government Debt Is the Worst in 200 Years," Newsmax, January 3, 2014,http://www.newsmax.com/t/newsmax/article/545071 ; Francine Lacqua, "An Insight, An Idea with Christine Lagarde," Bloomberg.com, January 31, 2014, http://www.bloomberg.com/news/videos/b/85e29297-56a2-45a9-b825-b924b861067a.

199. Troy Anderson, "Are We About to See Another Great Recession or a Great Awakening?", CharismaNews.com, December 12, 2015, http://www.charismanews.com/us/53934-are-we-about-to-see-another-great-recession-or-a-great-awakening.

200. Troy Anderson, "Is the Global Economy Following the 'Classic Crash Formula?', CharismaNews.com, November 6, 2015, http://www.charismanews.com/world/53035-is-the-global-economy-following-the-classic-crash-formula.

201. Peter Schiff, telephone interview by Troy Anderson, June 12, 2015.

202. Leo Hohmann, "Elites Preparing Last Phase of New World Order?" WND.com, August 28, 2015, http://www.wnd.com/2015/08/elites-preparing-last-phase-of-new-world-order; *Encyclopedia Britannica*, "Philosopher king," http://www.britannica.com/topic/philosopher-king.

203. Jim Marrs, *Rule by Secrecy: The Hidden History That Connects the Trilateral Commission, the Freemasons, and the Great Pyramids,* (Perennial, 2000), p. 239–240.

204. .J. Eric Oliver and Thomas J. Wood, "Conspiracy Theories, Magical Thinking, and the Paranoid Style(s) of Mass Opinion," University of Chicago Department of Political Science, June 2012, 20–21; Marrs, *Rule by Secrecy*, 242.

205. Jeff Sessions, "Sessions on TPP: 'My Fears Confirmed'; Shut Down Fast-Track Now," November 5, 2015, http://www.sessions.senate.gov/public/index.cfm/news-releases?ID=711D14A5-8B65-4E4B-AAE1-7DCAA93EE60B; Jeff Sessions, "Sessions: Fast-Track Guarantees Three Mammoth Global Pacts Encompassing Up To 90% of World GDP," June 17, 2015, http://www.sessions.senate.gov/public/index.cfm/news-releases?ID=5D45FE75-3EEB-46B1-AF2E-CB2466162A0F ; Jeff Sessions, "Critical Alert: Fast-Track Would Pre-Approve Formation Of Sweeping Transnational Union," June 11, 2015.

206. Greg Laurie, telephone interview by Troy Anderson, May 21, 2015.

207. Lt. Gen. William G. "Jerry" Boykin, telephone interview with Troy Anderson, June 25, 2015.

208. Chuck Missler, telephone interview with Troy Anderson, June 24, 2015.

209. YouTube video of Dr. Raymond Kurzweil speaking to the students at Singularity University may be viewed here: https://www.youtube.com/watch?v=uHg0FIilK0E, accessed on October 19, 2015.

210. Kathleen Miles, "Ray Kurzweil: In the 2030s, Nanobots in Our Brains Will Make Us 'Godlike'", *Huffington Post,* via http://www.huffingtonpost.com/entry/ray-kurzweil-nanobots-brain-godlike_560555a0e4b0af3706dbe1e2?fw29, accessed on Oct. 19, 2015.

211. "The Dalai Lama Supports 2045's Avatar Project," posted online at http://2045.com/dialogue/29819.html, accessed Oct. 19, 2015.

212. Andrew Couts, "How One Russian Millionaire Wants to Save the World… With Immortal Cyborgs," published on March 28, 2013 at http://www.digitaltrends.com/cool-tech/dmitry-itskov-2045-initiative/, accessed on October 21, 2015.

213. Sebastian Anthony, "DARPA Reveals Avatar Program, Robot Soldiers Incoming," ExtremeTech.com, http://www.extremetech.com/extreme/118773-darpa-reveals-avatar-program-robot-soldiers-incoming, accessed Oct. 19, 2015.

214. Annie Jacobsen, *The Pentagon's Brain: An Uncensored History of DARPA, America's Top-Secret Military Research Agency,* 1st ed. (Little Brown, and Co., 2015) 427, ISBN 0316371769, Kindle Version.

215. BRAIN Initiative Website's 'About Us' page is located at http://braininitiative.nih.gov/about.htm, accessed October 19, 2015.

216. Staff, "Russian Skynet to Lead Military Robots on the Battlefield," published on Oct. 19, 2015 at https://www.rt.com/news/319082-russia-military-artificial-intelligence/, accessed on October, 20, 2015.

217. Miguel Helft, "Google Goes DARPA," published on August 14, 2014 at http://fortune.com/2014/08/14/google-goes-darpa/, accessed October 21, 2015.

218. Melissa Dykes, "Google Patents Creepy New Toys that Spy on Your Kids, Controls Smart Devices in Your Home," published on May 24, 2015 at http://www.activistpost.com/2015/05/google-patents-creepy-new-toys-that-spy.html, accessed December 8, 2015.

219. Rupert Sheldrake, "Morphic Resonance and Morphic Fields: Collective Memory and Habits of Nature." published on May 11, 2012 at http://www.newdawnmagazine.com/articles/morphic-resonance-morphic-fields-collective-memory-the-habits-of-nature, accessed October 23, 2015.

220. For more on the concept of the Divine Council and how God apportioned the nations to the rule of seventy "sons of God," read Michael Heiser, "Deuteronomy 32:8 and the Sons of God," pdf available online via http://www.thedivinecouncil.com/DT32BibSac.pdf, accessed October 23, 2015.

221. Ted Bundy comment taken from transcript of "Fatal Addiction: Ted Bundy's Final Interview," available online via http://www.pureintimacy.org/f/fatal-addiction-ted-bundys-final-interview/, accessed October 23, 2015.

222. Editorial by Charles B. Davenport, "Eugenics, A Subject for Investigation Rather than Instruction." *American Breeders Magazine*, Vol. 1, Issue 1, 68, published in 1910 by The American Breeders Association, digital version accessed via Google Books, https://books.google.com/books?id=YLwUAAAAYAAJ&dq=American%20Breeders%20Magazine&pg=PP1#v=onepage&q&f=false, accessed October 21, 2015.

223. David Starr Jordan's "Beliefs Regarding Race," available via http://dsjeugenics.weebly.com/basic-ideology.html, (accessed October 21, 2015.

224. Rob Waugh, "Genetic Scientists Could Try to Create a Unicorn, or a Dragon," published December 9, 2015 at The Metro, http://metro.co.uk/2015/12/09/genetic-scientists-could-try-to-create-a-unicorn-or-a-dragon-report-warns-5554830/, accessed December 9, 2015.